THE SUPERFERRY CHRONICLES

Also by Jerry Mander

Paradigm Wars: Indigenous Peoples' Resistance to Globalization, with Victoria Tauli-Corpuz (2007).

Alternatives to Economic Globalization: A Better World Is Possible, with John Cavanagh (2003).

The Case Against the Global Economy, and for a Turn Toward the Local, with Edward Goldsmith (1997).

In the Absence of the Sacred: The Failure of Technology and the Survival of the Indian Nations (1991).

Four Arguments for the Elimination of Television (1977).

The Great International Paper Airplane Book, with Howard Gossage and George Dippel (1967).

NOTE ABOUT THE COVER:
The goddess on the cover, *Mamala the Surfrider*, drawn by Mayumi Oda, is a Hawaiian chiefess known for her extraordinary surfing prowess. She is also a *kupua*, a nature-spirit capable of magically assuming any form. Using her many gifts, she prevails over her foes.

THE SUPERFERRY CHRONICLES

*Hawaii's Uprising Against Militarism,
Commercialism, and the Desecration of the Earth*

KOOHAN PAIK AND JERRY MANDER

With Contributions from
Hannah Bernard, Joan Conrow, Daniel Hempey,
Lance Holter, Gary Hooser, Kyle Kajihiro, Michael Shooltz,
Teri Shore, Philip Taubman, and Haunani-Kay Trask.

koa books

Ashevill, North Carolina

Koa Books is a book imprint of Chiron Publications
www.koabooks.com / www.chironpublications.com

© 2016 by Chiron Publications. All rights reserved. No part of this publication may be reproduced, stored in a retrieval system, or transmitted, in any form by any means, electronic, mechanical, photocopying, recording, or otherwise, without the prior written permission of the publisher, Chiron Publications, 932 Hendersonville Road, Suite 104, Asheville, North Carolina 28803.

Copyright © 2009 by Koohan Paik and Jerry Mander
Cover drawing, *Mamala the Surfrider*, ©1985 by Mayumi Oda,
used with permission of the artist.
The background Superferry was drawn by Neil Shigley.

Cover and book design © 2009 by Daniela Sklan | Hummingbird Design
Printed in the United States of America
For information, news, and updates, visit www.superferrychronicles.com

ISBN 978-1-935646-17-4 - paperback
ISBN 978-1-935646-18-1 - hardcover
ISBN 978-1-935646-19-8 - electronic

Pubisher's Cataloging-in-Publication

Paik, Koohan.

The SuperFerry chronicles : Hawaii's uprising against militarism, commercialism, and the desecration of the Earth / Koohan Paik and Jerry Mander ; with contributions from Hannah Bernard ... [et al.].
Kihei, Hawai'i : Koa Books, ©2009.
    p. ; cm.

    ISBN: 978-0-9773338-9-9
    Includes index.

    1. Environmental degradation. 2. Political corruption-Hawaii. 3. Culture and globalization. 4. Indigenous peoples-Civil rights-Hawaii. 5. Civil-military relations. 6. Militarism-Pacific area. I. Mander, Jerry. II. Bernard, Hannah J. III. Title.

GE140 .P35 2008
363.7/00973-dc22   0811

1 2 3 4 5 6 7 8 9 / 12 11 10 09 08

Contents

Introduction

1. Superferry, the Movie *Jerry Mander*	3
2. Does Hawai'i Matter? *Koohan Paik and Jerry Mander*	22

Part One
BOILING POINT

3. Incident at Nawiliwili Harbor *Koohan Paik*	41
4. Governor Lingle Visits Kaua'i *Testimonies of the Citizens*	56
Box: Letter from a Republican, *Scott Mijares*	70
Box: Is Superferry "Good" for Small Businesses? *John Sydney Yamane*	77
5. In the Water *Michael Shooltz*	92
6. The Sham Public Hearings *Further Testimonies*	97
Box: Thoughts from an Old-Timer, *Lloyd Miyashiro*	116

Part Two
EVOLUTION OF A BOONDOGGLE:
HISTORY AND CHRONOLOGY

7. Before Nawiliwili: 2001 to September 2007   129
   Koohan Paik and Jerry Mander

8. After Nawiliwili: October 2007 to October 2008   173
   Koohan Paik and Jerry Mander

Part Three
INSIDE REPORTS

ENVIRONMENT

9. How Superferry Threatens Life in the Oceans   209
   Hannah Bernard

   Box: The Latest Findings on Vessel-Whale Collisions   215
   Manuel Carrillo and Fabian Ritter

10. A Global Problem: Whale Collisions with Fast, Large Boats, *Teri Shore*   217

11. The Parable of the Rocks: Threats to Hawai'i's Ecosystems   220
    Lance Holter

    Box: The Oversight Task Force, *Koohan Paik*   226

LAW

12. Summary Report on the Legal Cases Involving Superferry   228
    Daniel Hempey

13. Floor Remarks on Act 2   236
    Senator Gary Hooser

MILITARIZATION

14. U.S. Navy: The New Role for Fast, Shallow-Water Vessels   244
    Joan Conrow

    Box: Is Superferry for Civilians? Studying the Numbers   252
    Koohan Paik

15. How Not to Build a Navy Ship *Philip Taubman*	255
16. Stealing Hawaiian Lands for the War Machine *Haunani-Kay Trask*	264
Box: Depleted Uranium on Hawai'i Island, *Koohan Paik*	270
17. No Peace in Paradise: The Military Presence in the Hawaiian Islands, *Kyle Kajihiro*	272
18. Radio Interview with Austal Workers *Katy Rose, Jimmy Trujillo, and Jonathan Jay*	284
EPILOGUE AND AFTERTHOUGHTS *Koohan Paik and Jerry Mander*	291

    1. Do We Hate Ferries?

    2. The Villain of the Piece

    3. Unanswered Questions

    4. The Spirit of Nawiliwili

Acknowledgments and Photo Credits	301
Index	303
About the Authors	315
About the Contributors	316
Koa Books	320

Introduction

Chapter One

SUPERFERRY, THE MOVIE

Jerry Mander

I AM ONE OF FEW CONTRIBUTORS to this book who does not live in Hawai'i, though I have spent a great deal of time there over the past several decades. Being on the mainland, however, provides me the chance to see how the rest of the country reacts to events in our fiftieth state. With a *blank stare*. Recently, for example, I was in New York at a party at the home of a well-known literary editor. I saw old colleagues and friends there. One of them greeted me this way:

"Hey Jerry, what are you working on these days? We haven't seen a book from you in a long while."

"Actually I am working on a book now, about the Hawaii Superferry."

(Blank stare) "What did you say? Hawaii what?"

"The Hawaii Superferry. Maybe you haven't heard about it. It's this gigantic, high-speed aluminum ferryboat, and they've started running it between the islands there. It's such a scam and lots of people are furious. There are really big protests."

"But ferries are good, no? People don't have to get on planes. That's a good thing."

"Well, yeah, I really love ferries, but not *this* one—it runs forty miles an hour in shallow water with these big catamaran blades slicing through zones teeming with whales and turtles, and the company will not slow it down. It's an environmental nightmare, and it also carries hundreds of cars out to these little islands that are choking from traffic already, and it moves all kinds of bad bugs and animals like mongoose—that eat up everything in sight—and anyway, it's owned by this really scary New York military-finance guy, John F. Lehman, one of the most aggressive, right-wing *neocon* war-promoter militarists, who worked for Nixon and Reagan and now McCain."

"Are airlines run by nicer people?"

"Well, no, maybe not, but look, there's all this weird scheming and double-dealing going on, including outrageous legal manipulations by the governor—who's got her eye on national office—and Senator Inouye is involved, and they've been *refusing* to do environmental impact reports, and it looks like it may all really be about a big military buildup of these kinds of boats in the Pacific to get ready for future battles with China, about who dominates the coastlines of Asia. People need to *know* about all this."

"Jerry, for chrissakes, you sound like some kind of paranoid, coffeehouse, antimilitary freak, like Dennis Kucinich or Chomsky or Ellsberg or somebody."

"Yes, well, they would probably get the idea right away. Maybe I should tell them."

"Come on, Jerry, it's Hawai'i! It's all about vacations and condo timeshares. Who cares? Nobody really lives in Hawai'i; it's not like New York or L.A. or D.C. Come home. Get back in the action."

"I *am* in the action. Hawai'i is the center of the Pacific. We're staring at Asia there! China, India, Korea, Japan, the Philippines, Australia. That's the future. *That's* where the action is, about trying to save the local environment, and about control of the Pacific—the military is everywhere in Hawai'i. In the next two decades these issues will get bigger and bigger. Where it's located, all the action passes through Hawai'i. And a lot of people there get that. They see this Superferry thing as a part of the problem; part of a whole century of corporate and military intervention and takeover in Hawai'i, and they're up in arms, and doing these really moving protests, like when the ship actually got blocked from entering the port—by *surfers*! It's amazing. We shouldn't ignore this. We should get behind it."

* * *

Maybe the story would be most convincing as a movie, a big Hollywood blockbuster. A movie in the spirit of *Michael Clayton* or *Wall Street* or *Syriana*. It has everything—high-level corporate arrogance; deep governmental collusion and deception; military maneuverings to prepare for a Pacific conflict the public knows nothing about; a sharp female governor, Republican, with passionate ambitions, eager to make compromising deals with power to get ahead; a few brave whistle-blowers inside government agencies who see what's going on and speak out about it; some smart local investigative reporters and bloggers trying to dig up the real story; grave dangers to the environment that are swept under the rug; direct connections to the upper levels of the Bush administration; and *scores* of fiery, colorful activists of all stripes, from surfers to small businesspeople, to Native Hawaiian elders.

And it has that one really powerful, right-wing character, the wealthy founder of a New York investment company that deals only in megamilitary projects. He's a former secretary of the Navy under Ronald Reagan, and in that role he ardently fought against peace deals and fiercely advocated for winnable nuclear war strategies. Now he's the prime mover of a local Hawai'i ferryboat enterprise, 6,000 miles away! *Why? Why on Earth is he doing this?* He enters the story midway, quickly buys his way to the reins of control, hooks the project to his military contacts, and drives off the naïfs who thought they were just running a normal, neighborly service. They were slowing him down.

But all this scheming? Just for a local transport business?

Then, suddenly, *uprising*—a peoples' revolt. The public gets wind of the bigger story. They realize the degree to which their charming governor, who has been hawking the project with all her might, is *also* embedded in the wheelings and dealings and has manipulated the circumvention of cherished environmental laws. The protesters see how she and the corporation have been ignoring their environmental concerns and misleading them about the company's intentions and connections. They get it that the owners of the project are no longer familiar *local* do-gooders, but instead are distant, global financiers, Pentagon players, and corporate suits, all with military agendas.

The locals protest, they reason, they petition, they block roads, they sue. In a key moment for the story, *August 26, 2007*, they spontaneously appear by the thousands at Nawiliwili Harbor on the small island of Kaua'i. They blockade the docks, they jump into the water, they put their *surfboards, boogie boards, canoes, and bodies in front of the oncoming colossus*, risking arrest, even risking their lives. Soon after, they speak and argue at public hearings, with great eloquence and spirit. They speak of the *'aina* (sacred lands) and the whales and the deterioration of life on the islands, trying to save what makes Hawai'i a sacred place. And amazingly, as we write this, so far they seem to be succeeding.

Those astonishing events, starting at Nawiliwili Harbor in Kaua'i, are the *genesis* of this book, its raison d'être. Four chapters of Part One are devoted to these eruptions and their causes, and the inspiring testimonies of the people.

But first, let's check out this movie.

Regime Change

It's the kind of story you usually hear about some banana republic in the Caribbean during colonial days. But no, it's in the heart of the Pacific, the glorious Hawaiian Islands, where the cheerful people are constantly displayed in hundred-million-dollar ad campaigns, joyfully welcoming each new invasion of tourists or real-estate developers or giant global industrial agriculture companies or cruise ships daily pouring out thousands of people wearing flowered shirts and toting cameras, onto the once-pristine rural landscape. All of them are dutifully greeted at ports or runways by smiling (hired) hula girls with leis, kisses, smiles, and ubiquitous *aloha spirit* brought to you by the Chamber of Commerce.

Even after a 150-year history of intervention, invasion, and cultural and economic abuse; even after sugar plantation barons started taking over where there used to be local taro farmers; even after Native languages were *banned* from schools for a century and scores of missionaries were in cahoots with plantation owners to *deliberately* undermine traditional culture and self-governance, while aggressively buying up nearly all the Native lands; even realizing that these first invaders became billionaires, several of whose descendents *still* own most of Hawai'i, their names *still* on buildings and signs—Castle, Cooke, Baldwin, Pflueger, *et. al.*—as they continue to dominate Hawai'i's lands today nearly as they had in the 1800s; *even so*, despite all this, most people in Hawai'i still try to express aloha, acceptance, and inclusion, often to their detriment.

The key moment in Hawai'i's history was back in 1893, when the U.S. military arrived in force. Summoned by Sanford Dole and other corporate sugar growers, they occupied the islands for five years, against President Grover Cleveland's demand to restore order. But Dole refused. He even jailed Hawai'i's leader, Queen Lili'uokalani. *Regime change.* Then, in 1898, a new U.S. president, William McKinley, signed the resolution annexing Hawai'i to the United States. A fiercely independent Hawaiian nation was suddenly forced by a military occupier to submit to colonial rule. *Stop speaking Hawaiian! Get off that land! Your leaders are in jail! Put some clothes on! Here comes democracy!*

From that point on, it was business 24/7/365: giant sugar and pineapple empires for global export; billions of dollars in tourism based on fantasies of freedom and paradise; high-rise hotels and vast real-estate developments climbing once-sacred, chiseled green mountains; all-out assaults on the 'aina—now commodified, objectified, bought, sold, developed.

No problem; come one and all. Get your piece of Hawai'i, packaged and sold like so many chocolate-covered macadamia nuts. *See the lovely hula girls. Meet the smiling, friendly natives*—that is, the people cleaning your hotel rooms—with the lowest income rate, the highest disease rate, the highest incarceration rate, and the lowest education and literacy rate of any cultural group within the state. Maybe it *is* a banana republic.

One more important part of the saga: The military that arrived in 1893 to help overthrow the government?—it never left. Hawai'i is occupied by one of the largest U.S. military presences anywhere off the U.S. mainland, though it's partly hidden under the soft aura of dancing Hawaiians and the luscious music of Braddah Iz. Well, everyone certainly *has* known about Pearl Harbor ever since the Japanese attack in 1941. Pearl Harbor has now become a mega-attraction for tourists, a kind of theme park of itself, and as our plane descends to Honolulu we see it: *huge*. Home of the Pacific fleet: aircraft carriers, battleships, submarines. Home of the jets that carry the big bombs toward Asia. And, home of the Stryker Brigade—hundreds of small tanks of the kind used in Iraq, shooting shells encased in uranium.

There are giant military bases on most of the Hawaiian Islands: the Barking Sands Pacific Missile Range Facility (on Kaua'i), out past the end of the road on the west side; the Pohakuloa Pacific Training Area (on the Big Island of Hawai'i), hidden up in the saddle between three mountains—that's where those Strykers will soon be transported en masse (by the Superferry!) for live-fire training with soldiers, leaving uranium dust to blow down the mountain onto tourist havens in Kona; and on O'ahu, 22 percent of the land is controlled by the military! *(For more on the history of militarization in Hawai'i, see Chapters 14–18.)*

The subtextual message to the world is clear enough. It's a statement to the countries of the Pacific Basin, particularly China, Russia, and North Korea: *Watch out*. We stand on the Pacific platform. We're in the exact middle of the ocean here. You can't get around us. And we're ready for anything.

And into all this geopolitical tension comes the little Hawaii Superferry. It is actually an enormous, sleek, aluminum-hulled catamaran with paintings of happy manta rays on the side. There will be two ships (one is already running; the other is scheduled for 2010), each the size of one-and-a-half football fields, five decks stacked one atop the other, with capacity for 866 people and 282 vehicles, and with *twin catamaran blades speeding through shallow waters at 40 miles per hour.*

The route goes through where humpback whales breed, areas home to giant sea turtles and colonies of sea mammals, many of which have evolved here over millennia and can be found nowhere else on Earth. *(Critics point out the practical impossibility that high-speed boats can avoid collisions, even with lookouts watching the waters ahead. We have reports on this in Chapter 9, by Hannah Bernard, and Chapter 10, by Teri Shore.)*

The Superferry promotes itself as a friendly, modern, *green* inter-island connector service—only three hours between islands. Smooth sailing, good for families wanting to visit their aunties on other islands; good for high school volleyball teams on Maui wanting to compete on Oʻahu; good for small local farmers wanting to take produce to another island to sell; good for tourists and tour groups who can take their rented cars on board with them and drive right onto the other islands. *Why should anyone be upset at this?* Back to the movie.

All-Star Cast

Let's review the central characters in this saga.

Timothy Dick. Small-scale independent Silicon Valley software entrepreneur, young, handsome, happy-go-lucky guy. He takes a vacation to Mallorca and sees high-speed catamaran ferries operating in the Mediterranean. Visiting Hawaiʻi, he sees no such thing. He has a big vision! If Spain can run high-speed ferries between Mallorca and Ibiza, then why shouldn't Hawaiʻi run them from Oʻahu to the outer islands? Tourists will love them. *He's excited.* He puts a business plan together in 2001, raises start-up money locally, starts HSF, Inc. (changed in 2004 to Hawaii Superferry, Inc.), and hires a new chief executive officer. He makes contracts with a shipbuilding company, Austal USA of Mobile, Alabama, to build two giant high-speed aluminum catamarans. (Curiously, this company makes a similar boat that the U.S. Navy leases for its Westpac Express transport program in the Pacific. And the design of the Superferry is unusually huge, with four big jet engines, seemingly way out of scale for its announced use as a local ferry service, yet little is made of this at the time.)

Later, as the financing gets trickier and additional markets need to be found, possible military options for the Superferry start to look increasingly attractive. In his application to the state Public Utilities Commission, Dick openly acknowledges that the Superferry will seek military contracts. In fact, he is already in touch with the state's Senator Daniel Inouye, who is earmarking Congressional funds toward accommodating Hawaiʻi's Stryker tank brigade; Dick tries to nail down a deal to shuttle the tanks back and forth between Oʻahu and the Big Island of Hawaiʻi, where live-fire training is planned.

And soon he starts going after *big* money, from New York investors connected to the military and government. But, alas, he opens a Pandora's box. The big-time New York bankers *do* know how to work government agencies, and they *do* have the connections to reach out for military contracts, and they *do* agree to invest money, but there's a catch: *They* come in with the money! They push their way in and soon take over Dick's board of directors, replacing most of its original members with a "rogues' gallery of former military commanders," as Joan Conrow puts it in Chapter 14. Soon, Timothy Dick, as well, is "relieved" of his role in the company.

John Garibaldi. Hired by Timothy Dick as the CEO of the new company, Garibaldi's prior position was CEO of Hawaiian Airlines, which went bankrupt on his watch. Charming, reassuring, and fun-loving in the back-slapping Italian way. A very good PR man, he explains how the Superferry will improve everyone's life in Hawai'i: bring together *'ohana* (Hawaiian for "family") and enable people to move with their cars from island to island. He talks about high school girls' sports teams and the small farmers who can use the ferries like highways, driving their trucks onto the boat to sell produce in Honolulu.

But soon, Garibaldi starts getting caught in controversial statements about how certain big investors and government agencies don't want any Environmental Impact Statements and that the (unnamed) investors will pull out of the deal if there's an EIS. He also denies any military connections or intentions, even denies the company's hopes to transport the Army's Stryker tanks. And he denies that the Superferry may eventually have a role as a prototype in the Navy's larger plan to deploy light, high-speed catamarans throughout the Pacific for its Littoral Combat Ship and Joint High Speed Vessel (JHSV) transport programs. (We only learn later that the Navy is putting out contracts to build ships for those programs, with the intention of maintaining a dominant U.S. presence in the Pacific.)

Governor Linda Lingle. Hawai'i's new Republican governor, elected in a Democratic state, from a family that owns one of the biggest automobile dealerships in the Hawaiian Islands, she was born in Missouri and raised in southern California. There, she began her career as a public information officer for the Teamsters Union, and then worked as an idealistic journalist on the mostly indigenous island of Moloka'i. She edited a community newspaper that supported many Native Hawaiian cultural and environmental issues. But she never strayed far from her family's business-first credo.

She eventually moves to Maui where her focus shifts to political power, serving five terms on the Maui County Council. She decides to run for mayor, with substantial backing from her family's colleagues and friends, and wins. True to her word, she pushes a grand economic investment and development scheme that brings in billions of dollars of outside financing from the global economy, and proudly helps transform much of that gorgeous island into a second Orlando, Florida. She becomes ever more conservative, and soon runs for governor on the platform "Hawai'i is open for business," becoming the first Republican governor of Hawai'i since 1962 and the state's first woman governor ever.

Early in her term, in 2004, she is chosen as part-time chair of the Republican National Convention. She's become a rising star on the national Republican scene, a close friend of the Bush family, with hopes she can ride her can-do business credentials to high national office.

As part of that vision, Lingle gets the state legislature to grant a $40 million loan to Hawaii Superferry, while working closely with the company to engineer the circumvention of state and federal laws such as the National Environmental Policy Act (NEPA) and the corresponding Hawai'i version (HEPA). She orders her state agencies to go out of their way to assist the Superferry's purposes, and she pressures her Department of Transportation to reverse the agencies' original strong demands that Superferry complete Environmental Impact Statements. In doing so, she ignores warnings from her own legal advisor, who strongly supports an EIS, while also shrugging off credible sources that report that the high-speed boat presents grave threats to whale calving grounds and sea turtle habitats, and can potentially wreak havoc by importing invasive species, thus accelerating the rapid decline of quality of life on the islands—already overdeveloped, polluted, and crowded.

It is those actions of Lingle's, more than anything else, that cause the public to rise in opposition. *(For details on the environmental issues related to the Superferry, see Chapters 9–11.)*

Outraged citizens take the case all the way to the Hawai'i Supreme Court, which rules unanimously that an Environmental Impact

Statement *must be performed before the Superferry sets sail.* Rather than honor the decision, Lingle defies it, giving the go-ahead to the company to begin operations. Then, in a spectacular act of will and hubris, Lingle bullies a weak-kneed legislature, dominated by Oahuans, into a special session whose only purpose is to officially override the Supreme Court ruling. In a direct slap at the court, they brazenly call it "Act 2."

Throughout all this, she refuses to allow the residents of the neighbor islands—Maui, Kaua'i, and the Big Island—the people whom she claimed this project was supposed to benefit—to have any say in whether it should proceed. Even after the Nawiliwili surfers, swimmers, and protestors successfully block the boat's entry to the harbor, she tells them, with characteristic arrogance, that the decisions about the project have already been finalized and that protestors will face *$10,000 fines and jail time* for violating "terrorism laws" should they protest inside the security zone established under federal Homeland Security law. She parries repeated questions about military connections and financing issues—taking a parallel line to Garibaldi's—and, like her spiritual mentors George Bush and Dick Cheney, refuses during the next months to turn over key background documents to legislators or for court proceedings, citing claims of "executive privilege" and "attorney-client privilege."

In all of this, Lingle's ultimate motives seem to be to gain favor with Republican powers and the rich mainland business interests and investors she will need for her national campaigns, and also to please Bush administration officials who want this project to succeed, for its military aspects. Like other Bush followers, she has learned to successfully emulate that smug, know-it-all style that characterizes the George W. Bush administration, while confidently smiling her way to great personal power. As we finish this book, Governor Lingle is extolling the virtues of Sarah Palin to reporters at the Republican National Convention.

John F. Lehman. Among the heavy characters in this story, this man is heaviest—the man who effectively owns the Superferry. Dynamic head of a powerful New York investment company, J. F. Lehman and Co. (no connection to Lehman Brothers), he is the leading equity investor in the Hawaii Superferry Corporation and, since 2005, has been chairman of its board. He installs five of his own corporate colleagues as directors—most of them with military backgrounds *(see Chapters 8 and 14 for details)*, thus completely controlling the board and all the company's activities. If this was ever a local project, as its promoters like to say, it isn't anymore. But that fact didn't prevent Lehman from telling a newspaper reporter that "what attracted us to the management is that they were citizens of Hawai'i, not carpetbaggers coming in from the outside" (*Pacific Business News*, April 8, 2005). Neither did it prevent him from *demoting* these folks and, in the case of Timothy Dick (also an advocate of faux localism), easing him out of the company.

Lehman is more than your run-of-the-mill aggressive businessman. He is a highly controversial public figure going back to his days as Assistant National Security Advisor to President Richard Nixon under Secretary of State Henry Kissinger, before joining Reagan, and most recently he was a member of the 9/11 Commission appointed by President George W. Bush. Lehman is a close intimate of some of the country's most powerful right-wing thinkers and players, including the neocon clique that brought us the Iraq War. While working for Reagan for some seven years, he was a strong opponent of the SALT disarmament agreement with the Soviet Union and an outspoken advocate for the idea of abandoning détente with the Soviet Union in favor of a policy promoting the nuclear first-strike option and winnable nuclear wars. He was famously quoted on nuclear war, saying, "Who gets to shoot first will have more to do with who wins, than any other factor" (*Washington Post*, June 23, 1984). And he has been a forceful, singular advocate for a vast expansion of the U.S. Navy fleet to maintain dominance over the world's oceans and "protect our vital interests worldwide."

Lehman was also an ardent member of the right-wing Committee on the Present Danger during the Nixon years, and to this day he remains closely associated with Richard Perle and other members of the Project for the New American Century, the neocon group that pushed hard for the invasion of Iraq and continues to press for military action against Iran, Syria, and North Korea. Lehman signed several letters to George W. Bush supporting such actions. And it has been just such ideas that have informed (and blessed) Lehman's military business and activities. As we write, Lehman also serves as one of John McCain's key military advisors, fund raisers, and, as predicted by the *New York Times*, the likely "chief of staff" in a McCain presidency.

All of Lehman's extensive contacts in government and within the Defense and Navy departments have certainly positioned Superferry to become a military contractor and asset, should such opportunities arise. Lehman's connections may also prove helpful for the designers of the catamaran, Austal USA, which is also a creditor of the Superferry, to become recipients of a potentially gigantic shipbuilding contract for the Navy. On balance, all that kind of activity seems to be far more Lehman's thing than does helping local families visit their 'ohana on a neighbor island.

As indicated, John Lehman doesn't enter the public story until several years after the company is founded, but by 2005, he has expanded his investment in Superferry to an estimated $80 million, becoming the largest single-equity investor in the company, its key player, and board chair. Yet he does this only after the U.S. Maritime Administration (MARAD) of the U.S. Department of Transportation, in a mysterious and controversial action, says it will violate its own internal rules to grant Superferry a *$140 million loan guarantee* that puts taxpayer dollars at high risk if the company does not succeed. One shocking condition of the loan is that there be no environmental review at any level, as normally required by the National Environmental Policy Act. MARAD itself will also decline to do a NEPA review, though most legal observers believe that its loan guarantee would automatically require an extensive Environmental Impact Statement.

In fact, at every turn of this story, environmental and other laws are routinely circumvented at both federal and state levels, despite considerable upset about this in certain government agencies.

Exactly how this process actually happened at high levels is an area under investigation by several keen Hawai'i state senators *(as reported in Chapter 8)*. The senators are demanding documents from Governor Lingle, but are being stonewalled.

(The fact that Lehman became active just after this peculiar MARAD loan guarantee leads observers to wonder whether it could have been Lehman himself, using his high-level contacts in the Bush administration, who orchestrated that unusual deal. It would certainly have been in his economic interests to do so, to protect his large investment while passing most risk on to the taxpayers.)

Soon after the MARAD announcement, Lehman also buys an enormous interest in a big ship production yard in Mobile, Alabama. It is directly adjacent to the facilities of Austal USA, the company that manufactures the Superferry and is also manufacturing nearly identical high-speed ships as prototypes for two U.S. Navy programs. If Austal should finally win the big Navy contract it is now seeking, to produce dozens more of these catamarans, then Lehman's *adjoining* production facility might be in a great position to collaborate on part of that production. So, the little Hawaii Superferry project begins to look far more like a test run for the seaworthiness of the fighting ship design than a simple plan to unite 'ohana and carry papayas across the interisland channels—endeavors that would seem far too measly for a global military finance magnate like John Lehman and his list of interlocking directors.

Admiral Thomas Fargo. If there was ever any doubt that the Superferry had turned the corner from a handy, modest, interisland transport to a far grander project, with its ambitions directed toward larger geopolitical issues, these were allayed in early 2008, when the company announced that its new CEO would be Admiral Thomas Fargo. (Former CEO John Garibaldi was a good *local* choice at the start, when the company needed to ingratiate itself to the island communities, but not a perfect choice for military maneuverings in the Pacific against China.)

Admiral Fargo served as commander in chief of the U.S. Pacific Fleet from October 1999 to May 2002, and then as commander of the U.S. Pacific Command from May 2002 to February 2005, reporting directly to Secretary of Defense Donald Rumsfeld and President Bush. In the latter capacity he commanded all military activities in the Pacific and Indian oceans, including the Navy, Air Force, and Marines. Fargo's office was at Camp Smith, Honolulu, where he was frequently photographed with his charming wife in local social-page newspaper stories. As the Navy's chief executive officer in the Pacific, he would doubtless have had a key role in helping to chart the U.S. defense strategy and apparatus in the region, including the buildup of the Littoral Combat Ship and the Joint High Speed Vessel programs *(see Chapter 14)* designed for flexible, fast action in the Pacific, and for which the Superferry design from Austal USA is now considered the lead prototype.

So, let's review. We have former Secretary of the Navy John Lehman, an aggressive militarist and a leading military finance expert, sitting at the helm of the Hawaii Superferry company; *plus*, a Superferry board of directors dominated by executives of Lehman's investment company (which is involved strictly in military investing); and *now* we have Thomas Fargo, the former head of all Pacific military operations, as the Superferry corporate CEO, the man who effectively supervised the very production contracts for the Navy's Littoral Combat Ship program, and the Joint High Speed Vessel, for which the Superferry's builder and creditor, Austal USA, is now competing. *Do you think they have a chance to win the contract?*

This seems to be one of the better examples of the infamous revolving door through which government and military officials move to positions where their insider status and years of intimate contact with military and government management can pay off bigtime as they cross over into the commercial world. Of course, Admiral Fargo says he has no such motives. For him, as quoted in the Superferry's own publication, his "great pleasure" is just becoming part of the "Hawaii Superferry 'ohana" helping to fulfill its "maritime mission to connect Hawai'i's 'ohana and islands by sea." No doubt those are Lehman's main motives, as well.

And, finally, let's not forget that we have that ambitious Republican governor to loyally carry towels and do the legal shenanigans for her influential friends in this commercial enterprise, bulldozing over public concerns, environmental protection laws, court decisions, and other roadblocks to make sure this project succeeds.

* * *

Our story also features some key supporting actors:

U.S. Senator Daniel Inouye, often called "The Godfather" of the Hawaiian Islands, has used his senate committee chairmanship to help steer hundreds of millions of dollars in congressional funds to Hawai'i to subsidize transportation and port facility "improvements," partly to facilitate the introduction of the Stryker Brigade to O'ahu and its primary training area on the Big Island. Millions of dollars also went toward new Superferry docks and facilities (also without EIS reports), new military roads, and new facilities on both O'ahu and the Big Island.

Then there's **Norman Mineta**, a longtime cabinet member under Presidents Clinton and Bush; head of the U.S. Department of Transportation (USDOT), which houses and supervises MARAD; an extremely vocal supporter of Superferry; and a friend of Governor Lingle. Mineta was likely the person who gave the "official" go-ahead for MARAD to issue its extraordinary $140 million loan guarantee, essentially a subsidy for an otherwise private business, thus opening the floodgates for big-time investors, such as John Lehman, while putting taxpayers on the hook to bail out any corporate failures.

No great drama is complete without its tragic figure—in this case, **Barry Fukunaga**, who served as assistant director of the Hawai'i Department of Transportation (DOT) at a key moment in this story. His first instinct in all this was *idealistic*. He adamantly demanded that Superferry follow all environmental laws of the state, including doing a broad, archipelago-wide Environmental Impact Statement *before* the ship would be allowed to run.

That's the end of the good news about Fukunaga. He was quickly shut down by higher-ups, including Lingle and her then-Chief of Staff **Bob Awana**, who had no intention of ever allowing an EIS to be prepared, at least not before the boat was in the water. Seeing the political handwriting on the wall, Fukunaga reversed course, withdrew his EIS demands, and became one of the project's biggest boosters. Soon after, he was rewarded with a promotion to head the DOT, and later to his present position as Lingle's chief of staff.

So far, this film contains no murders and no sex. Maybe Hollywood will change that during preproduction. However, there *are* plenty of heroes.

Local Heroes

The *Honolulu Advertiser*, the islands' biggest newspaper, published a series of excellent exposés about the Superferry over the last four years. In one, it reported the actions of two federal government bureaucrats who saw the irregularities that were going on and tried to stop them.

The reporters were particularly focused on MARAD's decision to give a $140 million loan guarantee to a private company without demanding an EIS, or at least what's called a "Section 7 consultation" on potential dangers to marine mammals, as *clearly* required by the Endangered Species Act. **David Cottingham** of the U.S. National Marine Fisheries Service and **Chris Yates** of the Office of Protected Resources for the Pacific Island Region wrote separate, and anguished, letters to MARAD demanding that it explain why it was not living up to these laws. Both men allowed themselves to be quoted by name in the *Advertiser* and in other news stories, at considerable risk to their public careers, though MARAD continues to stonewall the situation to this day.

Speaking of the *Honolulu Advertiser*, **Christie Wilson**, who wrote the story about MARAD cited above, and **Derrick DePledge**, who prepared the key report on Fukunaga's shocking turnabout and several other exposés, definitely deserve commendation for their reporting. They should also be praised for apparently persuading the usually conservative newspaper to publish a series of tough investigative reports that uncovered a blizzard of hidden crosscurrents, lies, and questionable dealings that have helped expose the project as the doubtful deal that it is.

Another hero, a former police chief from Iowa named **Rich Hoeppner**, founded a 6,000-person citizens' group on Kaua'i to petition against the Superferry. In 2006, he and six others took the petition to Honolulu to hand deliver it to Governor Lingle, who refused a meeting, refused to accept the petition, and refused even to provide a staff person to talk to. The group was then hustled out by a huge guard in an aloha shirt. Hoeppner has been involved in every protest since. (In the movie, let's put Tom Hanks in that role.)

A few outstanding government representatives deserve special praise. These include State Representative **Hermina Morita**, who filed a complaint, early on, with the Public Utilities Commission for granting the Hawaii Superferry a certificate to operate without requiring the company to comply with environmental law. There is also **JoAnn Yukimura**, a member of the Kaua'i County Council and a former Kaua'i mayor, who on every crucial occasion has made inspiring speeches. When Governor Lingle showed up on Kaua'i that fateful day, Yukimura was first to directly challenge her to finally tell the truth.

And then there are State Senators **Gary Hooser** (Kaua'i), **Shan Tsutsui** (Maui), **Roz Baker** (Maui), **Kalani English** (Maui), and

Russell Kokubun (Big Island), as well as eleven state representatives, who were the only lawmakers who voted against the passage of Act 2, which legislated Hawaii Superferry out of having to follow the Hawaiʻi Environmental Policy Act. *(See Chapter 8; October 2007: "House Passes Act 2.")* Hooser, Tsutsui, and English, in particular, have been at the forefront of the statewide community-driven movement asking for an EIS, and they have demanded at every opportunity in the legislature that Lingle and her agencies come clean about what was going on and start listening to the people. They also initiated the series of senate investigations that Lingle continues to stall.

The State of Hawaiʻi Environmental Council, a citizens board, showed great courage when it resisted pressure from both Superferry and state attorneys to remain silent on the EIS issue. Instead, its members determined that the ship should *never* have been exempted from environmental review, a decision which carried weight in the later Supreme Court ruling.

There is also the bevy of local bloggers and YouTubers that put out a steady stream of information about what was going on, where, and when. **Joan Conrow** (Kauaʻi) and **Kyle Kajihiro** (Oʻahu) brilliantly covered the many military angles. Both have written articles in Part Three of this book, where we delve more deeply into specific issues, like militarism, environmental impacts, and law. **Juan Wilson** (Kauaʻi), **Karen Chun** (Maui), and **John Tyler Craig** (Kauaʻi) kept tabs on local and state moods and reactions. **Richard Diamond** (Kauaʻi), through his online newsletter, provided the latest updates on public hearings and relevant senate bills. Researcher and blogger **Brad Parsons** (Maui), **Ian Lind** (Oʻahu), and **Dick Mayer** (Maui), the latter a former college history professor with an uncanny knack for locating pithy archives and government reports, have been constantly digging up previously unknown details about the Superferry.

Other researchers who have played a big role include **Larry Geller** (Oʻahu), **Jeff Sacher** (Big Island), and **Lee Tepley** (Big Island). All these people keep us riveted to the story. And a tiny local Kauaʻi nonprofit radio station, **KKCR**, a seemingly amateurish, hippyish, laid-back operation that usually favors local gossip, surf reports, reggae, both New Age and Hawaiian music, was suddenly thrown into the role of media central, a key rallying point for the protesters; the station's leading voices in its Superferry coverage include **Kaʻiulani Edens-Huff, Mahelani Sylva, Katy Rose, Jimmy Trujillo,** and **Karlos deTreaux.**

A big role has also been well played by an extraordinary group of Native Hawaiians from Kauaʻi, who have formed the **Polynesian Kingdom of Atooi.** They have been working to gain recognition and attention for the fact that the Hawaiian Kingdom was illegally invaded and overthrown and, therefore, is still illegally occupied. For them, the Superferry is just a continuation of the same unlawful process.

At the time of Kauaʻi's Nawiliwili Harbor protests, they took the role of an alternative local police and, most impressively, helped maintain calm, while also voicing their own case against the Superferry. Two of them were rewarded for this peacekeeping effort by being arrested by the Kauaʻi police.

Then there's a coterie of underpaid idealistic legal advocates like **Isaac Hall** on Maui, **Dan Hempey** on Kauaʻi, and the organization **Earthjustice** in Honolulu, each carving out a piece of the complex mosaic of appalling illegalities, secrets, and federal and Hawaiian government malfeasances, and who may yet produce the ultimate win in court. Hall, for example, representing four leading environmental groups on Maui—**Maui Tomorrow,** the **Sierra Club,** the **Kahului Harbor Coalition,** and **Friends of Haleakala National Park**—has already won the profound State Supreme Court ruling that called the Lingle waiver of the Environmental Impact Statement illegal.

Everyone thought this might kill the Superferry, which could probably not survive a good EIS, as opined by attorney Hall. But then, in an in-your-face move worthy of Dick Cheney, Lingle coerced the legislature to make a new state law that overrode the State Supreme Court. This cynical subversion of legal processes, perhaps more than any other single act, incited the outrage that burst forth at Nawiliwili and was the start of all that followed.

Tranquility

The above recitation of heroes doesn't begin to cover all the players. The greatest heroes, as you will read in Part One, "Boiling Point," were the people of the outer islands, notably those on Kauaʻi, the small island best known for its spectacular, lush, folded green mountains, and its quiet, pristine beauty—its tranquility.

As the protests revealed, it was a tranquility that was daily tested by pressures from tourism, mindless development, increasing pollution, shrinking open spaces, and the destruction of pristine rivers and streams that nourished a wonderland of biodiversity—all diminishing the very characteristics that had given the Garden Island its nickname. It was also sorely tested by the disdain, opacity, and simple rudeness of top government officials.

At least for now, the Hawaii Superferry does not go to Kaua'i, and the Nawiliwili protests have achieved legendary status on the islands. That turn of events would have made the perfect climax for our movie, but alas, this isn't a movie. This is real. And there is no sure victory yet.

At this moment, October 2008, the boat *is* still running to Maui, as legal battles continue. The so-called Environmental Impact Statement mandated last year by a special session of the state legislature is in process, though it is merely a disclosure document (unlike a real EIS under federal or state law), one that will not require the company to actually mitigate any environmental concerns. *(The fraudulent nature of the Lingle EIS will be discussed further in Chapter 2.)*

Superferry has announced that it will begin runs to the Big Island in 2010. As for the pending big military deals for Austal USA, at this date, they are not final. The future is unclear. The saga is still unfolding.

Chapter Two

Does Hawai'i Matter?

Koohan Paik and Jerry Mander

IN AUGUST 2008, while we were completing this book, Senator Barack Obama took a break from his presidential campaigning for a brief vacation in Hawai'i. This led to harsh criticism by certain mainstream media pundits, particularly Cokie Roberts of ABC-TV's *This Week*, who said, "I know his grandmother lives there, and I know Hawai'i is a state, but it has the look of him going off to some sort of foreign, exotic place. ... He should be in Myrtle Beach if he's going to take a vacation at this time."

In reaction, Hawai'i's two U.S. Senators, Daniel Akaka and Daniel Inouye, apparently feeling insulted on behalf of both themselves and their state, particularly by the "foreign" label being applied to Hawai'i's citizens, each issued a forceful statement reminding Roberts and ABC that Hawai'i is part of the United States and that its citizens are Americans.

"The question comes up," remarked Inouye, "what is America, and who is American? I would resent anyone suggesting that my roots are not American."

Indeed! Daniel Inouye has been Hawai'i's U.S. Senator since statehood a half century ago. He lost an arm fighting for the United States in World War II (as part of the *segregated* Nisei 442nd Battalion, the Army's most decorated unit in history). And he has been a leader in the senate in furthering U.S. military policy. In Chapter 1, we noted that he has been an ardent backer of Stryker tanks and the Superferry to transport them. (One *could* make the case that Inouye is so pro-U.S. military that he might actually be overcompensating for the humiliations suffered by Japanese-Americans interned during

World War II.) But in any case, to imply that he, or any of Hawai'i's citizens, are somehow "foreign" or "exotic" or "other"—and that Barack Obama should avoid them (though he is himself from Hawai'i)—well, exactly *what* is Cokie Roberts thinking? Is Hawai'i really less American than Myrtle Beach? Is Daniel Inouye less patriotic than Cokie Roberts? What puts the state in this more dubious category, as far as American-ness goes?

Remarks like Roberts's are all too familiar to Hawai'i's residents, who may rightfully ask whether the central problem isn't simply that 75 percent of Hawai'i's population is not of European descent.

Hawai'i is mostly composed of a mix of Native Hawaiians, plus descendents of immigrants from Asian countries—the Philippines, Japan, Korea, and China—many of whom came over to work on the sugar plantations at the turn of the 19th century, along with Portuguese, Puerto Ricans, and others. *And* Pacific islanders from Micronesia, Tahiti, Samoa, and elsewhere. Hawai'i is the most racially mixed state. Is *that* why it's less American? Less like *"us"*?

What Is Hawai'i?

Hawai'i is the one state in the union that exists in most people's minds entirely as a tourist/vacation "product," promoted and sold by tens of millions of advertising dollars. Hula girls, white sandy beaches, flower leis, big-wave surfing, Diamond Head, Don Ho, Day-Glo cocktails, tiki torches. As the man said in the first chapter, "Nobody lives in Hawai'i," save those who serve as background "color," or waiters.

Of course, people who have actually visited Hawai'i carry other visions—those of lush green mountains, velvety trade winds, waterfalls, rainbows, whales frolicking on the horizon, and the richest biodiversity on Earth, with life bursting from every pore: a true paradise. And, if you're *really* rich like a movie star, Pierce Brosnan for example, or Michelle Pfeiffer or Clint Eastwood or a global arms dealer like Adnan Khashoggi or one of the many other billionaires who now own property here, you may want to *buy* a chunk of it, to turn your visit into a real-estate shopping experience, choosing a fat slice of paradise that had once been Native Hawaiian taro fields or a pristine river valley or unfenced open space, as it mostly was until quite recently. For other newcomers, it's a *spiritual* haven for seekers of every persuasion, including Buddhists, Hindus, and thousands of New Age *haoles* who arrive every year to experience the vibrations of a place that feels like Shangri La.

But whether it's the tiki torch or the let's-buy-up-this-paradise mindset or meditation retreats, there is precious little awareness of the history of this land or its people or that Hawai'i is a place of monumental geopolitical and military import. It's the *frontier*, the westernmost outpost of U.S. expansion, the first line of U.S. defense, the launchpad for U.S. movement in the Pacific and toward Asia. That's all Hawai'i, too.

For the majority of Hawai'i residents, there is yet another reality. They might remember the days when their parents or grandparents toiled in difficult jobs for sugar growers in an era of racial segregation, though life was made more bearable by the incredible beauty and abundance of the place: reefs teeming with fish, wild pig in the mountains, fields of taro, and exotics that thrive in the subtropical climate—oranges, papayas, lychees, longans, and other succulent fruit. Yet, out of that segregation, it has become a place that embodies the American ideal of racial multiplicity.

Hawai'i is home to a diversity of cultures found nowhere else to this degree in the United States, albeit in the broader context of a growing tourist economy where *absentee* owners have taken the place of the *plantation* owners as the central economic overseers. Giant chain hotels, housing developments rolling up the sides of the hills, big-box stores, and John Lehman's Superferry are all expressions of that, with Governor Lingle as the eager facilitator. And, beyond development stands the ever-expanding military, facing west.

Local people know that only a generation ago, Hawai'i was entirely different. All the islands, O'ahu included, were once unfenced mountains, forests, and beaches, with no "private property" signs, no freeways, no shopping malls, no car lots, no big-box stores. Where there was once a generous mango tree, there's now a Whole Foods being built that will sell organic mangoes imported from Mexico for seven dollars a pound.

If you grew up in Hawai'i, you remember certain turning points, when the old Hawai'i was run over by the new Hawai'i. Suddenly, you saw daily traffic jams on tiny islands, river and ocean pollution, military exercises, missile firings, disastrous explosions of overdevelopment—all hints of the greater coming malaise. In 2004, two hundred melon-headed whales stranded themselves on the beach at Hanalei Bay, Kaua'i, their only escape from cerebellum-numbing vibrations of the Navy's "low-frequency" sonar experiments. In 2006, a man died after falling into Honolulu's Ala Wai Canal, after 48 million gallons of raw sewage flowed from Waikiki hotels into the waterway.

In 2008, Hanama'ulu Beach in Kaua'i was ranked the tenth most polluted beach in America. And what about those experimental agriculture test plots, growing genetically modified (GMO) crops; thousands of acres of techno-cornstalks and other plants, sprayed with terrible pesticides that the winds carry to neighborhoods and schoolyards; living laboratory experiments where new genetic plant life is created for corporate patenting? Astonishing—that Hawai'i, the home of sacred taro, the place of wild abundance, has become ground zero for corporate mad-scientist experiments to redesign and control the world's food supply, right here on these tiny islands, the most remote land masses in the world. How could our government let this all happen? Well. Hawai'i is a "company town," as much now as when sugar barons ran it.

For Native Hawaiians, some memories are especially bitter. Some still carry hard stones inside themselves from sorrowful stories of grandparents being beaten in school for speaking Hawaiian, or the shame on the family when a relative was forcibly banished to the leprosy settlement on Moloka'i. They may have painful memories of the great-uncle who lost his land when his signature on a transfer deed was forged; or, more recently, they may have been displaced by unaffordable housing or astronomical taxes to pay for the big new highways, so that tourists and military tanks can get around faster.

But still, Hawaiian culture has mostly held together, and it remains the soul of the islands. As with indigenous peoples everywhere, traditional Hawaiian culture is rooted in relationships with nature and each other, which is expressed in everyday activity: family gatherings at the beach that last for days and nights, *lu'au* for baby's first birthday, spear-fishing under the stars, hikes *mauka*[1] through forests to collect medicinal herbs or fragrant leaves and flowers for *lei*-making, or to hunt for wild pig to bake in the *imu*[2].

---

[1] *Mauka*: upland.
[2] *Imu*: pit oven.

All this activity, and others, becomes more difficult as open land is progressively impacted by development and as new fences appear.

Meanwhile, in parts of the islands where nature is still dominant, viable, and strong, people have lately sensed a strong negative shift. They feel upset about all the recent compromises to the islands' quality of life. Farmers now find it hard to farm, as they battle housing developments and biotech corporations. Surfers, swimmers, and fishers have to deal face to face with the increased pollution; and Native Hawaiians, as well as the descendants of plantation laborers, face ever-increasing pressure from unbridled property taxes to sell off their lands. *Haole*[3] newcomers, especially the New Agers, start to wonder, when did their nirvana disappear? Even the billionaires — those who've moved here and bought up huge land parcels—are not so sure they made the right move. *"Wouldn't we get more paradise per dollar on some small island off Belize? Or Madagascar?"*

So, what is Hawai'i? All of the above. It is a multiverse, an anthropological kaleidoscope. To some, it's a former colony; to others, it's still a colony. It's also a model for social relations in a globalized world, a place where genuine aloha has survived. And it's a battleground pitting overdevelopment—largely by absentee owners—against the local people and the environment. It's the western frontier of an expansionist society, still asserting its Manifest Destiny. It's a playground, and a wonder of nature. And, as we discuss later in this chapter, it *could* also become a model for sustainability before the world heads over the brink.

Given Hawai'i's amazing complexity and diversity, it is all the more remarkable that throngs of its citizens—at least those on the outer islands, where an intimacy with cultural roots, and with nature, is still an everyday experience—showed up, *spontaneously, yet in concert*, seeking to turn the Superferry back.

Earth Island

Admittedly, the Superferry cannot be blamed for most of the ills we've been describing. It is only one new expression of a century-long commodification process that has assaulted nature and local economies and cultures throughout the United States and, actually, the whole world. But in Hawai'i, especially among the neighbor islands of

---

[3] *Haole*: foreigner, usually a Caucasian. Literally: without breath.

Kaua'i, Maui, Moloka'i, and the Big Island, the Superferry tends to be viewed as a particularly galling expression of outside invasiveness, intrusion, fake altruism, soulless capitalism, globalization, commercialism, and false friendship. Its pompous displays of entitlement, the insider manipulations of local government, and, now, the disguised advance toward yet more *militarism*. The Superferry has struck a nerve on these islands. Lots of local people don't like it. They're frustrated and angry. They feel that things have now gone too far. They feel they've been ignored for decades by the powers-that-be, in particular about this project. They feel they've been had. This is a nerve only rarely struck here, so used to laissez-faire, where cultural training in aloha seems always to have allowed acceptance of corporate and military entries. Not this time. The protestors offer an uncomplicated message: *Pay attention to what we're saying, stop intruding in this place, stop manipulating us and the law, leave our island alone. No aloha for the Superferry!*

Has something shifted?

The great ecological leader of the 20th century, David Brower, executive director of the Sierra Club and founder of Friends of the Earth, frequently said, "We *all* live on islands." The Earth itself is an island oasis in space. Later in his life, Brower formed another organization, Earth Island Institute, as a monument to that idea and to spreading the "consciousness" of Earth as an island.

Brower argued that people on islands have, for the most part, instinctively grasped the absurdity of unlimited expansionist views. They see the limits of their own resources every day, limits that are everywhere apparent. The shoreline is there, right in front of you. You can drive around the island in an hour. You can only stuff so many sardines into a tiny can. The same reality applies to the whole Earth. There are limits to how much stuff can be mined or cut or removed or shipped, how much waste is possible, how much poison can be sprayed. And with climate change and the vast resources crises of our times, the boundaries of the Earth's capacities are clearly in view.

On the other hand, people still come to islands who *don't* see limits; they see opportunity, that is, commercial opportunity, profits. And there lies the crux of the problem. Absentee owners are not interested in local self-sufficiency or sustainability. And politicians like Linda Lingle have opened the gates of development for them.

She acts as if serving corporate growth is the ultimate purpose of her governorship. As she proclaimed at her inauguration, "Hawai'i is now open for business."

Most people who have spent their lives on islands have an extra sense. For survival's sake they have embodied a keener, innate awareness of *limits* than those of us who live on giant continents, where limits are hard to discern or imagine. Of course, there are some historical examples of island peoples who failed to abide by limits—the infamous Easter Island catastrophe, for example—and died because of it.[4] Yet that's not the typical case. Peoples of the Pacific, by and large, have managed to live comfortably and survive for millennia on often *very* tiny islands. They have trapped fish in the plentiful lagoons; they have stewarded the offerings of nature; they have grown and used what they needed. They have been sustained and guided by their cultural training, community involvement, and spiritual teachings that celebrate such indigenous values as reciprocity with nature; economies of limits and balance; the primary importance of *local* community and cooperation; and the integration and sense of kinship with nature and its beings. They have usually developed compatible political systems, as well, that encourage protection of and fair use of the natural commons.

The same could be said of most indigenous peoples everywhere on the planet, cognizant of natural limits, who are effectively treating their immediate environments *as if* they were islands, living within the natural offerings of a defined small region, eschewing expansionism, knowing that to survive well, over time, requires a respect for the limits of a place. Those who lose that awareness of and respect for limits do not survive. That certainly seems to be what's going on now in the wider world.

*   *   *

The great ecological crises of the dominant society today—climate change and the global depletion of some of the most crucial resources (fuels, freshwater, forests, fish in the seas, arable soils, key minerals like zinc, phosphorous, coltan, and so on) are caused by one central

---

[4] In just a few centuries, due to unclear causes that may have involved external pressures, the people of Easter Island wiped out their forest, drove their plants and animals to extinction, and saw their complex society spiral into chaos.

problem: the abandonment of the awareness that we live on a finite planet. There are limits. Yet the very idea of limits is, by definition, anathema to capitalist systems that require ever-increasing resource use and ever-increasing markets to sustain themselves. Modern society remains mentally encased in the prevailing economic paradigm that takes a view that is the polar opposite of the indigenous worldview. Modern economics is based on *no* limits, ever-increasing economic growth, constantly expanding commercial activity, and uncontrolled consumption of planetary resources, continuing non-stop forever.

Economic growth and expansionism are the fundamental bases of our economic system, its lifeblood. Corporate growth is the ultimate measure of corporate success; it determines stock values, profits, ability to attract investments, and CEO salaries. Candidates running for elected office get chosen or not based on whether they convince the public they can accelerate growth, while avoiding the reality that never-ending growth requires never-ending supplies of resources, a standard that is obviously preposterous—*insane*—on a finite planet. It's little wonder that after a century of this philosophy, the planet faces its greatest ecological crises ever. The entire prevailing global economic model is based on this utterly false premise.

The advancing ecological crises in Hawai'i are a microcosm of similar problems everywhere on Earth, caused by the same set of economic misassumptions. In Hawai'i we now see the death of the coral reefs, the loss of arable soils from pesticide poisoning, and the acceleration of species extinctions. Hawai'i is the endangered species capital of the world, with 379 entries on the endangered species list.

With the ecological limits of the whole Earth suddenly obvious, it is also obvious that the economic model based on *never-ending growth* cannot continue. Judging by the global financial crisis, which is partly caused by rising prices of scarce resources, from oil to arable soils, it may already be over. The most basic economic operating assumptions of the modern world are now subject to question. People who live on islands, where self-sufficiency equals survival, understand this instinctively. The prevailing modern practice of relying on materials and products that must flow endlessly from distant sources is a tenuous basis for survival.

We are facing a *systemic* crisis. And a crisis of consciousness. But, even as we are blaming the absurdities of the prevailing system, we do not absolve from blame the myriad individual corporate players who steer and execute their plans. The Superferry is one of those plans. The folks who run such companies are either oblivious to the bigger picture or indifferent. In any case, they continue to do their thing in Hawai'i, and everywhere else they can. They must be opposed, locally and globally.

* * *

The uprising on Kaua'i at Nawiliwili Harbor offers an excellent example of the empowering results of effective local direct action. The protesters understood the ecological limits of their fragile island. But, in the modern world of communications, they were also aware of wider implications, and *painfully* aware of the steady decline of our planet's health. They couldn't do much about the whole world, but they were not about to let their little corner of the planet fall sway to further global commercial and military invasions, at least not without a struggle. In Hawaiian, *kuleana* is the word for fulfilling one's responsibility. The protesters were acting on their kuleana. Thinking globally, acting locally.

Formidable segments of the Kaua'i community also act in other effective ways, such as by advancing a thriving, local, food self-sufficiency movement that seeks ultimately to feed the island's people without depending on imports. There are also growing movements to eliminate GMO agriculture and to revive traditional sustainable farming practices, particularly of ancient taro. And, very importantly, a broad cross section of the community has allied itself with Native Hawaiians seeking to reignite interest in their rights struggles, including the protection of traditional lands and burial grounds, now threatened by outside real-estate investment. On Kaua'i, the island has lately come alive on these matters.

The ecology of the planet is like a giant tapestry. When everyone takes responsibility to reweave his or her own threads in one small part of the tapestry, it has a chance to be whole again. The protesters at Nawiliwili came together to reweave their part of the tapestry. By standing up for a return to local control, local self-sufficiency, and local resource protection, and by turning the giant Superferry back, they became an unwitting model for community action in other places. When everyone acts in the interests of their local community, the global tapestry will be whole again. One of the purposes of this book is to try to assist that process.

Back-Story:
The Pacific, an "American Lake"

When we first started researching this project, certain colleagues in Hawai'i told us that the more they learned about the main issues involving the Superferry, the more they thought the biggest part of the story was its *military* aspect. The boat was just masking as public transportation in Hawaii, they said, so that it could perform live test runs on the open ocean to impress the U.S. Navy and help get a piece of the military contract for these kinds of high-speed catamarans that would be worth billions, as part of the Navy's plans to control Pacific Basin coastlines, especially in Asia. The addition of so many former high-ranking U.S. military leaders to the board of Superferry, and its very ownership, have clearly reinforced that point of view.

At first, we didn't want to believe such arguments. "It's mainly an environmental issue," we replied. And of course, it is also that. Yet the military aspects are obviously bigger than we'd realized and have been kept under wraps. It's a crucial part of the back-story, the deep roots of current events.

The United States has asserted its dominance throughout the Pacific Basin since at least the late 1800s. Projections of U.S. self-interest and authority in the Pacific began in earnest with the Spanish-American War, fought simultaneously in the Pacific and in the Caribbean. This led to the U.S. occupation of the Philippines, Cuba, Puerto Rico, and Guam in 1898, the same year as Hawai'i's annexation, with other islands soon to follow.

By the mid-20th century, Japan was advancing through the region, challenging U.S. commercial and military hegemony, leading eventually to the attack on Pearl Harbor and the giant Pacific war. During World War II, U.S. forces hopscotched across Pacific islands like Saipan, Midway, Wake, Tarawa, Iwo Jima, and Okinawa, and throughout the Micronesian islands, which cover an area the size of the continental United States and include the Marianas, the Marshalls, and the Carolines, which soon became a sprawling strategic U.S. Trust Territory.

The United States' military forces also notoriously occupied Bikini and Enewetok atolls, uprooting entire populations—which had supported themselves for centuries by reef fishing in the bountiful lagoons—moving the residents hundreds of miles away to uninhabited, reefless sandbars that offered little opportunity for the people to continue to sustain themselves without U.S. handouts of Spam, rice, and condensed milk, which have become the "local cuisine" for the entire Pacific. The purpose of the Bikini and Enewetok occupations was to test atomic bombs far away from the U.S. mainland. More than sixty years later, what remains of those islands is uninhabitable because of radiation fallout.

More recently, the United States took over and moved the people of Kwajalein, in the northern Marshall Islands, off their homelands to the island of Ebeye, yet another bare, inhospitable place without a fishing reef. From there, workers from Ebeye were daily taken by boat to their U.S. military jobs on Kwajalein and back. Meanwhile, the military did its best to convert the base on Kwajalein into a place where American military personnel would find the comforts of home; there is a golf course, a bowling alley, a movie theater—and a military base dedicated to our Star Wars missile program. That program remains highly active to this day, though there is scandalously little reporting about it.

The United States continues to maintain military bases spread all over the Pacific, especially in Guam and the rest of Micronesia, where nuclear airplanes and submarines are based, and which were key staging grounds for the Vietnam War. Hawai'i remains *Central Command* for all this, and is home to more than thirty military facilities, occupying about 5 percent of the total land area of the archipelago. Now, the military is advocating that the uninhabited Northwest Hawaiian Islands—whose last pristine coral reef stretches across an area larger than the state of California, and which was recently designated a National Monument—be used simultaneously for chemical warfare simulations, sonar activities, and new Navy missile interceptions, yet more appalling preparations of U.S. forces for protection of the nation's long-term (but unsustainable) commercial and military interests in the Pacific.[5]

---

[5] See Joseph Gerson and Bruce Birchard, *The Sun Never Sets* (Boston: South End Press, 1999), and Peter Hayes, Lyuba Zarsky, and Walden Bello, *American Lake* (New York: Penguin, 1986).

It is in the context of that history, as well as recent indications of preparations for conflict with China, that a future military role for the Hawaii Superferry (especially given the identity of its ownership and management) seems more plausible than not.

USS SUPERFERRY?

Over the last decade, according to U.S. military reports, China has been developing a fleet of high-speed boats to operate quickly, flexibly, and efficiently in and out of the countless inlets and bays found along its coastline, from North Korea, past Taiwan, and down to Vietnam. If there were to be future military actions in the Pacific region, the U.S. Navy believed it needed similar boats. So, a Pacific high-speed vessel *arms race* began.

That was the precipitating cause of the Navy's rush toward a Joint High Speed Vessel transport program, and the Littoral (shallow water) Combat Ship program being developed during Thomas Fargo's tenure as head of the U.S. Pacific Command—which contemplated having fifty-five or more ships deployed in the Pacific as soon as possible.

As pointed out by Joan Conrow and Philip Taubman in Part Three, the question for the Navy became this: *Where could it find an operational, fast, shallow-water vessel that could carry large numbers of troops, tanks and equipment in the Pacific and could also be quickly outfitted into a fighting vessel?* The answer was to adapt *existing* high-speed, shallow-water catamaran designs that had been used for civilian purposes. It would be fast and relatively inexpensive, compared with the exorbitant costs of building traditional warships. After the proven success of the Navy's use of an Austal catamaran as the Westpac Express, the Superferry design suddenly became quite valuable. For the Hawaii Superferry company, it may have looked like an opportunity to combine patriotic service with its overall mandate.

A few years ago, the U.S. Navy announced its formal competition for contracts for the Joint High Speed Vessel and the Littoral Combat Ship programs, as well as for continuation of the Westpac Express transportation program. In the two competitions, the Superferry's basic aluminum catamaran design—as manufactured by Austal USA—was among the finalists.

Subverting Legal Trivia: the EIS Saga

If Austal USA's Superferry design were to establish its viability as a successful prototype for the Navy contracts, one task remained—to get the vessel operational and into the water quickly. Meanwhile, the Superferry Company, increasingly indebted to Austal for its production work, had a parallel interest in getting the boat up and running, in order to establish itself commercially and satisfy investors. So, it was important to both companies that any legal "trivia" that might come up be minimal and not get in the way. The urgency of these concerns was expressed over and over through the years by Superferry CEO Garibaldi and Governor Lingle—particularly their demand that no time-consuming Environmental Impact Statements be required.

Garibaldi and Lingle usually blamed their anti-EIS position on Superferry investors who might withdraw if there were delays. They never named any specific investor, but in retrospect, we know there was only one dominant investor: John Lehman. Since his days as Navy secretary, Lehman has been an outspoken supporter of an expanded Navy Pacific fleet, and of programs like the Navy's LCS and JHSV programs, for which Austal was now competing for contracts. For all these reasons, the pressure for fast deployment was strong.

(In addition, as we mentioned in Chapter 1, Lehman's 2006 purchase of Atlantic Marine Holding Co., a shipyard adjacent to Austal in Mobile, Alabama, raised some conjecture that an Austal contract with the Navy might have some secondary benefits for Atlantic Marine.) But whether it was on behalf of Austal's vying for military contracts, long-range visions of a powerful Navy, or short-term commercial reasons, to slow the Superferry's rapid deployment in order to satisfy mandated federal or state Environmental Impact Statement requirements would have been beyond inconvenient. Especially as public concerns were rapidly rising about dangers to whales, dolphins, and sea turtles, as well as the transit of invasive species. Lawsuits were being filed; mass demonstrations had begun. A boat in the water could help make this a fait accompli, trumping any continued opposition.

Fortunately for the Superferry company and its causes, Hawai'i's governor was happy to accommodate influential individuals who could help enhance her position on the national stage. Governor Lingle, who had already received significant campaign donations from Superferry executives, joined by subservient state legislators, many of whom had also been subjects of corporate largesse, repeatedly saved the day. After years of public wrath, lawsuits, and a State Supreme Court ruling that the vessel could not sail before an EIS was complete, the governor and legislature still managed to get the ship in the water. Linda Lingle had proven equal to the task.

Only after she pushed through Act 2 did she finally permit the state to start preparing its own Environmental Impact Statement, though it was one that had been custom-tailored to suit Superferry's specific needs and was not nearly in conformance with previous environmental protection statutes. Federal and state environmental law had already defined an EIS as containing certain specific features, most notably a "no action alternative," which could have the effect of preventing the project from proceeding. But Act 2's new definition of an EIS eliminated the "no action alternative," and other features found in the bona fide EIS reports of the National Environmental Policy Act (NEPA) and its Hawai'i equivalent, HEPA.

Instead, Act 2 was written with the specific intent of allowing the vessel to continue operating, even as the study proceeded. It had no power at all to stop the boat, no matter how disastrous the environmental impacts might be. Although they call this invention an "EIS," it's not a real EIS at all, but rather a subversion of the goals of both NEPA and HEPA. It's a *fake* EIS. *(See Chapter 6, "The Sham Public Hearings," and also Chapter 12, by attorney Daniel Hempey.)*

So, in the end, without an EIS, as ordered by the Supreme Court, and with the boat in the water, Austal USA got to study and fix any kinks in its design, and the Navy got to see the ship as operational, thus helping Austal's chances for the lucrative Navy contracts. And the Superferry company got to start commercial service and retain the commitment of their unnamed investors. For Governor Lingle, excluding the public from meaningful input was just an unfortunate necessity to advance three higher causes: Superferry's financial viability, new military options in the Pacific, and her own career track in Republican national political circles. Hawai'i, it seems was just a pawn in the game. The citizens, excluded from major decisions—once again—were furious. We will hear directly from them in later chapters.

Note on the Shape of This Book

The body of this book is divided into three Parts. Part One, "Boiling Point," focuses on the uprisings at Nawiliwili Harbor on Kaua'i on August 26 and 27, 2007. The eruption gave birth to a movement, and it also gave birth to this book—and remains its first focus. How did it happen? Who were the individuals who rose up to stop the Superferry from docking on their shores? What was in their heads? Chapter 3 describes those events in detail.

Three weeks later came the next key moment, the monumental visit to Kaua'i by Governor Lingle, who attempted to squelch public reactions to her appalling and illegal behavior, and instead set them aflame. In Chapter 4, we present many of the most inspiring testimonies from that day, along with photos of most of the people speaking. Chapter 5, by former banker Michael Shooltz, describes the personal metamorphosis of his own perceptions, feelings, and actions as he evolved from observer to participant, finally joining dozens of others in the water at Nawiliwili on that landmark day.

Resistance to the Superferry is not confined to Kaua'i. Chapter 6 presents testimonies from people on Maui, the Big Island of Hawai'i, and Moloka'i at various *sham* public meetings that were required by law, but did not take the citizens' concerns seriously.

Especially interesting in this history is how each island emphasizes issues unique to its character: Maui presents well-organized, professional examinations of environmental issues, especially the problem of invasive species; the Big Island's focus is mostly on the possible drift of uranium from the Stryker war games; and on Moloka'i, the people are deeply worried about the lives of the whales and turtles, and also about the impact on the traditional cultural life of the islanders, most of them Native Hawaiians.

Part Two of the book, "Evolution of a Boondoggle: History and Chronology," presents in two chapters a detailed, month-by-month history of the key events in the development of Superferry, from its inception in 2001 to the moment we go to press in October 2008.

We came to realize that a detailed history of the myriad overlapping narratives would be helpful both to us and to any other journalists or scholars interested in figuring out what has really been going on in this story. For those readers who have the patience to go through it in detail, slowly—there are several hundred entries, and it reads rather like a puzzle waiting to be solved—there are surprises and rewards. As far as we know, no similar narrative time line, wrought to this degree of detail, exists. If you don't need that kind of detail, skip forward.

Part Three, "Insider Reports," presents in-depth reporting about some of the most significant issues concerning the environment, the law, and militarization. First, there are three chapters on the key environmental questions—by Hannah Bernard, a Hawai'i marine biologist and activist, who has studied the traumas caused by ships to whales in this region; by mainland journalist Teri Shore, who presents a similar report on the broader global problem of the dangers of high-speed ocean vessels to whale populations; and by the Sierra Club's Lance Holter, whose focus is invasive species and the opportunities for them made possible by the Superferry.

The next set of articles deals with legal issues. Attorney Dan Hempey, the lead advocate in Kaua'i's litigation, reviews the state of play for several of the cases related to the Superferry, and the strategies that the company and the governor used to thwart them. State Senator Gary Hooser (one of the few senators who consistently stood up against the Superferry) provides his reasoning in his speech opposing the Act 2 law, now being challenged in the courts.

Finally, we present five articles on the military dimensions of this story. Journalist Joan Conrow explains the Navy's plans for its expanded Pacific fleet, and the role of the Superferry in those plans. Philip Taubman, of the *New York Times*, gives the history of the Navy's extremely troubled efforts to get a boat built, which reads like a Keystone Cops adventure in bad boat-construction practices. Two articles follow, by Hawai'i activists Haunani-Kay Trask and Kyle Kajihiro, on the history of militarism in Hawai'i. Finally, we present the transcript of a shocking interview from radio station KKCR, on Kaua'i, with workers at Austal USA, in Mobile, Alabama, one of whom has been building the second Superferry vessel, and the military prototype boats, as well. Their discomforting message is that the vessels may not be altogether safe.

Part One

Boiling Point

Chapter Three

Incident at Nawiliwili Harbor

Koohan Paik

August 26, 2007

The Superferry appeared on the horizon, headed straight at us. One-and-a-half times the length of a football field, five stories high, the uninvited menace had burned nearly 6,000 gallons of diesel from Honolulu to Kauaʻi. This was its maiden voyage. The ultimate mission would be to deliver as many as 282 vehicles and 866 passengers daily onto the increasingly crowded and polluted shores of our tiny, still-wonderful island of Kauaʻi.

Built for maximum speed, and with the efficiency of a giant samurai sword, the ship's enormous catamaran blades slice through ancient calving and birthing grounds for thousands of whales, areas rich with dolphins, monk seals, sea turtles, and other marine life. The ship is also certain to transport an array of invasive species to exquisite and fragile ecosystems already in crisis. *No way.* We could not let it happen. We *would not* let it happen.

This voyage to Kauaʻi is an act of aggression. We believed that when the Kauaʻi County Council unanimously passed a resolution to require Hawaii Superferry Corporation to prepare an Environmental Impact Statement (EIS), it would have carried some weight. We believed that when 10 percent of our island's population signed a petition *demanding* an EIS, our voices would count for something. Then when state senators arrived to collect testimonies from a room spilling over with citizens demanding, "EIS First!" we believed an impact statement would be required, but the bill never got out of committee. And, finally—following a *unanimous* State

Supreme Court ruling to *require* an EIS—we thought we had won. But Governor Linda Lingle and her Department of Transportation ignored the Supreme Court ruling and greenlighted the Superferry to move its launch date *forward* by several days. It was as though our elected leaders had turned on us. For those of us who still believed in the principles of democracy, it was a nightmare coming to life.

So, when we saw this gigantic catamaran enter the harbor, specifically sized to transport heavy military vehicles (as we later discovered), racing headlong toward us in flagrant disregard of all our efforts, we were *outraged*. About 1,500 of us *spontaneously* gathered at the dock to try once again to make clear what our state officials had refused to hear: We would *not* allow this luxury monstrosity on our shores until an EIS had been satisfactorily completed. We chanted, sang, and beat drums. We brandished banners and waved *ti* leaves, the sacred plant that wards off evil while calling in good.

In that moment, all the remnants of the old sugar-era manipulations that had pitted race against race, class against class, vanished. Shoulder-to-shoulder stood Native Hawaiians; Japanese-, Filipino-, Portuguese-, and Chinese-American descendents of plantation workers; descendents of American missionaries; and transplants from North America who have been calling Kaua'i home for as long as forty years and as short as six months. Lawyers, musicians, small farmers, students, doctors, college professors, politicians, writers, New Age haoles, woodworkers, social workers, nurses, mechanics, architects—every part of Kaua'i's community was represented.

The coup de grâce came from a few dozen surfers who suddenly leaped from the jetty's rocky edge to paddle out toward the mouth of Nawiliwili Harbor. Most were kids. There they sat, straddling their boards, looking as small as mice, in comparison to the skyscraper-high ship, yet they blocked it from moving forward—a sort of Tiananmen Square challenge in the waters of Kaua'i! It was dangerous; they went right up under the bow of the mammoth boat. Then dozens more swimmers jumped into the water, some with boogie boards, and headed out toward the ship, despite the strident warnings from officials in Coast Guard and police boats. No one was killed, but they could have been.

As for the rest of us, we lined the dock, many hoisting signs and shouting, "GO HOME" and "EIS FIRST!"

Afterward, a passenger on the Superferry, when interviewed by a Honolulu TV station, said that when she saw the crowd waiting on the pier, she mistook it for a *welcoming* party of Natives, the kind mythologized in the early days of Hawai'i tourism. Only when she was in earshot of the angry slogans did she realize she was on a ship headed for trouble.

Until that moment, that passenger from Honolulu had had no idea whatsoever of the concerns and growing anger and resistance to the ship that had been rising up on the "outer islands" of Kaua'i, Maui, and the Big Island. We on Kaua'i had been pushing petitions, writing letters, filing lawsuits, and testifying to the legislature demanding an EIS, a full report on how this alien vessel would impact our already environmentally stressed island. But to state officials, we seemed not to exist. We were *equally* invisible to an O'ahu-centric media. Our voices had been effectively silenced. The rest of the archipelago knew nothing of our discontent, and we knew little of theirs—until the Kaua'i protests.

When the community turned out to block the boat, our protest was briefly covered by the North American media, including the *New York Times* and *Los Angeles Times*, with a degree of admiration. But the local press remained disdainful and sloppy. One oft-broadcast video clip, claiming to show "violent" protesters pounding on the hood of an SUV that had just disembarked the Superferry, was both humiliating and infuriating to us—and *wrong*. Actually, the people slamming the car were trying to draw the driver's attention to a man who, in an act of nonviolent resistance, lay down in the path of the vehicle's front tires. This was never revealed by the mainstream media. Kip Goodwin, an eyewitness, later described it:

> When someone opened the gate to let cars off the Superferry, the first vehicle out, an SUV, was faced with a crowd of protesters. The driver, who was tensely chewing gum at seemingly a mile a minute, nosed forward, his white knuckles gripping the steering wheel, while a man lay down on the pavement in front of the tires, prompting hysteria and yelling. Some protesters surrounded the vehicle shouting warnings to the driver about the man only three feet in front, but the noise was too loud to hear anything. Others grabbed the man on the

ground and pulled him to safety. Trying to get the driver's attention, a woman batted her paper poster at the windshield and a man slapped on the hood with his hands.

It was hardly violent, but it became the prevalent television encapsulation of the event, repeated on news shows for weeks, as if it were the World Trade Center twin towers tumbling down.

The Superferry did eventually dock that night, but before it could, it had to hover on the ocean horizon for two hours, while a tense standoff took place between surfers and Coast Guard boats festooned with M16 rifles. Finally, the Coast Guard managed to herd away the surfers like goats, clearing a path for the ship to enter. The passengers waited late into the night for the angry crowd to disperse, persuaded by SWAT teams. The weary travelers finally disembarked around nine in the evening. As the ship slunk away into the distance, a shooting star arc'd green through the sky, fizzling to nothing just above the harbor. The Hawaiians cheered, "*Hoʻailona!*"—a good omen.

August 27, 2007

The next evening, the vessel returned, and the number of people in the water doubled. Protesters in kayaks and traditional Hawaiian outrigger canoes joined those on surfboards to form a human blockade. Onshore were SWAT teams from Oʻahu holding back German shepherds. A handful of arrests were made, which included four children, but they could not clear away the citizens in the water. After three hours, the boat was forced to back out of the harbor and return to Oʻahu. A second hoʻailona—the smoky-orange orb of a full lunar eclipse—glowed over Nawiliwili like a Chinese lantern.

Onshore, someone thanked one of the surfers for staying the course in the cold water, as the hours dragged on. The surfer responded that they never could have done it without the *mana*, the spirit, of those on the shore. "Us guys were the arrow. You guys were the bow." Bow and arrow needed each other to successfully hit the mark. The Superferry has not returned to Kauaʻi since.

Without any individual leaders calling us forward, but sharing a mutual sense of alarm, Kauaʻi's people spontaneously showed up, in the thousands. It was a seminal moment.

* * *

As discussed in the introductory chapters, this eruption had been developing for decades. It's as though people were just waiting for the right stimulus to act. The Superferry itself was not the most egregious example of commercial or military excess, but it came after decades of frustration and humiliation, as the people saw their island steadily diminish in character and mood, while their pleadings had been ignored by the powers-that-be. As for the governor over in Honolulu?—she may as well have lived 5,000 miles away in New York, sharing tea with John F. Lehman. Lingle had shown only haughtiness and unconcern when people tried to raise issues.

By the time the Superferry showed up, displaying its own high degree of entitlement and ignorance of local concerns, it was seen as a foreign monster, a prime example of corporate soullessness that may not have been unique in Hawaiian history, but had arrived at the wrong moment. The people knew what to do. The mood of the island shifted. It marked the turning point of consciousness, political will, and self-determination. The citizens on Kaua'i were transformed.

Feverish protests also took place on Maui, and people voiced strong opposition on the Big Island and Moloka'i, too, but Kaua'i's sudden uprising was the vanguard—a unified outburst from a full cross section of the kinds of people and groups that rarely find themselves fighting on the same side: old-time residents, including Japanese and Filipino farmers; bureaucrats who sadly expressed the feeling that the quality of life in the islands is suffering from crowding, noise, and traffic; haole environmentalists aghast at the island's overdevelopment; newcomers who had come to realize that the beautiful island they fled to is being destroyed by tourism and commerce that is overrunning the landscape; Native Hawaiians striving to retain the integrity of the 'aina and their culture; school kids joining their parents and teachers; and *surfers*, leaping into the water as human shields against the juggernaut. This level of shared commitment to a common cause had not been seen for a generation on this laid-back island normally described as "paradise," the greenest island in all Hawai'i.

The images of surfers in the water blocking the boat and protesters on land blocking the tourists, while shouting, "Save the whales!"

and "Protect the 'aina!" and the *demands* that the governor and the ferry company honor the Supreme Court ruling, were *not* good public relations for a Superferry project whose legal authority to operate was sketchy, at best. Worst of all, it was obviously *spontaneous* and *leaderless*: ordinary people exploding in frustration against willful corporations and collusive government leaders. And it all came *before* the full awareness, then developing, that there were also significant military dimensions to the story.

Three weeks after the events at Nawiliwili Harbor, there was a third fateful date. That was September 20, 2007, when Governor Lingle made her one greatest mistake, rooted in her own blind arrogance, by descending upon Kaua'i to declare that her decisions were final, and to threaten the protesters with fines and imprisonment. The people were outraged, and poured forth three hours of eloquent testimonies, which form the centerpiece—the heart and soul—of this book.

The Hijacking of Aloha

An important subtext weaves its way almost invisibly through much of this story: the prevailing Hawai'i etiquette to always show "aloha spirit." As a result, *any* public protest in Hawai'i has been considered quixotic at best, offensive at worst, and always in poor taste as a transgression against the spirit of aloha. The ancient, culturally rooted aloha spirit has in recent years been appropriated and perverted by the "hospitality industry" to commercially package the Hawaiians as the most loving, welcoming people in the world, and, regrettably, it has evolved into a kind of shackle against Hawaiian self-defense. If challenged—by the absence of a smile, or refusal to welcome every stranger (or megahotel or real-estate developer or biotech agricultural corporation or Superferry) that rolls in—it gives rise to criticism from those in control of Hawai'i's economy, and also from some locals. It's as though we are all suffering from a gigantic case of Stockholm Syndrome, in which the victim comes to identify with the forces working against him or her. Others call it "plantation mentality."

The Hawaiians' genuine and sublime quality of aloha—*the quality of loving openness, welcoming, receptiveness, inclusion, love*—has been cynically twisted and effectively used against the Hawaiian people themselves. The sugar industry first exploited it to gain easy entry, and later, the tourism industry turned *aloha* into a kind of brand. Today, aloha is a term that insinuates itself into every aspect of daily life, endlessly parroted in sales pitches for condos, helicopter tours, timeshares—and, of course, Superferries. Anyone who stands against these intrusions is seen as not showing enough aloha. Where there are *not* tourist promotions in Hawaii, the aloha spirit is quickly offered to the world's biggest laboratory experiments for biotech agriculture—Monsanto, Pioneer, Syngenta, and others—sucking even sacred taro into the machine, the ancient staple of culture, economy, and diet, now alienated from its roots, now *patented*, owned, and controlled by giant megacorporations. As a result, all challenges against any scale of economic or cultural invasion are deemed *not in the aloha spirit*.

The perennial Hawai'i newspaper headline declaring the status of tourism dollars sets a climate in which the perpetuation of any image other than that of a profitably welcoming paradise is considered sacrilege. God forbid if photos go out over the Internet showing throngs of angry residents on the pier, shaking their fists and beating their chests at an approaching Superferry. God forbid that the natives might be restless. In fact, in a private meeting with Kaua'i activists after the fact, Superferry's then-CEO John Garibaldi indicated that nothing could have been a worse PR disaster for the company than precisely that. But the protests also created schisms within communities, as "not being in the aloha spirit." Cleverly, Governor Lingle and the Superferry Corporation repeated that charge over and over—regrettably, with some effect. The implication was that no protest is acceptable.

Defending the Rural Soul

September 20, 2007

We finished our prayers at the County Building grounds and marched solemnly toward the auditorium. Many held up "EIS First!" signs, many wore T-shirts with slogans, and many waved ti leaves. Although we were a multifarious throng, we shared a controlled deliberation in every step we took, a vigilance that united and strengthened us. One of the Native Hawaiian elders advised us,

"Once we are inside the auditorium, we will wait until Governor Lingle asks for permission to enter. Then we will welcome her. That is Hawaiian protocol." Although this elder had admonished against any belligerence, there was no ambiguity to her message: It was we, Kaua'i's people, who must be in control of this meeting.

Well, things don't always turn out as planned. By the time we passed strategically positioned police officers and sat down in the auditorium, Governor Lingle was already milling around and shaking hands, trailed by bodyguards and television crews. She had come to tell us, in no uncertain terms, that the Superferry *would* return to Kaua'i, and when it did, we would not be allowed within a large, newly designated "security zone." Anyone violating these new boundaries would be subject to arrest under federal antiterrorism law, carrying a fine of up to $10,000 and imprisonment up to ten years.

Quickly, a sense of agitation, as tangible and slippery as a mongoose, gripped the room. Within minutes, the police locked the doors to any latecomers, even after more seats became available. People outside, climbing up to the windows to hear, were driven off by the officers. Inside, the genuine aloha that had flowed only an hour earlier at the County Building yielded to the urgency of dire community concerns.

The governor had apparently intended the meeting to serve as a signal that she was bringing the full weight of her office to bear in enforcing the new security zone, which would enable the Superferry to enter Nawiliwili without protest or confrontation. What instead unfolded was a dramatic reversal of roles—instead of the governor speaking *down* to her subjects, it was the people speaking powerfully to her—in a cavalcade of brilliant, heartfelt oratory. Most spoke spontaneously, "shooting from the hip" with very little preparation (we were given only two days' notice of the meeting), in passionate defense of their 'aina, of their civil rights, of marine life, and of the island's rural soul.

Every testimony burst with intensity. Every speaker knew that the interests of the Superferry, of the state, of the military-industrial complex, and of the citizens of Kaua'i were all converging at this particular point in time and space where we were given a shot—just one shot—to penetrate Lingle's robotic demeanor. The speeches exploded forth in a rainbow of dialects and language. Some were Shakespearean in power. Others were simpler but equally impassioned and revealing. Altogether, they told a timeless story, the story of a community that would stop at nothing to defend their ʻaina and their rights.

The next morning, I hurried to the newsstand to read how impressed the Honolulu papers must have been with our homegrown orators. How naive I was. I should have realized that the front page would trumpet only the sensational: GOVERNOR HECKLED OVER HAWAII SUPERFERRY. Corporate media were painting us as a fringe of unruly louts and NIMBY-minded mainlanders. Anti-aloha spirit!

The good news was that Superferry had, once again, postponed service to Kauaʻi indefinitely. The reason? Our "outlandish" behavior. No, I thought, that could not have been the whole reason. It had to have been more; it had to have been the words themselves—what people were actually saying—that haunted Governor Lingle later that evening. In sober retrospect, however, it is clear that our victory was most likely rooted in the fear that more news reports showing angry protesters would, alas, shatter the lucrative image of Hawaiʻi as the aloha-spirited Shangri-La. That's a line the paradise brokers will not cross.

The Distinct Character of Each Island

A year has passed and the Superferry still has not dared to again set sail for Kauaʻi. Meanwhile, the vessel invades Maui daily—twice on some days. The question begs examining: Why were we so successful on Kauaʻi? Whenever I visit a neighbor isle, I am consistently lauded with "You guys rock!" referencing the Nawiliwili incident. But seriously, if Kauaʻi could stave off the ship, why couldn't Maui? Maui has more than double our population, plus an impressive coalition of environmental institutions that had hired a lawyer with a proven track record. And they even won their case in the State Supreme Court!

Each island has its own separate, singular identity. Maui is different from Kauaʻi, and both are distinct from Oʻahu. The same goes for the Big Island. Each island responds to any given situation uniquely.

One prominent resident of Maui gave me her thoughts. She felt that because Maui's high-profile environmental institutions—Maui Tomorrow, Sierra Club, Friends of Kahului Harbor—had been working since 2005 on Superferry resistance, and had filed highly promising lawsuits, the public there may have felt a false sense of security that "things were being taken care of" by "professionals." By contrast, Kaua'i's residents, for the most part, knew nothing of the new venture until a year later, in 2006. They had no sense of security, false or otherwise, that anyone had been advocating on their behalf. So when the ship actually set sail for Kaua'i, panic set in. Then rage. In the end, Kaua'i's residents had only their bodies to block the behemoth from docking.

Kaua'i did have two specific advantages. The first was KKCR, the volunteer-run community radio station that would broadcast up-to-the-minute news, call-in shows, and commentary as each episode of the Superferry saga unfolded. It kept the story present, immediate, and very alive. Everyone heard viewpoints that they would have never, ever heard otherwise. As the radio station informed the island's residents of meetings and rallies, it also created a cohesion across race and class lines by providing a discussion space over the airwaves in which ideas could be introduced, pondered, and developed, regardless of demographics. No other island had a station like this, and it could never have happened in commercial radio, nor on continent-oriented National Public Radio.

The second key factor in the success of Kaua'i's solidarity was the proactive work of the Polynesian Kingdom of Atooi, a Native Hawaiian sovereignty group whose members make it a point to be racially inclusive. Their commitment to bridge-building shone at Nawiliwili, as Atooi marshals tended to the needs (water, food, transportation, and the defusing of tension) of a feisty crowd that might have otherwise strayed into chaos. No favoritism was based on Hawaiian-ness.

Yet the bottom line was this: The Superferry stayed away for the simple reason that *there is power in direct action*. We saw it firsthand. In this case, dozens of citizens jumping on surfboards may actually have worked better than a triumph in court, especially considering that the governor ultimately abrogated the legal decision, anyway. *People power* was what delivered the message so compellingly on Kaua'i. It was a message that Hawaii Superferry Corporation heard, loud and clear.

There are also the more remote islands, Moloka'i and Lana'i. You'd have to drag Moloka'i's people kicking and screaming to part with that island's sweeping rural landscapes, dotted with livestock, and its neighborhoods studded with old fruit trees and small gardens. On Molokaʻi, functioning traditional Hawaiian fishponds still feed people, using ancient, sophisticated aquaculture techniques. Molokaʻi elder Ruth Manu expressed her island's connection to the natural world at a hearing for Governor Lingle's sham EIS *(see Chapter 6)* in this way:

> To me, the ferry don't even belong here. ... If you think you goin' do that on the island of Molokaʻi, I object to it. One hundred percent. We don't need it. ... Sustainability is very important on the island of Molokaʻi. Even if you don't have enough jobs, we're making a way where we can still feed our family and stay as an ʻohana.

It's no surprise that, in a similar situation several years ago when cruise ships were trying to make Molokaʻi a port of call, the islanders there rallied at the docks and permanently turned away the first (and last) cruise ship.

And finally, there is Oʻahu, whose principal city and the state capital, Honolulu, is a kind of Manhattan of the Pacific. Dubbed the Gathering Place, the island has largely given itself over to tourism, development, urbanism, and globalization, so it's par for the course that on Oʻahu, the Superferry would elicit a high degree of indifference, and even enthusiasm. Unlike on Molokaʻi, the needs of Oʻahu's residents are not met by the land under their feet or the sea that surrounds them, but instead through long-distance shipping. Fresh milk, meat, eggs, vegetables—even seafood—all come from thousands of miles away. The Superferry fits perfectly into Oʻahu's economic paradigm of expanding markets and global connectivity, at the unfortunate expense of environmental health and indigenous culture.

The Superferry controversy has brought into stark relief the contrast between Oʻahu's and Kauaʻi's economic paradigms, and has led to an uncomfortable schism in the archipelago that reflects those who swear by an economy dependent on growth, versus those who believe it rests on sustainability. For the past several years, Kauaʻi's people have been working to shape their destiny in a very specific way: The island boasts the most diverse and abundant farmers' markets of all the islands, selling everything from kale to mangosteens to chocolate; independent citizens are working to set up alternative energy sources from wind, waves, and even hamburger grease; small-scale farmers supply residents with beef, chicken, pork, and goat cheese; scores of well-attended workshops are conducted on organic, biodynamic, and traditional Hawaiian farming; community gardens are popping up everywhere, including in schoolyards; and a growing movement is mounting opposition to the fields of experimental GMO test plots spread over the landscape like a horrible patchwork quilt. Kaua'i's grassroots activists have been on a path toward self-reliance that was not about to be disrupted by some Superferry.

Longing for *Hanabata* Days

To Kaua'i's people, the Superferry is a direct threat to all they've worked for and the fully sustainable island they wish to be. But to O'ahu's people, those on Kaua'i seem negative, if not downright prehistoric, for not embracing an "opportunity" like the Superferry that would connect them with all the goodies offered by the outside world. Anytime a news story pops up on the Internet about the Superferry, hundreds of *anti*-protester comments from Oahuans direct cyber vitriol toward Kaua'i. It all seems strangely excessive.

Some theorize that the overreaction stems from a certain envy and admiration for the outer islands, in view of how they have retained many of the values and much of the nature that O'ahu has lost in recent years. Oahuans, this view holds, want to "have it all," but also to have the option of stepping back to simpler days through a handy three-hour boat ride (with their SUVs) to charming outer islands, which still have the qualities they gave up.

So, here come a couple of thousand Kaua'i people saying, *No. It doesn't work that way. We are the ones who live here. We are protecting this place. You can't bring over hundreds of cars at a time, trampling the forests, reefs, and beaches, carrying invasive species, endangering whales, especially without having conducted a legal environmental review.* For many people of O'ahu, it isn't just their vacations that are being denied them; it's their childhood, when O'ahu had more in common with the outer islands than with San Jose, California, as it does today.

Maui resident Karen Chun had this insightful explanation for the unusually inflamed reactions from Oʻahu:

> You know, Oʻahu's so changed now, so urban. People there have a real longing for *hanabata* days.[6] They view the outer islands as a bit of their lost past. So when the outer-islands guys say they don't want the Superferry bringing over the Oʻahu people, the people from Oʻahu respond with pure emotion. They feel as if the outer islands folks have actually stolen something very precious from them. It is such an emotional thing, it's about their lost past. And they're beyond being reasoned with.

The clash of economic paradigms lies at the root of the schism between Oʻahu, Kauaʻi, and the rest of the islands. But actually *all* the islands share the common experience of rapid, continual development and the social as well as emotional upheaval that comes with it. Throughout the islands, Superferry has served as a flashpoint, triggering deeply felt reactions.

THE PIKO

Ancient lore refers to Hawaiʻi as the *piko*—the navel—of the Pacific. Polynesians to this day recognize the islands as an important geographic pressure point. And in some cosmic irony, the U.S. military also recognizes the archipelago's significance. From an American geopolitical perspective, Hawaiʻi's purpose has always been to function as *mission control* for its military endeavors. And who could ask for better positioning? Just as a castle is surrounded by a protective moat, Hawaiʻi is protected by the widest moat in the world—the Pacific Ocean. It is from here that U.S. imperial actions advance, and it is back here again that they retreat. Stryker tanks and troops train at Pohakuloa on the Big Island, travel to Iraq to throw U.S. weight around in deadly ways, then return back to the Aloha State. Kyle Kajihiro of the American Friends Service Committee aptly compares the U.S. military to a giant octopus with its brain in Hawaiʻi and tentacles outstretched to every corner of the planet.

---

[6] In Hawaiʻi's local lexicon, *hanabata days* means one's childhood, derived from the Japanese word for nose (*hana*) and the Pidgin English word for butter (*bata*). In other words, "the days of runny noses."

As lucrative as the industries of tourism and real estate are, they are secondary to Hawai'i's foremost function for U.S. interests. Conveniently, those glitzy ads of hula girls have so successfully trivialized these islands that, even in the minds of the most conspiracy-seeking radicals, not to mention Cokie Roberts, Hawai'i remains little more than a frivolity. In fact, nothing could be further from the truth, considering that the state's federal defense funding, vast population of military personnel, mammoth tracts of military-controlled land, and volume of high-tech classified weaponry all exceed those of any other state. Marketing has triumphed to disguise the *real* agenda of the U.S. military presence in Hawai'i, a phenomenon that continues with the Superferry. Fun-for-the-whole-family advertising has obfuscated the layers of military agenda floating barely submerged beneath the Hawaii Superferry, making it the perfect metaphor for Hawai'i's shadow role in imperial stagings.

Both military tacticians and Polynesian *kahuna*[7] acknowledge that what happens in Hawai'i *energetically* affects the rest of the world. Singer/songwriter Liko Martin, an elder with the Kingdom of Atooi, elaborates on how the scales can tip one way or the other: "If Hawai'i stays oppressed," he points out, "that oppression emanates throughout the whole planet. If Hawai'i is free, then aloha spreads out over the Earth. Because it's the piko."

Holding Actions

Most of the people who showed up on the docks to beat away the big boat would not call themselves activists. We showed up because we simply couldn't stomach another ignored attempt to be heard through traditional channels, and we had nothing left but our bodies and voices and nonviolent protest. Only in retrospect have we been able to digest that what we did is called direct-action activism and that it has a long, illustrious history of effecting positive political change. With no political pull, no mainstream media influence, and no funding whatsoever, we miraculously prevailed over the undemocratic agenda of both the governor and the Hawaii Superferry Corporation, with its hundreds of thousands of dollars in lobbying and campaign donations and its owner's influence at the Pentagon.

---

[7] *Kahuna*: priest, sorcerer, magician, minister, or expert in any field.

We learned a valuable lesson: All we needed to do was stand—or rather, surf—*together*.

No, it wasn't a "done deal" after all, as they had told us again and again.

As we go to press, however, one year after that pivotal night at Nawiliwili, the company is again making overtures toward Kaua'i. CEO Tom Fargo has begun his campaign to "talk story" (his imitation of Hawaiian homey jargon) with the island's three mayoral candidates and the head of the Chamber of Commerce, to scope out community sentiment, before strategizing Superferry's next penetration. Now that we're dealing with an admiral here—a military tactician—the battle will get tougher. As environmentalist David Brower always said, "There are no ultimate victories, only holding actions. They always come back." The struggle to stave off the relentless violations to government ethics and our natural resources sometimes seems daunting. But rather than give in to defeatism in the face of the challenges clearly ahead, we can draw inspiration from the August 2007 uprising on Kaua'i.

In the following chapter, that inspiration is expressed in the testimonies directed to Governor Lingle when she took the stage in Kaua'i, three weeks after the incident at Nawiliwili Harbor.

Chapter Four

Governor Lingle Visits Kaua'i

Testimonies of the Citizens

THIS CHAPTER PRESENTS *many of the testimonies given three weeks after the harbor protests, when Governor Lingle came to Lihu'e to have a word with Kaua'i's residents. She did not give much notice, only forty-eight hours'. Neither did she announce that the singular purpose of this meeting was to tell the public that they would be heavily penalized with fines and jail for further protests in violation of newly imposed security rules.*

* * *

Despite the short notice, some 1,500 people filled the hall to capacity, and dozens more were turned away by police surrounding the building. The mood of the room was festive but outraged.

As the community members entered the auditorium, they were handed two documents summarizing the "Consequences for Violation" of the new security zone at Nawiliwili Harbor. The documents were prepared by the U.S. Coast Guard and the State of Hawai'i. They defined the boundaries of the security zone, in the waters of the harbor and on the land near where the boat would dock.

The criminal penalties enumerated for failing to comply "with orders related to the security zone" included "imprisonment for up to 10 years" and fines of "up to $10,000." Violations could also bring confiscation of any canoes, kayaks, or surfboards used in the protests, as well as civil fines of up to $32,500 per day.

Governor Lingle mounted the stage with what she militaristically called her "Unified Command."

If the purpose of the Unified Command was to scare away future protests with the severity of its penalties, the purpose of the 1,500 people in the room was to tell the powers-that-be that if the ship would not comply with Hawai'i environmental law, it would not dock in their port again. It made for a wild evening. Thirty-three people gave formal testimonies at the public meeting. Thirty-one were against the ferry; two were in favor. In this chapter, we present nineteen of the speeches. In Chapter 6, we present testimonies from other meetings.

The evening begins with welcome 'oli[8] delivered by Native cultural practitioner Sabra Kauka, along with schoolchildren from Kanuikapono Hawaiian Charter School and members of the community. A Christian prayer follows. Then, Barry Fukunaga, followed by Rear Admiral Sally Brice-O'Hara, formally delivers the Unified Command's admonitions about penalties.

Neither Fukunaga nor Brice-O'Hara can be heard over the shouts of protest from the audience. In fact, as Brice-O'Hara turns on her heel to leave the podium, the rumblings in the audience build into a thunderous chant of the words "EIS! EIS!" (Environmental Impact Statement), for several long minutes. The Unified Command glance from corner to corner of the auditorium, like confused poultry in a chicken trap. Kaua'i County

GOVERNOR LINDA LINGLE WITH HER "UNIFIED COMMAND," LIHU'E, KAUA'I—SEPTEMBER 20, 2007

Pictured, from left to right: Department of Transportation Director Barry Fukunaga, Captain Vince Atkins, Rear Admiral Sally Brice-O'Hara, Interim Kaua'i Chief of Police Clayton Arinaga, Kaua'i Mayor Bryan Baptiste, Governor Linda Lingle. (Not pictured: Interim Director of Department of Land and Natural Resources Laura Thielen and First Deputy Attorney General Lisa Ginoza.) Standing: Cultural practitioner Sabra Kauka (not with Unified Command).

---

[8] *Oli:* traditional Hawaiian chants.

Councilwoman JoAnn Yukimura stands up from the audience and holds out her arms, schoolteacher-style, to quiet everyone down. It takes a moment, but she succeeds. Soon after, she takes her place at the microphone to offer her remarks. She and all the other speakers direct most of their comments to the governor, who also acts as moderator.

JoAnn Yukimura

JoAnn Yukimura has championed sustainability, conservation, and affordable housing ever since she began her political career in the 1970s. In 1988, she was elected mayor of Kaua'i, the first female mayor of Japanese ancestry in the United States. Her grandmother, Takayo Masuda Yoshioka, whose family was from Hiroshima, was born on a sugar plantation at Makaweli on Kaua'i's west side.

Aloha, Governor Lingle and members of the panel. Welcome to Kaua'i. I mean that. Welcome to Kaua'i. *Mahalo nui loa.*[9] Mahalo nui loa for coming to our island to hear our *mana'o*[10] about the Superferry. We welcome you with aloha. We know you bear the heavy burden of leadership. Being governor is not an easy job. Especially when there is an island like Kaua'i. *[Many people in the room chuckle.]* We give thanks for your willingness to do the job.

Yet, even as we welcome you with compassion and aloha, we want you to know that we cannot and *will not* hold back on the hard questions. There is too much at stake for our island not to speak up. But it is our intention to speak with respect and aloha, and *[turning to the audience]* I ask each one of you tonight to speak with aloha.

It is our prayer and vision that what unfolds tonight will lead to the highest good for our island and the state. When you make decisions on our behalf, we expect our leaders to be thorough, thoughtful, fair, and far-sighted. Full of discernment, as Haunani Apoliona would say. We expect our leaders to consult with us—those who stand to be the most affected by the Superferry—and I acknowledge that you're here tonight to listen with a genuine understanding that our comments, our concerns, and proposed solutions are important, have value, and can help in making the right decision.

---

[9] *Mahalo nui loa*: Thank you very much.
[10] *Mana'o*: thoughts, knowledge.

In return, we pledge to listen carefully, to listen with care and openness to seeing you, our leaders, outside the boxes of our judgments and assumptions. We will strive to be intellectually honest, to change our opinions in the light of new evidence and thinking. We will respect and acknowledge that you may have to deal with things that we know nothing or little about. But we do expect you to explain these things to us, and we hope that you will be open to changing your thinking as well. Now, to the questions:

Question number one: Governor, you have said that you were passionate about following the law. That must mean that you are also committed to the spirit of the law, not just the technicality of it. Why then, has the state, under your leadership, fought against doing an EIS on the Superferry from the beginning?

Because—if you understand the spirit and the intention of the Hawai'i Environmental Policy Act—you must know that the act is not designed to protect only environmentalists; it is designed to protect all of us here today, ranging from the businessperson to the artist, to the worker and the parent. It is designed to protect succeeding generations, our children and our grandchildren. And it is designed to protect our economy, our beauty, our culture, and our social fabric, things that we all value deeply. The EIS law attempts to instill and incorporate into our public decision-making process procedures that will increase the probability that the decisions we make as a community will be sound decisions, good decisions. It tries to ensure that we will have considered all potential impacts and ways to mitigate negative impacts, so that the resulting project will give us the benefits, without the negative and often unintended consequences.

Governor, we who love Kaua'i feel that at a minimum, we need an EIS. The law requires it, but more important than the law, it is the right thing to do in making a major decision that will affect many people.

Question number two: Why is the state not letting the legal process run its course in determining the legality of the Superferry?[11] In determining the legality of the Superferry operating while the EA/EIS [EA: Environmental Assessment] is being done,

---

[11] Councilwoman Yukimura is referring to two cases—one on Maui and one on Kaua'i—demanding that Superferry prepare an EIS before resuming operation. Despite this, Governor Lingle and the Department of Transportation had given the green light for Superferry to resume service just a few days following this gathering.

why will you not recognize that the Circuit Court is not the final say as to the law? Even as the Maui Circuit Court's decision declaring the Superferry exempt from the EIS law was not the final say. What if Judge Valenciano denies a preliminary injunction tomorrow?[12] The Superferry proceeds to enter Nawiliwili Harbor next Wednesday. Someone gets terribly hurt, and then Judge Valenciano's decision is overturned by the Hawai'i Supreme Court, which rules that a preliminary injunction should have been granted.

We are already reeling from the first misinterpretation of the law. Why risk even more dire possibilities of a second misinterpretation? And why is the state siding with the Superferry in interpreting state law? Why is the state not aligning itself with the People for the Preservation of Kaua'i?

In following the law, which says, "Acceptance of a required final EIS shall be a condition *precedent* to implementation of the proposed action," since an EA needs to be done before an EIS, it stands to reason that an EA process is condition precedent as well. And then there's the PUC approval, which was a condition of full compliance with environmental requirements. Why should the Superferry operations, as a matter of law, not be prohibited?

Question number three: What is the reason for pushing the Kaua'i route so intensely? You cannot tell us that it will make any real difference in the Superferry's financial situation. Is there another reason? Please be straight with us.

And lastly, question number four. What, if anything, does the Superferry have to do with national security?

If it does have something to do with that, why weren't we told up front? Especially when the taxpayers of Hawai'i are being asked to provide $40 million in state money. That was a major deception, perpetrated against the people of Hawai'i and the state legislature. Why wasn't the national security budget used to fund the Superferry instead, and *[speaking with great intensity]* why wasn't an EIS process part of this national security action in the same way that EISs are being done for PMRF [Pacific Missile Range Facility] and for Makua Valley?[13]

---

[12] Kaua'i Circuit Court Judge Randal Valenciano was scheduled, the next day, to grant or deny the request by People for the Preservation of Kaua'i for a preliminary injunction to prevent the Superferry from landing at Nawiliwili Harbor until the completion of an EIS.

[13] See Chapter 17.

Dear Governor, we implore you to consider these logical, legitimate questions and to reconsider your decision to support resumption of the Superferry operations in Nawiliwili, Kaua'i. Our state motto gives guidance to this: *Ua mau ka ea o ka 'aina i ka pono.* (The life of the land is perpetuated in righteousness.) We call on you. We count on you to choose life and to choose righteousness. Mahalo nui loa and may God guide you and bless you.

LINDA LINGLE

Thank you, Councilwoman Yukimura. Let me start by saying that my answers may not be the ones that you want to hear, and I just accept that. Because we can tell from the room tonight, there are obviously people who have differing opinions. But I would like to be clear on one point. We're not here tonight to make a decision about when the Superferry comes in, because we've made that decision already.

[The audience bursts into a rumble of discontent, punctuated by angry heckling.]

I'd like to address the question, why are we pushing the Superferry. Because it certainly can't survive just coming to Kaua'i. From my perspective, Superferry has a legal right to come into the harbor. There has been no legal opinion at this point to stop them.[14] *[Hecklers call out, "EIS!"]* So our responsibility is to make certain that that vessel is allowed to come in, and, of course, we're very concerned that all people be safe during this time.

The second question I wanted to address was, "What does Superferry have to do with national security?" I don't know of any issue that the Superferry has to do with national security. *[The crowd boos loudly.]* So the statement that was made that it was a major

---

[14] What the governor does not reveal is that a series of meetings had taken place as early as 2004 among her office, the state's Department of Transportation, and Superferry, with the purpose of massaging Superferry's wish list of proposed harbor accommodations until the corporation could squeak through to qualify for an EIS exemption. In addition, an email from a DOT design engineer to a project consultant around that time suggests that the deputy attorney general did, in fact, support environmental review. *(See Chapter 8, January 2008 entry: "Governor's Push for Exemption Exposed" and June 2008 entry: "Lingle Stonewalls; Cites Attorney-Client Privilege.")*

deception to ask the legislature for the $40 million is simply not a true statement. We didn't deceive the legislature. We went down—Superferry went and talked to legislators. We answered all questions that were posed to us, and keep in mind, and this is not trying to blame someone else, we're just trying to keep clear on what the process was. I could not, on my own, have made these improvements. I could not on my own have spent $40 million on improvements throughout the state so that the people could have this option available to them, although I believe it's a great option and I support it very strongly,

We would not have been able to proceed with the project had the members of the legislature not voted to allow us to spend that money, and I want to make one point on the money. The money was approved by the legislature in the form of reimbursable general obligation bonds. And what that means is that the Superferry has to pay money to the state in order to pay back the bondholders. So that the impact on us as the government and as taxpayers is—we made an obligation when we sold those bonds—that we would pay those bondholders with interest, and now we're obligated to do that.

[Despite many hecklers, she continues.] The final question was, why have we aligned ourselves against the People for the Preservation of Kaua'i? I think, as you can see tonight, there's a difference of opinion, and it's not unusual to this island or to this issue. But, my decision in this initially when the idea came up, I was very enthusiastic, and I remain enthusiastic, because I believed, and I still believe, it's an important option to have, to be able to travel. *[The audience responds with a long and passionate symphony of boos.]*

RICH HOEPPNER

Richard Hoeppner was born and raised on a farm in southwest Iowa almost seventy years ago. After marrying, raising two sons, and completing a twenty-year law-enforcement career, he retired, traveled through North America and Mexico, and finally moved to Kaua'i in 2002. According to Hoeppner, his love for the land and culture, combined with the lack of democratic process he witnessed as the Superferry Corporation pushed its agenda through, gal-

vanized him to become an activist for the first time in his life. Hoeppner spearheaded the campaign to require an Environmental Impact Statement.

Thank you, Governor, for hearing me. Hello, Mayor. Hello, Chief. Admiral. My name is Rich Hoeppner. A year and three months ago I listened to Superferry come in here and tell us what they were going to do. They didn't ask us any questions. They said, "We got $140 million from the federal government, the ferries are being built, we've got $40 million from the state and we are coming in." No questions asked. Come hell or high water, our opinions didn't matter.

I said at one of the meetings, "That's wrong, and I'm going to start a petition to get an Environmental Impact Statement." They said they weren't going to do it. I was immediately surrounded by people who wanted to sign my petition. I said, "I haven't done it yet; I just thought of it."

So I composed a petition. And we circulated it for several months. We got over 6,000 signatures from the people of Kaua'i requesting an EIS.

I went through protocol, trying to get a meeting with you. You refused to see us. We held a meeting at the capitol last September. We invited you, through protocol, filled out all the forms, invited you to that meeting. We had seven speakers, it had press coverage, television coverage. You refused to come. We went to your office the next morning. There were seven of us. I talked to the receptionist. Said I wanted to see your planning director first. She went back through the big door, came back out, and said, "I'm sorry, she's not available." I said, "Then I would like five minutes of the Governor's time. I'm representing 6,000 people from Kaua'i. I want five minutes of the Governor's time to present the petitions." She went back through the big door and came out, and she said, "I'm sorry, the Governor can't see you." I then asked to see one of your senior aides to present the petitions, so they could get it to you. She went through the big door again, then came out, and said, "I'm sorry, there's nobody to see you." There was a large man in an aloha shirt, who then said the meeting is over, and we were about to get thrown out of your office.

I have those petitions tonight. *[Hoeppner holds up a stack of white paper the thickness of two phone books, bound together theatrically with a large red ribbon tied in a bow. The auditorium applauds the delivery of their signatures.]*

I would like to present them to you. And the question of an EIS is moot. Because the Hawai'i Supreme Court has said what we've been saying for fifteen months now, that an EIS, an EA is required, and an EA, I'll guarantee you, will lead to an EIS. It's a moot point, because the Supreme Court has already decided on it. As I see it, you're trying to turn HEPA (Hawai'i Environmental Policy Act) upside down. Because HEPA says anytime state money is spent or state property is used, an Environmental Assessment is required, *before* they start operations. Now there's a big legal dispute on that. But if you'll read it, and read the Supreme Court, how could we *possibly* have the Superferry operating for two years, while the EIS is done, without turning HEPA on its head!? Because the damage will already be done by the time the EIS is done! *[The crowd crows in agreement.]*

When the Supreme Court came out with their decision and Superferry decided they were going to move their operating date up two days, it was a big mistake. Because people who had said to me that they were all for the ferry came and said, "I've changed my mind. This act is illegal."

[The audience cheers heartily.]

You and Mr. Fukunaga gave your approval to have them operate before the EA is accomplished. Now, if that's a violation of law, you were sworn to uphold state law. *[Amidst the cheers, someone calls out, "Yes!"]* You were sworn to do that. If you were in consort with Superferry to violate state law, is that an impeachable offense? *[The word* impeachment *elicits squeals from the audience.]* I don't know.

[The room is stirred up in a frenzy of howls, jeers, and boos against the governor and Fukunaga.]

I'm asking questions. I don't know the answer to that. But I've had people come to me and ask that. So I've got this for ya.

[The governor takes the petitions as people cheer.]

And, Governor, we've collected several thousand more in two days. So there are probably eight to nine thousand signatures and of all the people I ask, if I ask a hundred people to sign the petition, eighty of them sign the petition. So when you say there's a small percentage on this island that is for the ferry, I'll guarantee ya there's 80–90 percent of the people on this island that want the EIS before the ferry starts running. *[Cheering and applause.]*

Lloyd Imuaikaika Pratt

Lloyd Imuaikaika Pratt, whose lineage dates back centuries in the famed Kalalau Valley, is one of Kauaʻi's most eminent practitioners of Hawaiian culture and spirituality. He helped found Kanuikapono Charter School, whose students he takes to various heiau *(ancient temples) where he gives hands-on instruction on traditions such as protocol and chanting. He is a* kahu[15] *in Hawaiian spirituality and has walked every ridge and valley of Kauaʻi. "For Polynesians, Kauaʻi is a walking bible," he says. "Every place has a name and a story which bring a person closest to God." Several years ago, while cleaning his ancestral heiau at Kalalau, Pratt was arrested and then incarcerated for twenty-seven days, for trespassing on state property.*

Good evening to the governor and also to the panel here. I have a lot of concerns here because I'm born and raised here. I'm fifty-six years old. I'm from the west side. I am a native of this land; my ancestors go way back, six centuries and back. And here you guys are making decisions for us when you don't even live here. You don't even see our lifestyle here. I eat the food that is in the ocean. I go up in the mountains to get things. People all know me here. I don't even know you guys, and you guys making decisions for us.

Now, I been to a lot of public hearings and a lot of the people who are on the panels either disregard us or look funny at us or laugh at us, and it's really unethical. No respect. We speak full *mana* to you folks, and we try to make you guys listen to us. Because we the one who is affected by it. But yet, you fraudulent people who are here as government, which is actually fictitious here, in our homelands, and trying to tell us that this is this, when actually it's all fictitious. You have nothing solid here. You have no *kapu*[16] over us. And yet you guys make decisions and put us away in jails.

Now you guys give us this paper. It's a terroristic paper to me.[17] You tellin' me, when the Superferry comin' here you cannot go in the

---

[15] *Kahu*: leader/priest.

[16] *Kapu*: taboo, prohibition, jurisdiction. *Also*, sacred.

[17] The speaker is referring to a document that was distributed at the meeting. The document describes the boundaries for the newly designated security zone at Nawiliwili Harbor, which, if violated, would result in arrest and prosecution under federal law.

water! And yet, my ancestors—if they were here? Oh wow, they would give you guys all scolding! *[Someone calls out,* I mua![18]*]*

It's really sad that you guys have the power that you say, by the gun of the policeman, by the U.S. Coast Guard, you know, county, state, federal. It's not in our homelands to do this. You go back to your homeland and do that. *[The audience cheers loudly.]* This is our home. We make decisions for us. We are very simple people, very civil. We speak by heart. You guys speak by fictitious. You guys say things to us to flower us, and then we find out, it's about money. It is not about land, what resources that we live here for. Now you gonna say, oh bring the Superferry so all Oʻahu people can come and pick up my *limu*.[19] And then go home and sell it, too! We already know Maui did the same thing. They picked up the *pohaku*.[20] And yet, this is our sacred grounds, not only of Hawaiʻi, but whole Pacific triangle. This is why this is the temple here. Our major temples are here on this island, and nowhere else. *[More cheers.]*

I got a question. I got a question for you, the panel, and also for the governor. Why aren't you listening to us? We telling you, that we don't want this ferry. Yes, the people that is in Oʻahu, love the ferry. But we don't want it. You guys all flower. You guys have decorated a really nice picture for us of the Superferry. And then we find out—oh! it's a *disaster* what gonna happen here. Now, I asking you guys a question. Why didn't you guys do this first? Good Luck! Environmental impact. For me, I don't want it, and why? Because you guys are all fictitious. You guys are actually conspirators to a fraud here! Conspirators to a fraud. We born and raised here. We love our ʻaina. We come from the ancestors. You guys don't. So you guys don't care. It is not your home. You can go somewhere else. Not us. I am from way back, before Kamehameha. Kamehameha is state side.[21] Yeah! Kamehameha. But what about the rest that lived before him? We are here! We're all royal bloods. Even though you say we not, we *are*! Aloha.

---

[18] *I mua!*: Go forth!

[19] *Limu*: seaweed.

[20] *Pohaku*: stones.

[21] Here the speaker refers to the historical independence of Kauaʻi, which, for centuries, was an unconquerable kingdom separate from the rest of the archipelago until it was unified by Kamehameha I with the threat of his newly procured arms. Because the submission of Kauaʻi resulted from Western contact, the speaker refers to Kamehameha as "state side."

Andrea Brower

Andrea Noelani Brower was born and raised in Kapaʻa Homesteads on the east side of Kauaʻi. In her twenty-three years, she left the island for five years, to earn a degree in feminist studies and environmental studies at the University of California, Santa Cruz, and to travel. She is employed at Malama Kauaʻi, a nonprofit organization working toward a sustainable Kauaʻi.

Aloha *kakou*.[22] Thank you. Mahalo, everybody, for being here tonight. I know there are a lot of different opinions in this room. And I hope we can just maintain the spirit of aloha. I know we're all feeling pretty passionate right now. My name is Andrea Noelani Brower. I was born and raised on Kauaʻi, and I have many questions, but since you guys are talking tonight about the new laws you've created and the new security zone, I would like to address that specifically. I was in the water on Monday night as a protester, with many, many other young Kauaians. There were over seventy of us in the water that night. There were lawyers, there were farmers, there were people who were landscaping, there were construction workers, there was a young woman who is getting her doctorate at Stanford, there was an engineer. These are all very important community members. My question to you is, do you really feel justified threatening these people with ten-year imprisonment in federal prisons? Do you really feel justified using violence against these people? Do you really feel justified sending Child Welfare Services after them for neglect of their children? *[Random calls of support from the audience.]*

These are people who have the conviction to stand up for something they believe in. To stand up against an unjust and unlawful government. Malama ʻAina!?[23] *[The audience goes crazy with cheers.]*

One more very, very quick question. I've seen a lot of numbers floating around; I'm curious. How much did the Superferry board of directors contribute to your campaign?

---

[22] *Kakou:* all of us.

[23] *Malama ʻAina!:* Care for the Land!

Torri Law

Sixteen-year-old Torri Law worked as a coffeehouse barista while finishing up at Island School, where she was active in the theater department. Since fall 2008, she has been at Occidental College in Los Angeles, studying biology and theater.

Hi, my name is Torri Law. I live in Wailua. I'm an Island School student. Why on Earth is Nawiliwili Harbor being turned into a security zone? The job of the Coast Guard of Hawai'i is to protect the people, to protect the people out at sea. I respect them for doing that. My dad is a fisherman; he's a free diver. If something happens to him, I'm trusting the Coast Guard to go and find him to bring him home to me, because he's important in my life. It's their job to protect the people. So why are you protecting the Superferry? *[The audience cheers.]* The Superferry is not a person. The Superferry is not in danger. Maybe their *business* is in danger. That's not the Coast Guard's job to protect that. *[Even bigger cheers burst from the crowd.]* What's really in danger is the people of Kaua'i and Kaua'i itself. You've got—*[An audience member yells out, "Power to the People!"]*—you've got a giant boat as tall and wide as this building here going forty miles an hour through the water, and we've got people protesting peacefully. They're sitting out in the water on their surfboards. They can't get out of the way. Whales can't get out of the way. The dolphins, the *honu*,[24] they can't get out of the way. We are the ones in danger. If that boat hits somebody, that's on the Coast Guard's head. That's their fault. Protect the people. Don't protect the Superferry. *They're* the threat. Protect *against them*. *[The audience cheers wildly.]*

As I said, I go to Island School. I've gone there my whole life. I've spent thirteen years at a very difficult school. My family has spent—I can't even count how much they have spent on my education. Do not think that just because I'm a child that I'm ignorant of what's going on. I understand. I understand what's going on. I've lived in Hawai'i my whole life. I've taken for granted the beauty and the pristineness of this island. And now that that's being threatened, I realize that, I can't take this for granted. I will fight tooth and nail to protect it. *[Huge applause from audience.]* Mahalo.

---

[24] *Honu*: Hawaiian green sea turtle, an endangered species.

Scott Mijares

Scott Mijares is the founder of a business that designs and manufactures surfboard-shaped wooden postcards. He and his wife of twenty-three years live in Kilauea with their eight-year-old daughter, Maile. The couple's two sons are students at San Diego State University. Mijares loves coaching Maile's soccer team and surfing, and has been active in community issues since moving to Kaua'i in 1999.

Good evening, Governor and members of the panel. My name is Scott Mijares. I think what gets people on Kaua'i the maddest is that we really don't feel like we were considered in this decision. We feel like you were pandering to the majority of the people in O'ahu and other places, and we really didn't have a say-so. We started a grassroots petition. We got some 6,000 signatures. I got a petition in the mail to sign if I was in favor of it. I know there was a petition drive and money spent to see what the support was, and I was curious about what the results would be, but we never saw them.

We do have our 6,000 signatures that says we'd like an EIS, but I don't know, you know, in the news we hear that overwhelmingly the people support it, and if they support it in O'ahu great, drive the Superferry around O'ahu. *[The audience laughs, cheers.]* But here on Kaua'i, we're a small island and feel very vulnerable, and we have tremendous concerns, and no one has yet to address those to our satisfaction at all. So, I think, that's what everybody's getting at.

One last note. I have prepared a heartfelt letter that I have written. I emailed it to you, but I wanted to present it to you in person. I took the time to etch it on wood.

LINGLE: Thank you, Scott. Happy to receive it.

Mijares walks up to the podium, handing Lingle a wooden board etched with words. She notices its fine craftsmanship, with apparent surprise.

LINGLE: He really did etch it. Thank you, Scott.

Letter from a Republican — Scott Mijares

This is the letter that Mijares handed to Governor Lingle.

September 17, 2007

Dear Governor Lingle,

My name is Scott Mijares and I am a resident of Kauaʻi. I am a father, a business owner, a soccer coach, a homeowner and, by all accounts, a conservative Republican. I voted for George Bush for President and for you as Governor of our State.

In my 47 years, I have never been a party to a demonstration or rally, never placed a bumper sticker on my car; never carried a sign for any cause.

On the afternoon of August 26, 2007, that all changed. Yes, I was there at Nawiliwili Harbor that late afternoon and I plan to be there again on September 26. I am not a dissident or a terrorist and do not wish to be characterized as such. I am only one of a growing number of good citizens who are desperate to have our voices heard by leaders like you. We are totally resolute in our belief that the Superferry should not be allowed to operate in Hawaiian waters until an EA is completed as prescribed by law.

I believe you are making a mistake by creating/enforcing a security zone for the Superferry when it comes to Kauaʻi. You are setting the stage for an inevitable confrontation between citizens and law enforcement to facilitate the safe passage of the Superferry as it enters Nawiliwili Harbor. In the best-case scenario, Kauaʻi will be seen by the world as a war zone with mothers, aunties, kupuna, and children being herded around by faceless officers in riot gear. The worst-case scenario will be that one or more citizens is badly hurt or even killed in the harbor waters. That would be devastating to our community and would certainly lead to extreme levels of civil unrest. Someone will have to be held responsible. If not you, then who?

I want you to know that I respect you and the authority that your office holds but I am concerned that you are underestimating the resolve of the people of Kauaʻi. This is not a small group of dissidents. This is a diverse group of citizens that includes Kanaka, entrepreneurs, doctors, lawyers, teachers, politicians, and others whose level of sacrifice has yet to be tested.

As a Republican and a supporter of our President, I find myself constantly engaged in interesting debates with my fellow citizens. Inevitably the question is asked, "Would you send your son to fight in the Iraq War?" My response has always been this. "My son is an adult and hopefully I have prepared him to make his own decisions. If he decided to enlist in the military, I would be very proud of him and I would support him 100%."

The other day I was talking with my oldest son, Ryan. He is a senior at San Diego State University and will be going off to med school next year. He has been following the drama here in Hawai'i via his computer and is truly saddened by what is happening. I told him that things are going to get pretty heavy here on September 26 and that I was contemplating entering the harbor. I told him that if I were arrested that he and his brother might have to leave college to care for their mother and sister. I was overwhelmed with emotion when he paused and said to me, "Dad, I love you and I respect you. I know you will do the right thing. If you decide to go through with this I will be proud of you and I will support you 100%." (Kids—they are amazing.)

Governor Lingle. If this issue can get a conservative Republican contemplating such a huge sacrifice, what do you think is going through the minds of the average Kauaian?

Please come to Kaua'i and talk to the people. Our concerns are real. The law seems very clear to us. If there is an emergency threat to our island and you have to suspend the law so that Superferry can protect us, explain that threat to us. On the other hand, if you are using your authority to give law enforcement officers orders to arrest good citizens; citizens who feel like they are being denied their right to gather in their parks and assemble, so a commercial enterprise can make some money while the courts decide their fate, then shame on you.

I look forward to meeting you again and hope that my perspective helps guide you in the future.

Sincerely,
Scott Mijares

Pua La'a Norwood

Aloha, Governor Linda Lingle and the honorable body of panel chairpersons. *'O Pua La'a Norwood ko'u inoa. 'O hanau wau ma Wailuku, Maui. 'O noho wau ma Waipake, Kaua'i. 'O Timoteo ko'u keiki kane.*[28]

We're imploring you to listen to the people. We're asking—demanding—an EIS. My first question to you: Would you be willing to put forth a law to protect our harbor and bar the Superferry from entering?

We are concerned for our resources of the island. We are concerned about invasive species and drugs and traffic. Our infrastructure here cannot handle the traffic that we currently have. The Department of Land and Natural Resources is not able to police our resources to make sure that harvesting of fish and natural resources is done in an environmentally protective way. Our police department is not able to fight the drugs on this island. We, as the people of Kaua'i, know that this is sacred 'aina. This is the Garden Island. We have a vision for this land and it is *sustainability. [The audience cheers with enthusiastic support.]*

We are currently fighting rampant, unchecked overdevelopment with a lack of foresight. We have agricultural lands being bought up and being made up into gated communities, homes for the ridiculously rich, while we, as a common people, are not represented; we have housing shortage. Our beaches, a lot of them don't have lifeguards, they don't have bathrooms, we have the highest drownings in the state. Are you gonna bring more people here and have that be more of a problem? We're just some of the residents here. Not everyone can make it. And not everyone has a voice. We also represent the whales, the dolphins, the honu, the manta ray.

[Cheering erupts from the crowd.]

You defended the Superferry and the lack of the EIS by saying that this has not been required before. A ship like this is *unprecedented.* There is no other vessel like that coming into our waters. That thing was going 40 miles per hour. That thing is superfast and

---

[28] Translation: My name is Pua La'a Norwood. I was born in Wailuku, Maui. I live at Waipake, Kaua'i. Timoteo is my son.

superscary. And we have mother whales birthing in these waters! They need to be protected! *[More cheering.]*

Initially, it was said, oh—we'll use sonar to detect the whales and that'll help us get out of the way. We know that even with sonar, you wouldn't be able to stop fast enough. We've seen pictures of the two hulls ramming through whales. But now you're saying you can't even use sonar, because the amount of sonar you would need would deafen the marine mammals. So we're speaking on their behalf.

We have a vision for Kaua'i, and I don't think you've been hearing it. I think that you've been listening to big businesses. *[More cheering.]*

I was in the water on Sunday, exercising my right to free speech and civil disobedience, and I am so grateful that we have the Coast Guard that helps us in times of need, but I'll be honest, they weren't being very nice in the water. They were actually being very rough to a lot of us. And threatening to gaff people in the water. And they tried to run me over with their Zodiac boat, and had I not been a strong swimmer, I would have suffered. I had to evade their maneuvering.

I am begging you to listen to the people of the island. We are speaking for seven generations in the future. We do not own this land. We are stewards of this land. And you may have been elected governor. You have a responsibility, a kuleana, *a kuleana,* to represent the people fairly and justly. Give us our 'aina. We saw what happened to Maui. We saw what happened to O'ahu. This is sacred land. Please hear our voices. *[The audience roars in approval.]*

CLAIRE HILL

Claire Hill is a licensed clinical social worker and registered nurse who has worked in the mental health field since 1975. The majority of her life as an adult has been spent in Alaska working with survivors of child abuse and domestic violence. She currently lives and works with children and families in the state of Hawai'i. Her proudest accomplishment has been to raise four compassionate and intelligent children who are contributing to their communities and to the world.

Good evening, my name is Claire Hill. We heard the word *respect* used a lot tonight; we heard the word *passion.*

I have to tell you that from the beginning, I've written letters to the editor of the *Honolulu Advertiser,* to the local *Garden Island* news, and to your office. The responses were not personal responses. I signed a petition. And I felt like I was never heard. So, my passion is partially driven by the fact that I'm a landowner here. I have a child who goes to school here. I work in a school myself. I work with families and the children in this community. What I see happening is that when we get to feeling so disrespected that people are not hearing our voices, anger comes up. And perhaps even bitterness. I'm old enough to have marched in the civil rights marches. And there's a part of this that feels like that. It feels like we're not being heard. The power to the people isn't there.

Hawai'i is a strange state, because we're all divided up into little places. Kaua'i is not like O'ahu, we're not like Maui, we're not like any of the other islands. We're very small. Our infrastructure has one major road that goes around the island, and it doesn't even go all the way around. When I first came here ten years ago, it took me twenty minutes to get to work from north Kapa'a into Lihue. Now I have to allow forty-five minutes because the traffic is so horrible. It might not sound like much if you're living in a big city, but for us here, it's not just the amount of time, it's the amount of congestion. And what I'm seeing on the road is increased road rage. And so part of my concern is what we're talking about here is bringing a number of cars onto this island that we do not have the infrastructure to support.

My second point has to do with business. We've heard many times over that the ferry—I refuse to call it the Superferry—that the ferry is just another business and should be allowed to operate on our island. All of our other businesses have a distinct building on a distinct piece of land that we can choose to go to or not. They are not bringing their product and putting it on our doorstep. When we have people coming from other islands, and I'm not suspecting that all persons are bad persons, but there is that element and you have to acknowledge it. Look at your homeless problem. Our beaches are already crowded. Last time we went to Ke'e Beach, we couldn't even find a place to park. We had to come home. Because the whole beach was packed out. When we have all these cars and if we got increased homelessness packed on our beaches, we are going to have problems. Yes, we already have drug problems on our island. We can't say we don't. We do. But that doesn't mean we need to bring more here.

We just had the recent example of the guys stealing rocks off of Maui—*[The crowd roars in confirmation]*—coming on the ferry. On *that* ferry. Okay, they took rocks they shouldn't have. But that's not all they can take. You know, we've always had a joke here about how one of the ways we keep our children in line is that we know they can't take from somebody else's home without us knowing, because everyone knows each other. And we also know that you can't steal something here and take it on the plane if it's a big item, because you're gonna get caught with it, right? Well, people bringing their cars over can take pretty much whatever they want.

My seventeen-year-old daughter—part of the reason we came here was because I felt safe. There are children running around, playing in neighborhoods. We didn't have to worry about people abducting our children. My seventeen-year-old daughter has to sit for a couple of hours outside her high school, to wait for me until I get out of work. I'm not gonna feel safe with that anymore, when half a mile up the road—or down the road, actually—is where the ferry is gonna disembark. I don't know who's gettin' off that ferry, I don't know if it's child molesters, I don't know who it is. *[The audience cheers.]*

My suggestion all along has been, I really believe each of the islands should have the people of their island vote as to whether they want the Superferry or not. We should all have equal say. If I get a vote, an equal vote with everybody in here, and I miss the vote, then I'm gonna have to adjust to it. But in the meantime, it makes me very bitter to think that I didn't even get a vote. And we're at risk. Our homes are at risk. Our children are at risk.

The last point I want to make is that the media has kind of portrayed us as ignorant, unemployed, kinda lowlife people who are protesting the ferry. I want you to know that I have three college degrees, I'm a professional woman. Everybody in here is educated. Educated enough to know what's going on and to be able to be articulate enough to speak it! *[The audience cheers and stomps, nodding. It appears that Kauaʻi's people have had enough of being misrepresented by the corporate media.]*

Before I finish, I would like to say that I am like the most patriotic person in the world. Everyone who knows me knows that I have great honor for our Coast Guard, our military, our policemen. We need them for safety. We need them for protection. But we do not need to have to fight them for civil rights! *[Huge roar of approval from the crowd.]*

I'm amazed at this kind of passion I feel. I came here with no notes, except what I scribbled on my hands a few minutes ago. I'm constantly reminded—I'm kind of a history buff—in the early days of our American colonies, we had government from afar, government that did not listen to the people, government that was taxing its citizens, who didn't want to be taxed. So those people became what we would now call anarchists. And they unloaded a bunch of tea into the harbor. The Boston Tea Party. I don't want to see that happen here. But we have to find a compromise that doesn't put us all at risk—our homes, our safety, our land, our environment. Thank you for your time.

Michael Fox

Michael Fox fell in love with Kauaʻi thirty-two years ago but didn't put down roots on-island until recently, when he was able to semiretire from running an educational nature and science store in Nevada City, California. On Kauaʻi, he is active in politics and community issues, serving on the board of Friends of Kamalani and Lydgate Park, and more recently as a delegate to the 2008 Democratic National Convention. Every Saturday morning he can be found at Lydgate Park for beach cleanup.

Good evening, Governor. My name is Michael Fox, and I'm a resident of Wailua. I wish you could have been at the meeting prior to this meeting. You would have seen the real heart and the real spirit of the Kauaʻi people. You would've been touched, and you would've felt connected to what we're talking about here tonight. You have seen lots of frustration; the frustration is because it's voices speaking into the wind. We don't feel we've been heard, and there has been no response from the state government. There is maybe 50 feet between us, but there might as well be 5,000. There is an invisible barrier. We talk at you. You talk at us. What really gets accomplished? The Superferry people came to our public meetings, because, by law, they had to. What did they take away from those meetings? What did we gain from those meetings? Were we heard at those meetings? No. Will we be heard tonight? I think not. I'd just like to say that America's founding fathers were thinking ahead when

Is Superferry "Good" for Small Businesses?

Letter to the Editor of Kaua'i's Garden Island *newspaper*
John Sydney Yamane

I am a small professional computer repair and information technology provider on the island of Kaua'i and have been operating successfully as a small, "one-man" business operation.

As you know, Kaua'i and all of the other islands have similar "small," one-man operations, and it is almost a basic living right that we do. The opening of the Pandora's Box of connecting the island with a so-called "ocean highway" that will allow the hundreds of smaller professional business operators in O'ahu to overlay their service areas to the outer islands is what I feel will be an irreversible "economic threat," and this is what I fear from the Superferry.

To me, as a small business operation, our business culture here on Kaua'i is protected in isolation, and I believe on each neighbor island, the way we do business is so very different from the business culture on O'ahu. We small "country" businessmen will not have a chance if you compare us with what O'ahu business counterparts will offer. Their business strengths will overcome our business model so easily and we will be overrun by hundreds of service vehicles coming from O'ahu to "scoop up" our business and then drive back to their home base in O'ahu.

I believe that Kaua'i has its own economic vitality because we are separated and isolated by ocean.

I may be a bit naive. May I ask, has there ever been an EIS done for the Superferry?

Our little island commerce is at stake. Why is the Kaua'i Chamber of Commerce not protecting our business haven?

they established strict regulations and laws limiting the power of corporations. They understood how the potential for contamination of the three branches of federal government through economically powerful corporations could do irreparable damage to our democratic system. Over the years, corporate lawyers have all but gutted those regulations, making it so a corporate takeover of America would be possible. Today we see our governor brazenly taking the lead, perpetuating the transition of a government of the people, by the people, and for the people, to a new paradigm, to a government of the corporation, by the corporation, and for the corporation.

[A big round of applause.]

Recently, on your weekly radio show, you accused Kaua'i's state legislators of illegal behavior, by inciting illegal behavior at the demonstrations. As someone who was there personally, I can tell you that it is your statement that is irresponsible.

[Cheers fill the room.]

Representative Morita was there strictly as an observer, and a representative of all the citizens of Kaua'i.

[Amid the cheering, someone yells out, "Right on!"]

We missed our mayor being there.

[Applause of acknowledgment.]

The mayor's position is neutrality on this thing, even though he signed the letter from our County Council. He was a signatory of the letter, saying that an EIS should be done. Since then, he's sort of disappeared. And his neutrality basically has said, no, I'm not neutral. I'm choosing politics over the people. *[Addressing Mayor Baptiste.]* And I'm sorry, Mayor.

[Applause.]

Arrogance from the Superferry corporation and the state government has created this mess. This started out with one person—Rich Hoeppner. One person, with a petition. And this has grown and grown and grown.

[More applause.]

We are a nation of law and order. Power does not give license to play loose with the rules. If the Superferry executives had to assure their investors in order to raise the capital to fund their venture that an Environmental Assessment would not be required and that the support of this governor and the Department of Transportation was a done deal, then something stinks. And it's not my feet!

George Inouye

After serving in Vietnam, George Inouye returned to his Kaua'i home, where he was employed as a heavy equipment operator at the Kekaha Sugar Mill until its closure in 2000. Throughout the 1980s, he was an avid fisherman, having at one time pulled in a record-breaking, 285-pound marlin. As a teen, he was the namesake for the surf spot called "G.I.'s," just north of the Waimea Pier, for having been the first person in recent history known to have surfed there. Today, Inouye can no longer fish, having been incapacitated by the delayed effects of exposure to Agent Orange. He is now active in the campaign against chemical toxins in the environment.

Good evening. My name is George Inouye. I'm a Vietnam veteran. I'm a Hawaiian in Hawai'i. I was born and raised over here. I against the Superferry because you guys don't think about the drugs and the traffic of the island and the robbery and the breaking in the houses. In the future, gonna be like this if you pass this law.

[The audience cheers loudly.]

Mahalo, my brothers and sisters. We have to back up Kaua'i. We have to leave it like this here, because we have too much hotels and we have plenny traffic. I live on the west side. It take hour-and-a-half to reach in Lihu'e. And if the Superferry gonna come, it might be two hours, two-and-a-half hours to reach in Lihu'e. So now, you folks getta look in the future. All these drug problem coming in on Kaua'i. And the robbery and everything gonna be more worse on the island. And it's too late to stop it.

[More cheers.]

Right now we have to step up and stop this Superferry coming onto Kaua'i. We don't need this on Kaua'i. Keep it the same way how we had it in the 1990s. Keep it original and a lot of aloha, not fighting with a lot of people.

The Hawaiian people of Kaua'i, we love our fishing. We love our 'aina. And the *'opihis*[29] on the rocks. And we go out to the beach and pick it up and eat it. Now, if the Superferry be coming in, maybe twice a day or three time a day, now harbor is gonna be a lot of oil in the water. Same like Na Pali coast. Now I don't eat the fish,

---

[29] *'Opihi*: Hawaiian limpets, a culinary delicacy since ancient times.

I don't eat the 'opihi in the Na Pali coast.[30] So right now, my brothers and sisters, you have to stop this Superferry from coming on Kaua'i. Big problem. Thank you very much.

Josephine Bonaparte

Josephine Bonaparte is the Kaua'i base manager for Air Service Hawai'i, which provides ground handling for private jets. She has worked in the visitor industry since 1976, first on Maui, and then on Kaua'i. In her younger years, she was a trophy-winning surfer, a sport she continues to enjoy in her daily life.

Good evening, Governor Lingle and panel. My name is Josephine Bonaparte. I live on the northeast side of Kaua'i, and I hope that you can see, Governor Lingle, that it's not just a small handful of people that are opposed to the Superferry, like you said on the news. *[The audience cheers in agreement.]* You know there's a lot of us that couldn't be here tonight.

My house in Kilauea has always had an open-door policy. I've never locked the door. It's always been open for my son and his friends to hang out. And I don't want to see that change. In Tahiti, they brought over a Superferry and all of a sudden people were going to another island and stealing things and leaving that evening. We're definitely afraid of that happening here.

Anyway, we are a large group of people opposed to this, and I hope you will recognize that. This was pretty much shoved down our throats. A panel came to Kaua'i last year to listen to testimony from people, but the panel was just yawning and not really listening. Their decision had already been made. We don't want it. It's nothing that we voted on. Even with the EIS, I am opposed to the Superferry. Thank you.

Abbie Lapetina

Abbie Lapetina, an elementary school teacher, fell in love with Kaua'i the moment she arrived twenty-two years ago. In that time, she has raised two

---

[32] Although the legendarily beautiful Na Pali coast is off limits to development, daily throngs of tourist boats have left a layer of oil on surrounding waters.

sons and enjoyed surfing, caring for dozens of stray animals, teaching special education, and pursuing numerous hobbies, including sewing, photography, carpentry, and Volkswagen repair.

I'd just like to take a little trip into the future here. Let's say, for the sake of argument, we do have the Superferry here next week. And let's say that eventually an Environmental Impact Statement is done. Who's gonna pay for all the impact that happens between now and the time that that statement comes out? Is the Superferry gonna be held accountable for that? Are our tax dollars gonna pay to get rid of the mongoose[31] and whatever else comes over here on the Superferry? Who's gonna pay for that after the fact, when the impact statement, as we all believe, will indicate that there's been significant negative impact to our island?

LINGLE: Thank you.

LAPETINA: Is there some answer to that?

LINGLE: I can let you know that these issues are what the judge is weighing on Maui right now. There is no process I know of to apportion liability in the sense of the state. As I told you earlier, we sold $40 million worth of reimbursable general obligation bonds. So if Superferry is not allowed to go forward, we still have an obligation to pay those bonds. *[The audience jeers and heckles.]*

LAPETINA: My point is that loss of revenue to the Superferry is recoverable. Loss to our environment is not. Therefore, logically, the environment should be put before the Superferry. Their finances are recoverable. Our environment is not. *[Huge cheers from the crowd.]*

UNIDENTIFIED MAN

I want to address the idea of respect. I don't think it's very respectful for you to come to people's homes and tell them what you're gonna do to them. You came here saying you wanted to hear from the people, but you've already made your decisions, and you're forcing them against the will of the people. And that's wrong. And

---

[31] The mongoose is a cat-like carnivore whose introduction to other Hawaiian islands has led to the decimation of many native species, particularly birds.

as far as your new rules—whoever passed the rules for Wednesday—I'm really scared about Wednesday,[32] because people here feel strongly about the sense of righteousness, and what is right and respecting this island and the people that live here and their way of life. And they don't care about your rules or your big boats or your cops or your Coast Guard, and I'm scared what's gonna happen. The guys on Maui, the second trip, they take rocks from a sacred river. That is wrong. And the only reason they got caught was because your boats were docked and those trucks were there for days, and finally someone looked and goes, "Wow, there's truckloads of rocks! What are those doing there?" That kind of lawlessness is going to be perpetrated over and over and over again. We feel violated, threatened, and I am really scared that people are gonna get hurt by YOU! And I want to ask the mayor a question: Are you scared for the people of Kaua'i on Wednesday? People are going to protest, Mayor. Are you scared for the safety of our children and our citizens? I'd like you to answer, please. *[The crowd is going wild, as the mayor has been invisible for months, throughout the entire Superferry controversy.]*

MAYOR BRYAN BAPTISTE *(Booming over raucous crowd)*: Excuse me! May I have some quiet! You yell out. You don't let people speak. *[His face furrowed in discomfort, he takes a moment to collect his thoughts.]* I worry every day about this situation.

UNIDENTIFIED MAN: Why won't you stop it? Because people are gonna protest, they're gonna put themselves at risk on Wednesday. Do you not know that that's gonna happen?

BAPTISTE: We have a situation where we don't have a legal decision on whether the Superferry can come here to Nawiliwili or not. The mayor of this island does not create the laws. *[The audience has been booing through Baptiste's speech.]*

UNIDENTIFIED MAN: My question was, do you not realize that people are going to be at risk on Wednesday? How do you feel about that? Your heart. Not your political answer. Your heart. I know you're from Kaua'i, and I know that you are a feeling person. How do you feel about the fact that people will be at risk on Wednesday?

LINGLE: Mayor? Mayor? May I say something?
[The audience booms out "NO!]

---

[32] The speaker is referring to the vessel's scheduled return date to Kaua'i.

UNIDENTIFIED MAN: I asked the mayor a question respectfully. I respectfully asked the mayor a question politely, and I respectfully asked him for his answer, not your answer.

LINGLE: Okay, I just wanted to share something with you about your per—

UNIDENTIFIED MAN: He can make his own answers, thank you.

BAPTISTE: I've said from ... I've said from the very beginning, with legal direction, I could stand by what is legally already, what is desired. Now, I am speaking for myself. And I'm speaking—yes, I worry. Every moment of the day I worry. That's why I've been trying to get sides together to come to some solution. Right at this point, we have a logjam. We have a community that has great passion. And at the same time, I don't have anything to legally say that the Superferry cannot come to Kaua'i.

KEN TAYLOR

After serving two years in the U.S. Navy, Ken Taylor owned a wholesale landscape nursery business in Santa Barbara, California. During that time, he witnessed the population of his community explode from 8,000 to 38,000, a phenomenon that galvanized him into lifelong involvement in community and environmental issues. In Santa Barbara, he worked for, and succeeded in passing, a moratorium on new water meters, as well as raising money to plant thousands of trees. He and his wife, environmentalist Jane Taylor, continue their activism in development and planning issues on Kaua'i.

Governor, thank you for being here tonight. Thank you to the panel for being here, giving us this opportunity to share our concerns. I do hope, I do hope you're really listening. Because I do believe what's brought us here tonight is you and your staff's lack of following the law. I have here Chapter 343 of the Hawai'i Revised Statutes, Environmental Impact Statement. I find nothing in here that says Superferries are exempt. I don't find anything in here that says how we treated other projects as to make the determination as to how we treat this project. What I do find in the statute, under 343-5, Applicability and Requirements: "Except as otherwise provided, an Environmental Assessment shall be required for actions that propose the use of State or County lands, or the use of State or County funds." Now that's pretty clear to me, that a requirement was needed to do an EA in the first place! *[The crowd applauds enthusiastically.]*

Why am I so concerned about an Environmental Impact report? In *The Creation: An Appeal to Save Life on Earth*, E. O. Wilson, a biologist at Harvard for five decades, writes, "Most of the world's losses of bird species occurred in Hawai'i, America's notorious extinction capital and one of Earth's most biologically ravaged hot spots." The Superferry must not sail without an EA. *[Cheers of approval and enthusiastic applause.]* I hear businesspeople and others saying, well, we can't stop the ferry because it's gonna cost them money. The Almighty Dollar is wonderful, but I tell ya what, without an environment, there is no buck. Thank you.

RAYMOND CATANIA

Raymond Catania lives in Puhi, Kaua'i, with his wife and two teenage daughters. He works for the State of Hawai'i as a social services assistant for Child Welfare Services.

Catania remembers vividly the fear and confusion he experienced as a ten-year-old, enduring the nightly sounds of exploding bombs and artillery from war games at the nearby military base on O'ahu, as well as the racist epithets slung at him and his friends by soldiers stationed there.

My name is Raymond Catania. I live in Puhi. I'm fifty-seven years old. And my whole life, I been standing up against stupid injustice like this. I have never seen a force of the military used against the people the way it is happening today. *[The crowd cheers.]*

My life began in Damon Tract on O'ahu, which was a farming and fishing community, and all us guys was kicked out to make room for the airport, and soon after that we had statehood. For all my life, I've seen nothing but development and destruction happening every day. And I tell you what—this is the first time that I have ever seen Child Welfare Services, which is a good agency to help with child abuse, being used against the people of Kaua'i because we standing up! *[The auditorium roars in support.]* I can say this, because *I WORK IN CHILD WELFARE SERVICES!* *[Seemingly impossible, the crowd cheers even more loudly.]*

And every stinkin' day, we gotta deal with drug addicts. We gotta deal with molestas. But I tell you what. Our families who permit their kids to go inside the water and stop that Superferry—these families should not be harassed—*[The audience cheers, applauds.]*—and have the threat of investigation over them. You seen all these young people that came here and they *wen testify*.[33] I don't see why their families should be put under investigation. They are good people. And this a real bad thing happening because the only thing we armed with is the *TRUTH* and the *PEOPLE!* And you guys get the guns! You know? *[The room's enthusiasm has approached a crescendo over which Catania yells in order to be heard.]*

YOU GET THE GUNS! And you guys don't give a *HOOT* if we *DIE*, okay? Or if we get injured. Because all you concerned about is letting the Superferry come through because it's more than just having my mother come over here with her car and bringing me manapua[34] from Chinatown! It's all about the Superferry bringing the Strykers! J. F. Lehman Corporation! The majority stockholders of the Superferry have deep ties into the Pentagon. And I want to hear you answer that, to tell us there is no military connection. Because there is. Sean Connaughton, with the Maritime Administration, admitted in Maui a few weeks ago, that America's national defense will be compromised if you don't get the Superferry through. Okay. So the military connection has been exposed. In Hawai'i, the *Pacific Business News* in 2005, J. F. Lehman himself said that the Superferry can carry Strykers from Pohakuloa on the Big Island to O'ahu. Hawai'i already has 300 Strykers training at O'ahu and Big Island, where depleted uranium has been measured. Now, are you gonna bring it to Kaua'i? Are they gonna bring depleted uranium practice to our island? We wanna know these kinds of things. I'm not saying that they will, but with an EIS, we can find out if the military will be using these ocean vessels to train on Kaua'i and where.

---

[33] *Wen testify*: Pidgin English for "went and testified."
[34] *Manapua*: Hawaiian for Chinese pork bun *(char siu bao)*.

Timoteo Hewlen

Aloha, my name is Timoteo Hewlen. I was born and raised on Kaua'i. I was one of the kids arrested for swimming in from the protest. The person who was watching over us called over one of the Coast Guard boats and asked if we could get a ride to the jetty without being taken into custody. They promised we wouldn't be taken into custody. Instead of taking us straight to the jetty, they brought us in the back where the Superferry docks. They handed us over to the police, and from there we were dropped off at the police department where they took down our name and all our information. *[Random audience members call out "Shame! Shame!"]*

I strongly disagree against the Superferry coming to this island. I think that we should have had an EIS before. And thank you for coming to hear what I have to say.

Kalalea Ka'uhane

Kalalea Kamahalonuiokalani Ka'uhane lives in a special place called Kalalea Uka in Anahola. He is twelve years old and the oldest of four boys in the family. Kalalea loves the 'aina, ocean, taro patch, fishing, music, and basketball. The most important things in his life are his love for his 'ohana and being pono.[35]

Aloha, Governor. My name is Kalalea Ka'uhane. I go to Kanuikapono Charter School. Before, you heard my friend talk about how we got arrested.

I'm mainly here to show my love for the 'aina ... the land. I live for the land. Me, my family, my kupuna. I'm here to tell all of you to do your homework, like I do. As leaders of our State of Hawai'i, you should be required to do a proper EIS before making decisions that will impact us, the next generation. I just have one question. Do all of you have aloha 'aina?[36] If you do, please say it: "I have aloha 'aina."

---

[35] *Pono*: righteous, with integrity.
[36] *Aloha 'aina*: love for the land.

[The governor says nothing, as hecklers urge her on: "Say it!"]
LINGLE: Thank you for coming tonight. Next.

ROBERT PA

Robert Pa is a Kingdom of Atooi Customary Chief and Konohiki,[37] *as well as a master canoe builder. He descends from both the Kamehameha and Kaumuali'i lines, and is a seventh-generation descendent of the Kahuna Kalaiwawa'a (master canoe builder) of the Big Island's Ka'u District. He himself has supervised the building of a twenty-four-foot authentic Polynesian sailing canoe, made entirely by hand and adze, and of natural materials, such as rope hand-woven from coconut fiber. It is the first canoe of its kind since the days of King Kaumuali'i, in 1818.*

Aloha, my name is Robert Pa, Customary Chief, and also Konohiki of the Halele'a District in Hanalei. I believe we all read the newspaper with the United Nations decision. The United Nations [Declaration on the Rights of Indigenous Peoples] decided to recognize First Nations. The State of Hawai'i ain't First Nation. The Polynesian Kingdom of Atooi[38] is First Nation. We have filed a cease-and-desist order with the company, the Superferry. They know about it. They have received it. So, respect the constitutional laws that we serve. As federal marshals from the Polynesian Kingdom of Atooi, we ask the state, you yourself, Bryan Baptiste, and the rest of the people to respect the First Nation, that is, the Polynesians on the island. The Coast Guard, the day that they came out, they conducted a very poor, and the most incredible outburst I've ever seen in my life. They have caused this, this chaos that happened down in Nawiliwili.[39] And every time that boat came into the harbor, there

---

[37] *Konohiki:* Supervisor of an *ahupua'a* (watershed land division) who, in precontact Hawai'i, controlled land, water, and fishing rights.

[38] *Atooi* is the earliest known name for the island now called Kaua'i. This was the designation inscribed on a map documenting Captain Cook's 1778 visit.

[39] The speaker, along with Atooi High Chief Dayne Aipoalani, were apprehended two months later, in November 2007, at a meeting concerning the disinterment by developers of Hawaiian ancestral bones. The two were charged with obstructing government operations and impersonating police officers by assuming their roles as "marshal" with the Kingdom of Atooi at the Superferry protests at Nawiliwili on August 27.

was an outburst of protest from the people. Now, the outburst comes with TROs [Temporary Restraining Orders] and laws; laws that you guys should all respect. Now, if you guys is gonna just come here and run this boat over us, you're badly mistaken. Because we are not gonna allow this to happen. We have to sit at the table and decide what is right for the people. Not right for the businessperson who's gonna make this money, who's gonna kill all our whales. 'Cause the first whale comes on the beach killed from that boat, I'm gonna drag it to Bryan Baptiste's office! *[An incredulous roar bursts from the crowd.]*

I will! The Polynesian Kingdom come with peace, and we come with respect. And we ask the same thing from your police officers, who have been treating us all our life like pieces of nothing. And the day I got arrested in Nawilili, an officer said to me that the people from Wai'anae's gonna come here and "take care" of us, the people from the Polynesian Kingdom. And that is the reason I got arrested that day.[40] They mighta made it out to seem something else, but lemme tell you one thing: We're taking this further, and we're taking it to the top. And it ain't the State of Hawai'i.[41] And your capitalism.

So, you know, remember one thing. Kaua'i is a special place. And we don't have things that other islands have. We don't want 'em. We don't want nothing from them. So, you know, one last thing to add with that. These companies have taken local and Polynesian people and gave 'em jobs, you know. The same Polynesian people, it kinda makes us all friction against each other. And that's the way the state wants us to be, is friction with each other. So we gotta be men, and we gotta be respectful people. So we all gotta come together as one and say NO to this boat.

---

[40] Wai'anae, on O'ahu, is reputed to be home to the archipelago's toughest Native Hawaiians. The speaker is demonstrating how the police officer was aiming to undermine his dignity with the specter of Polynesians pitted against one another, a particularly humiliating scenario to Hawaiian sovereignty activists. The real reason for the arrest, according to the speaker, is that the officer felt threatened by his claim of national sovereignty.

[41] The speaker is referring to international law's recognition of Hawai'i as a sovereign nation currently under occupation by the United States.

Nicolai Barca

Nicolai Barca grew up hunting and fishing on the north shore of Kaua'i, where he also coproduced a cable-access program on hunting. He has since graduated from Hawai'i Community College, Hilo, with a degree in tropical forest ecosystem and agroforestry management and currently works with The Nature Conservancy, protecting the remaining native forest ecosystems in Kaua'i's watershed areas.

Howzit? My name is Nicolai Barca. I'm twenty-three years old and a Kilauea resident. I'm also a hunter and a fisherman. My main concern is natural resources and invasive species. I'm also concerned with crime and crowding. But it seems to me that the people who are making these decisions are in O'ahu. An' y'know, O'ahu has nothing to lose from the Superferry. It's the outer islands who have stuff to lose. We're gonna have people here from the ferry with their trucks, all their fishing gear, all their hunting gear. They're gonna be comin' over here, exhausting our resources, picking our *maile*,[42] pickin our 'opihi, fishin' the reefs, diving. And they're gonna be takin' all that back to O'ahu. It's the outer islands, it's Kaua'i and Maui and Big Island. That's the places that really got a lot to lose from the Superferry. It just seems like it's getting shoved down our throats.

Anne Punohu

Anne Punohu is the education outreach director at the Kaua'i Museum. She is also a political activist, as well as a practitioner of Native Hawaiian culture, including 'oli, hula, politics, and ethnobotany. Her kumu[43] include Aunties Helena Maka Santos, Rachel Mahuiki, Poni Kama'u, Inoa Nahe, and many more. She has two daughters: Kaulana, seventeen, and Kanani, thirteen.

Aloha, my name is Anne Punohu. And I want to say aloha to all of the Superferry workers that are here, because I know a lot of you

---

[42] *Maile*: a fragrant vine found in the upland forests, prized by lei makers.

[43] *Kumu*: mentor, teacher, source.

personally. And I just want to show you something about Kaua'i people: You can divide us, you can't conquer us, but you can try to divide us. You can divide us along racial lines, you can say whatever you want about us, but when it all comes down to it, we gotta know each other when this is over. Now I'm gonna say a few comments, and then I have some questions for everybody.

My first question is to the Coast Guard. I fish down the jetty. And it's something that relaxes me, because I'm kind of a stressed-out person, so I enjoy that. When I called the Coast Guard and asked them for information on how I go and apply for a variance, I got all the way up the Public Information Officer, who was very nice. The Public Information Officer could not give me any information about how I needed to apply for a variance. We were told, and I'm not sure if this is wrong information for the people of Kaua'i, that all of us needed to go to the Coast Guard if we wanted to use the ferry area or that zone in the future and apply for a variance.

What is gonna be the procedure for people like myself who have a reason for being down at the ferry? My next question is, why are all of you ready to bring a ferry in to an area that has, number one, no stoplight! And is one-eighth of a mile from a public high school! You guys just had an incident on O'ahu, where a girl was walking to school, a man drove up in O'ahu, and tried to grab her and throw her in the car.

[Angry supporters call out in agreement, as Punohu's voice hardens with sternness.]

My question is, is my daughter gonna be safe at Kaua'i High that is an eighth of a mile away and easy access to somebody coming in when the ferry's gonna run at its regular time, which is five to nine P.M., in the dark? Are they gonna come and grab my kid and take her to O'ahu? I'm a mother. These are my concerns.

I feel personally that this is ill-conceived. It is the wrong time. It is the wrong thing. And I am the person that should be on the Superferry. And I'll tell you why. Because I am afraid to fly. I have not been off the island in eleven years! So, my situation is, I should be the first one gung ho on the ferry. And I *was* for the ferry. Until I started to think about it for a minute. When I heard they were gonna need an EIS I thought, that's great, they'll do the EIS, we'll come out, we'll make our comments, they'll put in a stoplight, we'll have good security, they won't have criminals or drugs on there, I won't have to worry about my daughter, all this will be taken care of because it'll be an EIS, we'll all be able to give public comments and it'll be done in a pono, correct, way. However, when I went down there and found out that you took our public-access pier, you denied the one few little happiness that I have in the world to put a little bamboo pole in the water and catch a little *manini*[44] fish!

Now, you have a million people on Oʻahu. I heard that 80 percent of the people on Oʻahu are for the Superferry and they want to come over here and—woo woo! Do you really think that 80 percent of the population of Oʻahu can squeeze onto Kauaʻi and we won't get pushed off?! We'll all be in the water on surfboards, because we won't have anywhere else to go!

---

[44] *Manini*: Reef surgeonfish *(Acanthurus triostegus)*, also called a convict tang in its adult stage.

Chapter Five

In the Water

Michael Shooltz

The fervor pouring out of the speakers during Governor Lingle's visit to Kauaʻi was powered by fresh memories of the showdown at Nawiliwili. Ire was at its zenith, not only because Superferry Corporation was bulldozing its way onto Kauaʻi regardless of public opinion, but also because the governor was bending over backward to accommodate the company, including calling out military reinforcements, replete with M16s. It was an insult to the democratic process that prompted many to take a stand. One such person was Michael Shooltz, a sixty-one-year-old semiretired banker. Here is his diary entry the morning after the vessel was turned away by citizens in the water.

Aloha ʻOhana,

Well, here it is, the morning after "Superferry: Day Two," and again I'm sitting here digesting last night's events.

I arrived at about 5:20 p.m. to see the Superferry already sitting there at the mouth of the harbor with the steadily growing crowds on the shoreline cheering on the surfers, swimmers, and kayakers filling the waters. While walking along the waterfront, I ran into a man who I'd met briefly at Sunday night's protests. As we chatted, a police officer stopped beside us, and we struck up a conversation. He asked us what our level of "commitment" was to the Superferry cause. He asked if we were willing to be arrested for the cause. He said that those surfers in the water had the courage of their commitment but accused us of being "just talkers." I agreed with him that I also found the courage and commitment of those in the water to be inspiring. When we asked him what he was "committed to" *he* was not willing to "commit" to an answer.

I moved on and ran into another friend who had a couple of large signs that needed to be held up along the water's edge, protesting the Superferry. So I hung the signs along the seawall and tended them for a while, joining in the cheering in support of those in the water. And then the canoe clubs arrived and began crossing back and forth across the harbor in front of the Superferry, bringing with them a wonderful surge in energy and support for both those in the water and those lining the shore. At that time I said to a friend, "I feel that I need to be there in the water." She said, "Go for it!"

I ran back across the park to buy a swimsuit and, on impulse, three large Snickers bars, then to my van to get my fins. As I crossed back across the street at the crosswalk, the police officer directing traffic noticed my fins and said, "You know, they are arresting those in the water." I said, "Mahalo," and continued on. When I got back to the seawall and got ready to get in the water, a stranger offered me a boogie board, which I gratefully accepted. Then another friend offered me their rash guard[45] to help stay warm, which was also a blessing. Then I entered the water with two surfers who were also heading out, as the cheers from those lining the shore supported our efforts. Gratitude swelled within me for all of those on shore and in the water. Within me was a clear knowing that the efforts of all of these ʻOhana were in support of some deep Truth that often lies buried deeply beneath the issues being wrestled with. Inside I prayed to hold the Light for everyone on all sides of these issues that our efforts together may bring to Light so much of what is happening in the world in the hope that it will all lead to a better, brighter place for all.

Being in the water was a beautiful experience. The full moon rising was magnificent. I gave chunks of the Snickers bars to many of those who had already been in the water for a couple of hours. They were received with laughter, joy, and appreciation. It was fun, kind of a boogie board "special delivery." The next hours floating in the water were filled with quiet conversations as folks got to know one another and expressed appreciation. I learned from a farmer from Moloaʻa about how the lettuce and broccoli are doing. Other bright young kids spoke of their concerns for the whales and dolphins.

---

[45] A type of athletic shirt made of spandex and nylon or polyester, used for light coverage to keep warm in the water.

Among the many Native Hawaiians, there were also folks from West Virginia, Santa Barbara, and the east coast, among other places. There were no leaders, merely a shared sense that this was the right thing to do and it needed to be done. There were many young people, and I found myself a bit humbled as I was addressed in the Hawaiian style as "Uncle" on a few occasions. As we were spread out across the harbor, there was one beautiful young woman on a board whom I only know by her voice as she would periodically lead us all in Hawaiian chants. I didn't know the words or the meaning, but the *mana* of the chants was strong, there on the water, under the full moon. And the periodic cheers from the distant shoreline warmed us and were a wonderful tonic for the thirst and occasional cramping that set in after awhile. At one point, we counted 71 of us in the water, plus the 30 or 40 who were paddling with the canoe clubs. We in the water would often break out in cheering of appreciation for those back on the shoreline whose support was so helpful and nurturing. The sense of camaraderie and shared purpose united us strongly.

Every so often, the Superferry would fire up its engines and begin to move toward us, kicking up its wake. I could always feel a surge of adrenaline go through the group on the water wondering what was to come next. Of course, always lurking around us was the presence of the Coast Guard and police boats, as they seemed to be probing and monitoring our level of commitment. I was told they weren't as aggressive as they had been the prior night, as there were many more of us in the water. We often greeted them with chants of *All Night Long!!*

On occasion, we would ask if they had anything to eat that they would share. They didn't. They shared that they were "just doing their jobs." I'd heard those same words from some of the police back on the pier. For years, whenever I hear those words, I have always been reminded of the question I used to wrestle with as a youngster when I first learned about the Holocaust in Nazi Germany: "How could a whole country of people allow something like the Holocaust to happen?" I just couldn't understand it. Now I see how much easier it is to "just do my job" than to take a stand that might bring much inconvenience into one's life; and how easy it really is for a whole society to slide into numbness and denial while "just doing my job." What is happening at Nawiliwili Harbor here on Kaua'i is about much, much more than the Superferry. It is a microcosm of how the military/corporate establishment is circumventing existing laws, totally trampling the well-being and constitutional rights of people everywhere. As in every other arena here on Kaua'i, they could care less about our environment, or the whales and the dolphins, or invasive species, or traffic and infrastructure problems, or drug trafficking, homeless people, or the local culture, let alone the rule of law. Our government's complicity in circumventing existing laws which very clearly require an Environmental Impact Study is so blatant. Those behind the scene have an insatiable thirst for power and control. I am told there is a new law that goes into effect on September 10th that will toughen the security areas around the Superferry, which will effectively mean that those beautiful young swimmers and surfers whom I met last night can then be arrested and treated as terrorists, as our government chooses instead to protect the Superferry Corporation and its CEO, former Secretary of the Navy Lehman, so that they can use this boat to transport their Stryker Brigades here to Kaua'i, all at taxpayer expense, and pursue their hidden agendas.

As I witnessed the conversations between the crews on the Coast Guard and police boats and those in the water, it struck me how those in the water were speaking Truth as best they knew it. And those in the boats spoke words containing intentional lies, other attempts at deception, or efforts to provoke fear. It struck me that if a person was going to be a peacekeeper, a fundamental requirement might be a willingness to speak the truth.

Of course those in the patrol boats were not from Kaua'i, while those in the water were attempting to protect their homes and way of life. The difference was almost startling when I realized it. The most glaring example was the Coast Guard's and police boats' offer to escort us back to shore "for our own protection" after the Superferry turned back to sea. Their escorting was actually herding, similar to our government's offers to protect us through the Patriot Act while herding us to a place of less and less freedom. Upon reaching shore, police then proceeded to arrest some of the escorted surfers, including a beautiful 12-year-old young man who had been out there for hours. Lies and deception always seem to be present at every level of the Superferry legacy and all that it represents. So much symbolism in the 12-year-old boy being greeted by police in riot gear.

The beauty and the courage of the ʻOhana together will stay in my heart. I wish I could do a search on this computer that would reveal the thoughts and feelings of each stalwart in the water as we watched the lights of the Superferry disappear over the horizon under the full moon. The thoughts were mixed, as we knew that the night before they had done a similar tactic and then returned to pull into the harbor. But it soon become clear that it was not going to return this night, and the mixture of joy, relief, accomplishment, and appreciation for one another and those on shore erupted in cheers, high fives, and slaps upon water and boards. In those moments, life was good and all was well on Kauaʻi. In seeming acknowledgment, a streaking meteorite flashed across the waters of Kalapaki Bay[46] as we turned back toward the breakwater and our ʻOhana cheered us on.

Swimming back to shore and being welcomed by the heartfelt cheers of family is sweet. The welcoming hands pulling surfboards and people back out over the seawall were so welcome. Knowing that some of those on shore were jumping into the water so that it would be more difficult for the police to identify swimmers and surfers was inspiring. They were giving us dry shirts and hats as we came out of the water to help disguise us from the SWAT team's efforts to arrest us. I never knew who provided my disguise, but later while walking across the park, a young Hawaiian man approached me and said, "You're wearing my cap." We exchanged Alohas and high fives, as I returned his cap with much appreciation.

Back at home, I treated myself to a hot shower and a cup of soup and then lay back out under our Kauaian night sky to witness the shooting stars and the unimaginable vastness of this universe within universes, wondering what the magic of this night's lunar eclipse holds for us all.

Today is another day, full of potentials and choices. Each is an opportunity to express our truth. May we have the wisdom to know what is right and the courage to do what is right, with peace in our hearts and love for one another.

Blessings, Michael

---

[46] Kalapaki Bay is adjacent to Nawiliwili Harbor.

Chapter Six

The Sham Public Hearings

Further Testimonies

THREE YEARS BEFORE GOVERNOR LINGLE *paid her infamous visit to Kauaʻi, the gears of the Hawaii Superferry machine locked into place and started to move. In January 2004, the company signed a contract to begin construction on two ferries. By spring, the state legislature passed a resolution to establish an interisland fast-ferry service. By summer, an application was filed with the Public Utilities Commission to secure a "Certificate of Public Convenience and Necessity." And, during the fall, PUC hearings took place on Oʻahu, Maui, Kauaʻi, and the Big Island. The hearings were a requirement for applying for the certificate, without which the ferry could not sail.*

Below are excerpts from some of the testimonies given at the Maui meeting, one of the earliest of many showings of concerned citizens demanding environmental review. The filled auditorium included canoe paddlers lining the back wall with placards urging an EIS. Even at this early stage, citizens were outraged by Superferry's attitude of being above environmental law. It was also here that the company first exhibited its pathology of citing arbitrary deadlines by which time bureaucratic processes had to be completed, lest the company lose its funding. This can be seen in the years that followed, as the company gave numerous shifting deadlines, ostensibly by which time they would lose funding, pressuring government agencies to expedite all processes.

Each of the following Maui testimonies forewarned of concerns that, all the way up until the time of this writing, were never resolved. Today, the Superferry sails between Oʻahu and Maui with insufficient screening for alien species, nonexistent whale protection, and no way to prohibit Superferry passengers from looting Maui's natural resources. In fact, in one month alone, in 2008, over 400 pounds of reef fish, 75 pounds of *'opihi*, and over 250 pounds of *limu* (seaweed) were taken from Maui's waters, discovered by inspectors in vehicles leaving Maui. As a result, many Maui residents have been panicked that their island will soon be stripped of its natural resources, with some species possibly plundered to extinction.

Following the Maui hearings are citizens' statements from more recent hearings on Kaua'i, the Big Island, and Moloka'i.

Public Utilities Commission Hearings — *Kahului, Maui, November 17, 2004*

Greg Kaufman — *Pacific Whale Foundation*

Good evening, Commissioners, my name is Greg Kaufman, I'm president of Pacific Whale Foundation, and I'm here this evening to testify on behalf of our over 225,000 supporters on this application. At the outset, we would request that you hold any action in abeyance on this application until a complete Environmental Impact Statement has been undertaken. Furthermore, since the application in its environmental address speaks to concerns on impacts of humpback whales and given the fact that there is federal money involved here, a Section 7 consultation with the National Marine Fisheries Service is required under the Endangered Species Act. The applicant has failed to include such a consultation in their application.

When I first started studying humpback whales here in the mid-'70s, there were an estimated 600 humpback whales in the entire North Pacific. I'm happy to tell you that today the number is estimated between 8,000 and 11,000. About 60 percent of those whales come to Hawai'i each year to mate, calve, and nurse their young. In the past four years, the whales have been arriving around between October 15 and October 20. This year they arrived on October 18. Last year they left Maui waters—the last sighting was July 3. This application states that there are only whales in Hawaiian waters from November to April. I don't know where they're getting their facts. But any water user can tell you differently.

The application tells you that this boat will cruise at 40 miles an hour. At 40 miles an hour, you move at a speed of 60 feet per second. Sixty feet per second. This boat is as big as—we all go to the Hula Bowl or the War Memorial Stadium—it's as big as that football field from end to end. From goal line to goal line. Imagine sitting on something that long moving 40 miles an hour. Imagine 900 people and 200 cars sitting on something that big, moving 40 miles an hour.

In Hawaiʻi, due in large part to the people of Maui County, we have the strictest approach regulations in the United States. In Hawaiʻi and Alaska, you cannot approach [a whale] any closer than 100 yards. In sanctuary waters, the fine for doing so is $125,000, potential impoundment of your vessel, and jail time. The Hawaii Superferry will close down 100 yards in less than five seconds. In less than five seconds, collision. That quick. Now, these folks in their application want to pretend under their Exhibit 10 that—they have this technical mumbo jumbo in there about Buck Rogers equipment that does not exist. Forward-looking sonar exists at speeds at eight to ten knots. You cannot stabilize it. The United States military cannot detect cetaceans. Yet these folks are purporting that they can detect cetaceans. Why is this an issue? Because deadly collisions occur at speeds in excess of 13 knots or about 17 miles an hour. This boat will be traveling at forty miles an hour through whale-rich waters.

Humpback whales don't care about geopolitical boundaries. They don't care about the National Marine Sanctuary boundaries. Humpback whales come here to mate, to calf, and to nurse their young. They are unpredictable. They are undetectable.

The National Oceanic and Atmospheric Administration (NOAA) whale guidelines for the East Coast say: "Within one to two miles of a whale, reduce speed to 13 knots." That's about 16 or 17 miles an hour. The minute they pull out of Honolulu Harbor, they cannot travel any faster than 13 knots, because there are whales all over that area within one to two miles.

It gets better: "From one mile to a half mile, reduce speeds to ten knots." Or about thirteen miles an hour. So these guys are saying that any time you're within a half mile to one mile of a whale, you immediately reduce your speed from forty miles an hour to twelve.

And it gets even better: "Half mile or less, no wake speed." Commissioners, if they live up to what they say, they are talking about a nineteen-hour one-way trip to Maui. Forget about how cheap their airfares are. Bring your sleeping bag. These fellows are saying anything they want and portraying anything they want to get this application considered. Just as they didn't talk to the scientific community as a representative, just as they didn't talk to the canoe club, just as they didn't talk to the people of Maui, just as they haven't addressed the socioeconomic issues, they have not addressed the environmental concerns and they have not addressed those of the endangered humpback whale which happens to be a multi-multi-million dollar contributor to Maui's economy. Approval [of] this application endangers whales and endangers our economy. Thank you.

Greg Westcott — *Farmer*

Hello, Commissioners. I'm a farmer here on the island of Maui. And I read the application and a number of the attachments, and, frankly, I was dismayed to see that there were no, *absolutely no*, environmental documents contained in this application. I can't understand how you would consider approving a project of this magnitude that affects all of the Hawaiian islands and could affect everybody living in Hawai'i without any kind of environmental review. An EIS is within your ability to impose upon this applicant, and it's the only way that you can have the facts that you need to make an informed decision. It's the only way that we, the members of the public, can participate in this decision in a meaningful way. This [meeting] is not adequate; one meeting at Maui Waena School is not enough, and you can't dismiss the public with such a small amount of participation. You wouldn't be able to tell from this application that the Hawaiian Islands are in the midst of an invasion of alien species. The Federal Office of Technology Assessment has said that Hawai'i's problem of alien species is the worst in the nation. The coordinating group on alien species, which is a joint group of federal and state agencies and environmental groups, has said that the number one threat to our economy, to the livelihood of our people is alien species. This new system, which they like to call H-4,[47] would in my opinion be an H-4 for alien species. How are we going to determine the risks posed by this system? If we don't have scientific data on how this system can affect the movement of

---

[47] "H-4" was a play on words based on the O'ahu freeway system ("H-1," "H-2," and "H-3") used by Hawai'i Superferry to promote its product. It was later abandoned after the outer islands made it clear that they did NOT want a freeway running from Honolulu to their islands.

alien species between the islands, then we cannot make an informed decision and we cannot assess the risks posed by this project.

There are a number of disastrous alien species that are now confined to individual islands. This H-4 will mean that they have a much greater likelihood of being transported to all the islands. The one that I fear most is on the island of O'ahu right now. It came in May. It's called the glassy-winged sharpshooter. It's an insect that attacks all plants and carries an incurable, fatal plant disease. It could mean the end of my livelihood as a farmer. It could threaten agriculture throughout the Hawaiian islands. If we don't examine this proposal in the light of the threat posed by this insect and by other equally dangerous insects on all the islands and snakes and chameleons and a host of other horrors that are waiting to spread among the islands, then we're doing a disservice. And you cannot make an informed decision unless you say there has to be an Environmental Impact Statement on this statewide system. It involves hundreds of millions of dollars, it involves state land and state facilities, all of the triggering mechanisms are there for EIS. And it furthermore would give us a chance to participate in a meaningful way. So thank you.

Jeffrey Parker — *Kahului Harbor Coalition*

Good evening, Chairman Caliboso and commissioners. Thank you for coming to our islands. I'm Jeffrey Parker and I'm representing the Kahului Harbor Coalition and my own business, Tropical Orchid Farm, Inc. I'm a farmer. I've been in business for almost thirty years. I'm a member of the Maui County Farm Bureau.

I get nervous when I hear the term "fast track," because sometimes it means limiting public participation. Throughout the application and exhibits, reference is made to the January deadline to satisfy the federal Title XI Loan Guarantee. I find this to be a completely specious argument. It is not the public's fault that the ferry partners may have wrongly estimated the time frame. And how do we know that this was not planned by the ferry partners as a way to put more pressure on you, the commissioners? In the application, it is even hinted at that a delay beyond January 1 would not totally sink the loan guarantee. In fact, I suspect that it would be just a matter of filing for an extension. I just cannot buy into the idea that we should ignore environmental review and other important issues simply because the ferry company has gotten itself into a time-frame problem.

I said that the application is weak in showing need. Much of the evidence presented in the exhibits is simply newspaper and magazine articles which are instigated in some degree by the ferry company itself. There is very little, if any, independent investigation or analysis in any of the articles I read. In some of the articles, it seems to be saying that one of the biggest benefits of the ferry is to move farm products to market. But after I raised the issue of increased pest movement interisland, a ferry spokesman at the big harbor meeting that we had about a month ago said, "We may be able to deal with your concerns by refusing to carry plants and produce altogether." So one of the main justifications for this permit in the application, that it will help farmers, may turn out to be a complete falsehood. This application is deficient. Where is the comment letter from the Department of Agriculture? We need to know if there will be inspections of vehicles and cargo, how will the inspector positions be filled, and where will the money come from to hire them? This application is deficient.

Now, what do I mean by major impacts? I can conclude shortly. The ferry system will ratchet up the whole alien species issue to a dangerous new level because now, any new pest species which is established on any island may rapidly spread to the other islands. But just as important are the cars, the pickup trucks, and vans that will potentially travel on every back road of every island, possibly dropping off seeds and eggs wherever they go. So rapid and efficient dispersal to every remote corner of every island is the new issue raised by this project. It's already been proven, for example, that coqui frog eggs can travel in mud splashed up underneath the vehicles. This project will overload the infrastructure of Maui with its daily disgorging of 800 passengers and 200 vehicles. By the way, Maui already has a critical shortage of campsites for visitors and locals. Where do all these people on holiday plan to camp? In the mall parking lot? As a key component of the larger DOT [Department of Transportation] harbor expansion, the ferry operations, together with the increased cruise ships and the resulting security zones, will eventually kick the canoe paddlers and the surfers out of the harbor. Native people have raised the issue that persons from other islands such as Oʻahu may now accompany their pickups and vans over to Maui for the specific purpose of harvesting our precious cultural and natural resources such as fish, ʻopihi, imu, maile, flowers, seeds, ʻawa,[48] etc. Can you imagine the fishing parties that will arrive in huge numbers from fished-out Oʻahu to plunder our relatively abundant fish stocks? Thank you.

Masako Westcott — *Flower Grower*

We have every reason to fear losing the home of the canoe clubs and our beloved surf spots. Where would the queue of embarking cars be at Holoa Park? We're concerned about the urbanization of the shoreline, the uglification of Kahului, and more pollution into the air and sea. We're concerned about the social impacts, more pressure on our beaches and parks, on fishing spots, on forest gathering. What are the plans for security? Will passengers be checked, baggage x-rayed? Who pays for this? Department of Transportation? Have they agreed? Where is the document? The memorandum of understanding. Will cars be inspected? Where are the studies about the possibility for smuggling prohibited plants, animals? What about drugs? Ice[49] isn't our only drug problem. Heroin from Afghanistan, cocaine from Colombia, they're imported. The ferry system sounds ideal for transporting drugs. Who will search the cars? Who will pay? I've heard the figure $200 million for this project. How is this figure arrived at if plans are not sufficiently developed to present to the public? How can the state involve us in a partnership without public review?

There are many more questions than answers. Approving this application without all the facts and without full public involvement is undemocratic. The applicant requests the PUC to review their application and issue the certificate within the time frame that meets their fund raising and financial needs, which they claim is the end of the year. This is my home. I am asking you to take all the time needed to conduct a genuine examination of the social, cultural, and environmental impacts of this project in a joint federal-state EIS. You are the Public Utility Commission and must act on behalf of the people. Mahalo.

---

[48] *ʻAwa*: kava root.
[49] Ice: street parlance for crystal methamphetamine, which is ingested by smoking.

Faith Mori — *Na Kai ʻEwalu Canoe Club*

Hi, my name is Faith Mori. I am president of Na Kai ʻEwalu Canoe Club and our *hale*[50] is in the Kahului Harbor alongside of Hawaiian Canoe Club. I'm sorry, but you're just newcomers to us. We live here. This is our home. This is our hale. When you supersede our needs because of some new person thinking that perhaps this is something that we want, I don't know why people don't listen to us. We live here. We're being shoved out of our home.

So please, I am pleading on behalf of the citizens of Maui that you look at us as residents of Maui, listen to our voices. We are the people who live here. Our grandchildren are going to grow up here. Our grandchildren are going to paddle, and it's going to go on for generations. So that's why we're here tonight—to plead with you to look at that social impact that the Superferry will have. I also come from Kula. And old-time Kula, we're all farming families. And the Superferry has a beautiful web site and one of the things that they are saying would be beneficial would be a farmer could load up his truck, drive to the Superferry, take his vegetables or his wares to market, and he could conceivably come home in the evening and be with his family again. Well, I say when you pack up your things and you get on the ferry and you're on until about 2 o'clock perhaps, you get off in Honolulu, you drive to the stores and all the receiving guys are closed. So maybe you can find somebody else to buy your stuff, turn around, get back on the ferry at four o'clock, be back on Maui by 7, home by 8, oh, yeah, great time to spend with your family. I don't think that this is viable. For farmers, small truck farmers, this is not a viable option.

Iokepa Naeole — *Hawaiian Canoe Club*

I just want to share with you my plans. I don't think you've taken time to listen to what we have planned for Kahului Harbor. In 2020, we will have tripled our fleet of canoes between Na Kai ʻEwalu and Hawaiian Canoe Club. We will have gone from 300 members to 1,000 members in 2020. In 2020, any given day of the week, Monday through Friday, you will see Kahului Harbor filled with canoes— one-man, two-man, three-man, and six-man—because people decided

---

[50] *Hale*: house, building.

to go paddle instead of eat their Happy Meal. In 2020, Kahului Harbor will look like Papeete, full of healthy people practicing their culture on the ocean and staying healthy. In 2020, the ice problem will have been eliminated, because all of those kids that we do have now paddling will spread the word on to their friends so they will all become part of our paddling, surfing, fishing community, recreational users, cultural users of the harbor, and ice will be a thing of the past. Domestic violence will be a thing of the past.

All the social ills that we see now that we have not really looked at curing in the past, we've been doing it at Kahului Harbor for fifty years. Hukilau, Maui Beach, Holoa Park will become a cultural attraction. And I'm not talking *dakine*[51] Feast at Lele, you know, hula show, I'm talking living, breathing culture. So what visitors do come to visit our islands, when they come to Kahului they will see a living, breathing culture with Hawaiians of every color, race, creed, religion, all applying their practices, being healthy, being Hawaiian.

In 2020, Kahului Harbor will host the first Olympic paddling event when Hawai'i has its first Olympic games held here in the summer, and we will host that event. In 2020, we will have replanted coral from outside of Kahului Harbor into Kahului Harbor to replenish the reef system that was once there and healthy. In 2020, the fisherman will be able to go into Kahului Harbor and, just like I did and my grandfather did when I was growing up, take enough food home to feed the street. In 2020, that little cove down by where Maui Beach Hotel is will become a fish pond again. So when the seas are rough, we don't need to go into the ocean, we can go right there and get our fish. That's our plans. If you ask me to give you this 2020 plan in a stack of paper, no, you come buy me some poi one day and something to drink and we sit down and we talk about it.

I'm representing not only Hawaiian Canoe Club but all the generations of paddlers before me and more importantly all the generations of paddlers that will come after me. If I have done my job, all of what I just shared with you will become reality. I'm not saying it cannot exist with the visitor industry and with the Superferry, although I do openly state that there should be a comprehensive EIS.

---

[51] *Dakine*: pidgin English for "the whatchamacallit."

What I'm saying is that's what we plan, okay, and how is your plan going to conflict with ours? Or could your plan possibly help ours? So keep that in mind. As a Hawaiian, one of the kuleana, your responsibility, is to be hospitable, to welcome strangers into your house, into your 'aina, and share aloha. We've been doing that, but now we're getting to the point where, wow, we've got to take care of ourselves, too. But I'm not willing to turn my back on any visitors coming off any ship or any ferry and say, you know what, *pau*[52] the aloha, no. I would stop being a Hawaiian like that. But you have to make sure you *malama*[53] us, too. But if you don't malama us, you know, might not be me, but in my generation or a couple generations from now, but the aloha will soon dissipate and disappear and then we will just look like Dallas, Texas—no offense to Texas.

Okay. So those are my plans. Those are the seeds that we plant in every child that comes to our canoe clubs, and we share with them this vision of how we can, you know, better our future socially, environmentally. My responsibility is to bring them up with big visions and empower them to pursue these visions and to say, you know what, you *can* do this. It doesn't always have to be, you know, like this with us. You know, historically it's been quality of life sacrificed for economic gain.

So put us first, invest in us, trust in us, that in the future it will be something that you will never see anywhere else on the planet. In 2020, the typical visitor will go home knowing that Hawai'i is the number one place to visit not because of the infrastructure provided for the visitor industry, but because of the people that are there and the way we feel about how to live on this planet. With aloha. So again, I request, I recommend, I insist on a full EIS. And I say put the community first, and I'm not talking just paddlers—fishermen, surfers, everybody—and it ends up becoming the whole community, because we get people that come and paddle for us from all ethnic backgrounds. Just put us first. Mahalo.

---

[52] *Pau*: no more, finished.
[53] *Malama*: consider, care for.

Belt Collins Visits the Islands
March 2008

FLASH FORWARD THREE YEARS from the Maui hearings. Governor Lingle has by now refused to accept a 5–0 ruling from the Hawai'i Supreme Court requiring an Environmental Impact Statement before the Superferry can sail. Instead, she has given Superferry her blessing to travel from Honolulu to the outer islands. And, in a direct challenge to the power of the court, in October 2007 the governor convened a special session of the state legislature. With the help of compliant O'ahu legislators (many of whom were targets of a fierce $379,000 lobbying campaign, sweetened with campaign donations from officials of both Superferry and J. F. Lehman and Co.), a new law was passed that effectively overrode the Supreme Court ruling. The amount spent in 2007 by Superferry on lobbying represented more than twice *the amount spent by any other company or organization seeking legislative outcomes. The new law, cynically called "Act 2," confirmed that an EIS would be undertaken, but it would be done while—rather than before—the Superferry continued operations. This in itself defeated the whole purpose of an EIS.*

Act 2 also mandated that, as part of this new EIS, hearings be conducted on all the islands for public input. This chapter presents testimonies from a few of those hearings, given on Kaua'i, the Big Island, and Moloka'i. Unfortunately, most people who testified were unaware of just how impotent their opinions were. They, like most people, had no idea that the new EIS was actually written to guarantee that the ship will sail, **regardless of any findings related to environmental impacts.**

For example, the legislature (pressured by Lingle and Superferry) made sure this new EIS did not provide what every authentic EIS offers: a "no action alternative," which allows the "accepting" entity (in this case, the state and the people of Hawai'i) to reject the proposed project. But this isn't the only difference between a normal EIS and its diametric opposite crafted by Lingle and the legislature.

As attorney Daniel Hempey points out in Chapter 12, the original EIS mandated by the Hawaii Environmental Policy Act (HEPA) had as its stated intent to protect "humanity's well-being." But under the new EIS within Act 2, the intent is "the establishment of interisland ferry service." Any findings at all related to environmental impact will have no real consequence whatsoever as to whether the ferry continues to operate or not! This is not a true EIS—this EIS is really toothless, advisory, merely *providing busywork for Belt Collins, the company chosen by the state to conduct the project. Whatever the findings, they would have no bearing on the operation of the company. All paid for by $1 million in tax dollars.*

The point of the EIS exercise was obviously not to protect humanity (that is, the public, or the environment) but to provide a public relations mask to protect the company, and the governor, and, most of all, to keep the ship in the water.

*   *   *

By this time, many people already felt so demoralized by the doublespeak of both Superferry and the Lingle administration that they chose to boycott the hearings altogether. Others, such as those on Oʻahu, where the meetings drew a total of twelve people, apparently didn't care. On Kauaʻi, however, sentiments remained as strong as they were the night the citizens jumped into the bay to block the ship.

At the start of the Kauaʻi hearing, before citizens were given the opportunity to speak, a graphic slide show listed potential impacts of the Superferry. No surprise that the presentation was rigged to steer a particular set of public responses: The military use of the Superferry was glaringly absent from the list, as was the option of "no action"—a requirement of every EIS. After the presentation, a panel of Department of Transportation and Belt Collins representatives sat at the front of the room, impassively and without speaking, as the public, one by one, poured out their frustration, anger, and sorrow.

Kauaʻi Hearings, Lihuʻe — *March 19, 2008*

Kauaʻi, which had been by far the most demonstrative of all the islands against the Superferry, drew sizable crowds to the Belt Collins scoping meetings when many on the other islands had thrown up their hands in frustration, after months of trying to navigate the Orwellian logic of Superferry and the Lingle administration. The following testimonies from Kauaʻi criticize the phony EIS process as much as they offer suggestions for protecting the environment.

Kaʻohu Harada

I'm a Hawaiian Studies student, but more importantly, I am a Hawaiian. Like many, I have had the privilege and responsibility of being raised here on Kaua'i with a family that understands the importance of our natural resources, a family that has depended on—and continues to depend on—our natural resources to feed and nurture our family and community. I was taught by my grandparents to stay within your area when you fish, hunt, and gather. Don't go *maha'oi*,[54] or take from other people's houses or their ice box without first being invited, and only leaving with what was given and shared with you by your host.

The Superferry has *no* invitation to Kaua'i, and yet, they insist on coming. How rude!

And now, to write up the mana'o [*she is referring to a handout distributed before the meeting*] that was brought to the opening of this *halawai*[55]: 'ohana, aloha, ho'ihi—respect. We should think, that the land was here before us. And like our kupuna, it has, in many ways, housed us, provided for our needs and luxuries. Now, it demands respect from its *mo'opuna*,[56] and the care and stewardship that is needed, returned.

[Earlier today,] I heard others share their concerns of cost, drug trafficking, public safety, manpower, military, and negative impact on our environment, such as invasive species. I do share the same concerns.

But what concerns me *more* than the invasive species is the invasive *mentality* of the Superferry! They have no understanding of what the true meaning of 'ohana, aloha or kuleana is. This mentality has done so much damage already and does not promote true progress of 'ohana, 'aina, our present or our future. How many times must we say no? No means no!

Keone Kealoha

Aloha, my name is Keone Kealoha. I work as executive director of Malama Kaua'i, a sustainability advocacy organization here on the island, but this evening, I'm testifying as a resident and individual.

I would like to bring attention to the fact of what is written here, and I'd like to read: "This EIS will not be governed by Chapter 343, Hawai'i Revised Statutes," as stated in Act 2.

---

[54] *Maha'oi*: to be presumptuous.

[55] *Halawai*: meeting.

[56] *Mo'opuna*: grandchildren.

Just to be clear, the process that is going on here is not an EIS. It is not an EIS. It says so right here *[pointing to a copy of Act 2 document in his hand]*. So just be clear, that throughout the rest of the documentation and the rest of the process as it is described as an EIS, it is not.

I would like to see, when you do produce the draft "EIS," that you clearly distinguish the differences between the HRS [Hawai'i Revised Statutes] 343 and *this* process. I'd like to see all of those.

I think part of the process that has gotten people so upset is that things have been done in a kind of sneaky and shady way. If you could at least put it right up front and say what's different about this process than the real HRS 343 EIS process, I think it'd be very clear and people could understand.

I have another question, and this goes to actually the next three questions, and I'll read from the handout that you gave: "This alternative mode of transportation would serve a wide range of users, including residents, visitors and various sectors, and emergency responders, and would support economic diversity." Is there a report anywhere that verifies or justifies that being stated in this document? I was at the Senate hearings on O'ahu when that question was asked of the representative from the Department of Economic Development. They said "no."

Second one. *[Again, he reads from the Act 2 document.]* "In times of natural or other disasters, large-capacity ferry vessel operations could provide the means to rapidly deploy disaster-relief personnel, equipment or supplies." Is there a study that can support that statement? Are there facts? It would seem to me, if there was a hurricane, that the ferry would likely be affected by that. Perhaps there might be some emergency services that might be needed to help the ferry, that might otherwise be taken away from residents and *their* needs.

[Reading] "The operations of the large-capacity ferry vessel would foster diversified agriculture." This question was also asked in the Senate hearings. There is no study or facts to support this from the state, from the DLNR [Department of Land and Natural Resources]. Barry Fukunaga was asked these same questions about carbon footprinting. There are no studies to support any of this.

And finally, a question about ... it says "description of action," action being evaluated here as being for harbor improvements for a large-capacity ferry. Is a large-capacity ferry really what Hawai'i needs? Have you done studies to look at *small*-capacity ferries? *[The crowd cheers.]* You're spending $350 million on harbor improvements on Maui for a ship that's taking less than a hundred people a trip. Maybe we could spend that money more wisely if we first did some research into what it is we really need by way of maritime transportation.

Juan Wilson

My name is Juan Wilson. I'm an architect and planner from Hanapepe. I represent www.islandbreath.org.

One of the things I spent a lot of time thinking about concerning the Superferry when it was first proposed was its connection to a Stryker Brigade and the transportation of military equipment between Oʻahu and the Big Island. It was of concern to me because I realized that the deck of the Superferry was going to be a common space that would be shared interweavingly between the public and the military. I am aware at looking at the equipment and the specifications for the equipment that the "Strykerferry" brigade is associated with, that the Superferry will be carrying machinery and weapons, ammunitions that are likely to either have been used in conjunction with depleted uranium, have depleted uranium particles or dust embedded in them, or be contaminated in one way or another. We know for a fact that the military has lied about DU at Schofield Barracks; they lied about DU on the Big Island; it's been discovered in both places. It's very likely under "emergency" or "security" or other reasons that the military will decide that it's best to have tests firing live ammunition, just like they're going to have in the field, or that they're going to be using machinery that has come back from Iraq or other places where depleted uranium has been heavily used, including all the personnel carriers—helicopters and all the other things that use depleted uranium munitions. It is a danger to the environment; it will be tracked back and forth from the harbor up into the test range; it'll be tracked from the deck of the Superferry, and ... those particles will be exchanged with public transportation and with private individuals—pickup trucks and coolers. There can be massive and universal contamination from the military equipment in this public space, which will be where all the cars park, spread out to every garage, every back cul-de-sac on every island.

So I think one of the things that this EIS should address is: What is the possible contamination and distribution of depleted uranium throughout the state as a result of the Superferry's EIS now saying that "we're going to be in Hawai'i" and the obvious use of the Superferry is to carry them around? Thank you very much.

Rick White

The de facto *governator* has gutted our environmental protection law by arbitrarily circumventing the will of the people and the well-being of the outer islands with the complicity of you, the DOT. The governor and her coalition of uselessness took the side of corporate special interest over the well-being and self-determination of the people of the outer islands; at their direct, indirect, and cumulative negative impacts.

You said in your opening statement … *that you found no substantial concerns*. Well, we have substantial concerns, and three minutes … it doesn't cut it. That's going to take *hours* for each person to speak today. Your process is flawed. You have stated that position—that you don't think there are substantial concerns (and this indicates that you have an obvious bias to start with toward corporate interest), and we don't want your urbanization; we don't want your militarization; and we don't want your exploitation. Not here. … It doesn't matter about your process. You need to get that, because we're going to fight this until you're old and gray.

I'll give you formal notice herewith that we the people of Kaua'i give the Department of Transportation and its conflicts of interest a vote of "no-confidence" on the EIS being done properly, and, likewise, with Belt Collins and its conflict of interest. Likewise, we give you notification here formally that you have a vote that we are giving you—we are giving the governor—a vote of no-confidence and her rubber-stamp legislature of O'ahu. We don't recognize them here as an authority, and if we're pushed, we'll make that formal also.

I respectfully submit your process as irrelevant. I'm the taxpayer. You're fired!

Raeamma Carter

I recently had a friend visiting here who lives on Bainbridge Island [in Washington state] and she used to live on the north shore—that's where I met her years ago. We were talking about the ferry and she said, "You know, in Washington that's how we get to and from the islands. We don't have planes on Bainbridge." And I said, "What is your ferry like?" and she said, "Well, I will tell you this much, we would *never* allow a ferry like you people have in Hawai'i." And I said, "Why?" and she said, "It's too large and it's too fast." She said they would consider it a threat to the environment up there. So I thought, they care more about their environment than [we do in] Hawai'i.

That's something to think about. Thank you.

Ned Whitlock

Hello, I'm Ned Whitlock. This morning I was cuttin' sugar cane for the fruit stand and, uh, I'm a full-time farmer and I've been farming most of my life. Each time you cut the cane down and you strip the leaves back, there's all ants all through there. You shake 'em out and put [the cane] on the ground, bundle 'em up, and carry 'em on your shoulder back to cut them up.

Well, it got me thinkin' about the little ... fire ant. The little fire ant is about a millimeter long. It comes from Central America, South America also. It has a very painful bite, and there's infestations on the Big Island where they estimate the population is 95 million ants *per acre*. These ants form "super colonies," they displace other ant species, and the University of Hawai'i, in their control efforts, were able to suppress them a bit, but as soon as they stopped the treatments the populations came right back. So just imagine the prospect of going from the pretty benign ant population we have here, to fire ants. It'll affect farming in a radical way. People who are working with plants everyday—there'll be a whole new element in their life. So in my perspective, anything that hastens the invasion of that little fire ant into Kaua'i has got to be stopped.

That's all I have to say.

David Dinner

I'm David Dinner, and I'm speaking for Thousand Friends of Kaua'i. ... Everybody knows that the fragile ecology and the infrastructure of Kaua'i cannot withstand even the development that's already here. The goose that lays the golden egg is not dead yet, but she has been mortally wounded by the deeds of the people who have developed the Superferry. Business and development interests are fighting over the golden eggs rather than working to save her.

The motives of the Superferry developers are hidden and deceptive, but they are clearly aimed at profit—at the cost of service and attention to the environment. Their methods have alienated the neighbor islands. Originally our main concern was a call for an EIS first, before the Superferry was launched. Now, though, it has become clear that this process is not simply a matter of expediency to avoid the EIS in order to save time for the passage of the ferry, the entire matter is more analogous to a bully pushing aside the considerations of the neighbor islands to get his way. The attitudes of the Superferry developers and, by association, the governor of Hawai'i, the Department of Transportation, and the legislature, have been unconscionable.

If you really want to protect the environment, then allow large businesses to enter our community only when they demonstrate a sincere effort to be forthright and caring about our islands. ... Hear us well, everybody knows that we will not do business with the Superferry developers, we will not allow the Superferry to pass a sham EIS without challenge, we will not have the Superferry come to Kaua'i.

Kim Potter

Aloha, I'm Kim Potter. Aloha, fellow concerned residents and friends. I'm here on behalf of the humpback whales. I am a contributing member of the Pacific Whale Foundation, and a huge humpback whale fan. I would like everyone to turn to the map that's on page three of the handout that we got at the door, Act 2: EIS.

There's a map in the insert of the State of Hawai'i. And the area that I'm concerned about is that area, that triangle which is part of the Hawaiian Islands Humpback Whale National Marine

Sanctuary. And I quote, "The vessel shall avoid operating within the Hawaiian Islands Humpback Whale National Marine Sanctuary, or in waters less than 100 fathoms from January 1 to April 30."

As a witness residing on the island of Molokaʻi, myself and several residents there have witnessed when the waves got too rough on the backside, or where the tallest sea cliffs in the world are, the way the Superferry is supposed to go, and everyone was getting sick and the boat was breaking down, *et cetera*, so they started cutting through that area. I've witnessed it. My friends have witnessed it, and this was *after* January 1. ... Well, pity the poor whales that come (as was in the paper this year) as early as October.

But I can tell you that during the time the Superferry was running, you did *not* see whales in that area. This is a WHALE sanctuary—it's like *whale soup* out there, folks! If you go 100 yards out, it's an ancient Hawaiian fishpond; beyond that it drops off, it's warm, calm waters. This is why the whales go there. We saw NO whales during the time that the Superferry was running there.

So, where are they going to go with their babies? I was out last week on the Na Pali; saw *nada* bringing up the newborn to the surface. What's going to happen? Anyway, I'm here for the *kohola*.[57] Please save the whales.

Katy Rose

First, I'd like to express my deep admiration for the August 27th brigade—the brave men and women, boys and girls, who stood fast in Nawiliwili Harbor and turned the Superferry around.

[Applause]

We owe them a debt of gratitude for using the time-honored practice of direct action and civil disobedience in keeping Hawaiʻi safe from the Superferry for the past seven months.

The intensity of the militarized response to our August protest told us here that there is much more at stake in the operation of the Hawaii Superferry than the provision of civilian travel. Hawaiʻi is a highly militarized area, and it is the staging area for much of the imperialist activity of the United States government.

I am here to insist that we, the people, be provided all the facts about the Superferry's intentions for use as a military carrier, the

---

[57] *Kohola*: humpback whales.

Thoughts from an Old-Timer

Letter to the Editor of Kaua'i's *Garden Island* newspaper
Lloyd Miyashiro

Some people saying only haoles protesing da Supaferry.

As not true. So if you born and raised preemuch, especially if you one ol taima, I like discuss dis issue wid you.

Kaua'i wen shua change yeh? I rememba, small keed time, when da choo choo trains used to pull cane between the houses in Waipouli an den cross da road right by wea Chevron service station stay now. I rememba when had rice growing in Wailua Valley, when da ony traffic light was in da Kekaha cane feel.

Rememba? When had plenny maile, mokihana an limu kohu, when had da small, sweet, purple lilikoi, Japanese family stoas and Filipino babas all ova.

Den pineapple an shuga stahted dying out. Tourism and hotels stahted coming up. Now get beeg stoas and beeg developments. Open space disappearing, traffic I no need tell you, infrastrukcha ovaloaded.

None of dis da Supaferry fault. But da Supaferry coming widout one EIS, as the last straw. As disrespectful to da ocean an da 'aina. Rememba da ol Hawaiian song, "Kaua'i, hemolele i ka malie," perfect in da calm? I no like Kaua'i come like eryplace else. So I going continue to, peacefully, protes da Supaferry, unless dey do da right ting.

How about you? Watchyootink?

Downtown Honolulu

scope of such use, if it is intended, and the impact on the people and the land of possible depleted-uranium contamination from the transport of such military equipment and vehicles as the Stryker Brigade. And while I know that this is far beyond your scope, unfortunately, I hope that you will keep in mind the ultimate victims of warfare and militarism. Thank you.

BIG ISLAND AND MOLOKAʻI

Below, in the testimonies from the Big Island of Hawaiʻi and from Molokaʻi, the character and concerns unique to each island are apparent. Radioactive waste ranks high among Big Island residents, while the people of Molokaʻi, the most rural of all the islands, are fastidiously protective of their whales, ecosystems, and natural resources.

HILO, BIG ISLAND — *March 26, 2008*

MOANIKEALA AKAKA

How would you like to have *your* child on that Superferry next to the Stryker Brigade, which has depleted uranium from Iraq on it?!! You know, we are sick and tired of being used and abused by the U.S. military in these islands. And there will be social impact. There will be much social impact.

My son is getting his master's degree in invasive species at the university. And there is a great deal of concern by that body about the invasive species, the natural resource extraction of our ʻaina, of our plants and resources. The ʻopihi, the koa wood, the fish that are rare on other islands. The plants. They will rape and run. They will take the plants over to Oʻahu and sell them, deplete us of our natural resources here. There's concern about the coqui, the transfer of the coqui frog. The transfer of invasive species, not only *from* here, but *to* here, as well. So there is a great deal of concern.

Also there is concern about the military-industrial complex, which has left many, many areas on this island from the Second World War, with their military *ʻopala*[58] and their munitions.

There are many people who do not want this Superferry on our neighbor islands. So keep 'em on ʻOʻahu where they belong. Mahalo.

---

[58] *ʻOpala*: garbage, waste.

Jim Albertini

I'm speaking on behalf of Malu 'Aina Center for Non-Violent Education and Action, in Curtistown, a local nonprofit peace-and-justice environmental organization. We've initiated depleted uranium, alpha radiation contamination on this island and Schofield Barracks. Alpha radiation is very difficult to detect. It's short wavelength. What procedures are going to be put in place to detect alpha radiation being transported on the Superferry on any military vehicles that go between Schofield Barracks and Pohakuloa? Who's going to be liable? Do the insurance policies of the Superferry cover radiation? Who's going to be liable for the spread of invasive species and all the economic damage that's been done related to those things? The bee mites coming to the Big Island. The coqui frogs spreading elsewhere. What about the civil rights of citizens and the martial law, gestapo-like tactics that have been used to block protesting on Kaua'i, Maui? What about the protection of natural resources? The *hapu'u* ferns being shipped off? This five-day comment period on what should be included on the EIS is far too short. The EIS should have been done years ago. And now that it is being enforced, you're pushing a five-day comment period. It's going to be in the newspaper tomorrow. It should be extended at least two to three weeks. And what about bankruptcy? When the Superferry goes bankrupt, how much does the taxpayer stand to lose?

John Ota

My name is John Ota. Born and raised on this island. ... I've attended quite a number of EIS meetings and it seems to me that this EIS also is addressing the same thing that the Navy did—using observers on board the ship. But how realistic is that—traveling at 50 knots? Ripples in the ocean surface, reflection from the sun, even with binoculars, anytime any observer is going to see a whale is when the tail sticks up above the surface of the water. There is NO man that can see underneath the water, who can see if a whale exists or not.

The keel of the catamaran—how deep is it? Will the captain of the ship know if the keel comes in contact with a whale? Why is the catamaran not equipped with sonar of some sort of fish finding devices so it can detect the fish? At speeds of 50 knots, even at 500 feet where it says ... they're supposed to maintain 500 feet away from whales, how many minutes does it take for a [ship traveling at] 50 knots to reach [stop before it is closer than] 500 feet?

Jet propulsion. I've worked with jet engines almost all my life. I do understand how jet engines work. Catamaran has four of these. Is the exhaust from the jet engine deposited directly into the ocean? If so, what happens to the carbon dioxide? What happens to all the chemicals that are added into jet fuel? What kind of pollutants do they create? How will the carbon dioxide be removed from the ocean? There are many questions that are not answered pertaining to pollution.

How long do the whales stay under the surface of the ocean? Does anyone know? The only time anyone can see a whale is when the tail comes up, or when the whales are giving birth.

Cory Harden

This EIS is probably illegal. An EIS is done *before* resources are committed and *before* harm is done—*not* on the fly.

The special law that allowed this EIS, and cut "the heart out of Hawai'i's environmental protections," as William Aila of O'ahu said, is probably illegal.

Our government calling out deadly force against unarmed surfers trying to stop a private corporation from breaking our environmental law is probably illegal.

Superferry should not sail until after this EIS is completed.

But this EIS, even if done illegally, can serve a purpose. It can answer questions that have been dodged for years.

Were the landing barges chosen mainly to avoid triggering an EIS? What happens if the EIS determines that the landing barges and other choices weren't the best choices?

Will sea animals be killed and maimed by collisions? Does underwater noise from the propulsion system impact sea animals by disrupting feeding, mating, caring for the young, and communication? What methods of protection will work, and who will foot the bill?

How will the military use the ferry? Will they bring hazardous material aboard? If it's classified, how will we know?

How does Superferry jive with the Sustainability Initiative and the new Harbors Master Plan? As Juan Wilson of Kaua'i put it, do we need a "40,000-horsepower, 40-mile-an-hour football field" or better small harbors for fishermen?

Who will check for fire ants, coquis, mongoose, fireweed, imu rocks, and other contraband? Superferry workers with one eye on the clock for lunch time? Or government workers? And then, will Superferry or the taxpayers foot the bill? Will the workers have enough training and enough time to catch everything? Will Superferry post a bond to cover the cost of dealing with any invasive species it spreads?

How will hundreds of people and cars from O'ahu impact neighbor island beaches, hiking areas, and rural lifestyles?

We await the court decision on the EIS. And we await answers that are long overdue. Mahalo.

Kona, Hawai'i Island — *March 27, 2008*

Gail Jackson

My name is Gail Jackson. A resident of Waikoloa. One thing I've been concerned about is, the humpback whale is an endangered species.

We took a whale cruise several weeks ago. … About twenty adults on board and twenty fifth graders, and a crew of course, and we were avidly looking for whales. We were about a mile out when we spotted a pod, and started to head that way, when a calf, mom, and escort surfaced about a hundred feet away.

If we'd been traveling at 25 or 37 knots, I doubt if a collision could've been avoided. I do have guidelines for whale protection and human safety from NOAA. One thing in the boater's section about avoiding collisions and disturbance is, "Watch your speed. NOAA recommends the vessels travel at a slow, safe speed in areas where a whale strike may occur." And of course, this is more than in just the marine sanctuary. The speed depends on vessel, time of days, sea conditions, and other factors. Research shows that collisions occurring at vessel speeds above 10 knots cause more whale deaths and serious injuries than collisions occurring at slower speeds.

James Karkheck

I understand the benefits of certain economic interests and to the military if the Superferry sails into Kawaihae, but I'm a taxpayer, and taxpayers will be subsidizing the Hawaii Superferry, and I would like to know, what would be the specific benefits to the average residents of this community? I haven't heard anything that strikes me as solid evidence. The only thing I've heard is people from Honolulu say, This is gonna help farmers. They're gonna be able to get their produce to market. I'm a farmer. Tell me how this is gonna help me get my product to market, because it's totally impractical.

Next question: what has the state ever done to ascertain whether this community wants its resources spent supporting the Hawaii Superferry?

I'm just a regular guy. I grow some coffee. I grow some fruit. I sell stuff. I teach kids. I want those kids to grow up and have good jobs, good opportunities. I'm for anything that's going to help our community without taking more out of our community than it gives to us. But I don't see the overall plan for integrating this operation to be something that truly provides community benefit. I'm sorry, I don't think we need to be subsidizing businesses that have plenty of resources. We should be subsidizing community needs, if anything. Thanks.

Kaunakakai, Moloka'i — *March 11, 2008*

Of all the islands' people, those from Moloka'i are the most unified and fiercely protective of their still-intact natural resources, from which many gain their livelihoods. Proof is in the poetry of the following testimonies, which were delivered mostly by a handful of Moloka'i elders. The kupuna women spoke slowly and mournfully, from deep in their guts. Below are a few speeches from the people of Moloka'i, all Native Hawaiian.

Note: At the end of Ruth Manu's testimony, she says, "You guys cannot answer us." She is referring to the meeting rule that no questions by the public would receive any response. The panel remained mute and impassive throughout.

Ruth Manu

Aloha, my name is Ruth Manu. I'm a kupuna from Molokaʻi. What I got to say ... truly ... I truly love the island of Molokaʻi. I want to die here. Molokaʻi love being the way we are. So when you're talking about ferry—fixin' the harbors! You want to come here on Molokaʻi to do that? This is ocean! Molokaʻi—and the whole islands in between—all the channels are different. Very, very different. We have waves! *Big nalus!*[59] ... To me, the ferry don't even belong here! What I'm saying is, if you think you goin' do that on the island of Molokaʻi, I object to it. One hundred percent. We don' need it. We gonna fight you all the way. In my heart, we know what we want. What we think. Us people who live here on this island, are surviving. And sustainability is very important on the island of Molokaʻi. Even if you don't have enough jobs, we're making a way where we can still feed our family and stay as an ʻohana, not fighting and bickering against each other. You see, like how my sister say, we're "the Friendly Island"—now come to be unfriendly, because there are so many issues that we are here to speak up on. If we don't speak out, they're gonna to run us over. But no, we have voice. We are the kupunas. We love Molokaʻi. We love *all* the islands. Whatever an island has, they fight for theirs, we fight for take care Molokaʻi, because we come from here. Thank you for coming and sharing your manaʻo. But our manaʻo is, that you guys cannot answer us. Next time you guys come, you come, you guys, and give us the answers to our questions. That is only pono. That's Hawaiian style. If you make meeting, when we have our Planning Commission, they answer our questions! Don't you leave us hanging like this. No! Pono is pono. You come over here, don't bring no greenhorns. Bring the guys that can tell us. That's the way it's supposed to be. That's honest, that's truth, and that's the way we are. Aloha.

Judy Caparida

Hello, you know what? We love Molokaʻi. I just need to say, that all of this looked good *[she refers to proposed EIS actions displayed on the walls]*, but this is an island that is set aside, different. Every island is different. Even if we have all the same things you have over there,

---

[59] *Nalus*: waves.

does it really matter to our life? [The Superferry] is something that people want to make for us so that we live by the way they want us to. We're so free because we're contented. We love what we have. We don't need to have all this stuff over here. It's all junk! It's all junk! What God has given us is free!

You know the problem today? Us, we have to pay taxes for everything. ... Our governor doesn't see the needs of the people; she sees the needs of *her* and *her* needs. We are the ones that put you guys in place. It was voting, we did it because that was the right way to do it. And for me, I say, wow; we have so many meetings, so many issues that pertain to life. Life is simple but that makes you *so* unfriendly! This is the Friendly Island but it makes you so unfriendly because it intrudes into your life, it makes you upset because everything you have is all you have! Because some people cannot afford to do *anything*! You work—all the money gone! For what? Taxes here, taxes there. Nobody put the truth. Nobody put how much cost, or what we gotta do to do this. ...

I was raised simple: you live off the ocean, you go get what you need, you go to the mountain, you get what you need, you plant, that's what you get. But this is a very unhappy thing for us to make plans for somebody else. We don't want the Superferry here, because we don't need 'em. They are going all over the islands takin' all the resources of our families out there! ... Make sure you guys get down to *life*—not fantasy, not make-believe. Who is the Blesser, and who the one that give us this Life, to want to live the simple and free Life? Him, He give us over here. The heart. The heart to live the way you want to live, and be really thankful that He's the one that provides for our needs. I need to share that to you guys because for me—hey, life is too short. You got to know where you're going to go one day. This is nothing you can take with you. All these things that is going on over there, is what? Taking away the blessings away from us! Taking away our life—it's killing us! That's what I need to share. Thank you.

Young Unidentified Man

Hello everybody, good evening. The only thing I'd like to share is that, I come here as a Moloka'i citizen and a local Hawaiian from Moloka'i. And I want to share with you guys my experience recently.

Me and my sons were at the beach and we went *holoholo*.[60] ... [T]he way Superferry is, is a sight to see. If any of you have actually seen it on the ocean, it's how the kids would say, "Ho, dad! check that boat out! How fast it moves!" I actually looked at my watch. It took less than 15 minutes from Halawa Point to Nakalele Point. Within 15 minutes!

In your EIS as we all know, the whales, the seals have more rights than us. They're protected by the federal government. If you go harm the whales—BIG FINE. You go jail! How about our Hawaiian seals? Same thing. So my only concern is that we're talking about the Superferry riding during whale season. *Impossible* for that Superferry to even feel something, to even see, turn their boat, in time to miss the whales. So if you goin' tell me that the whales is protected, then it's a lie, if you going that fast. I looked at my watch, and I watched it outside of Halawa Point and Nakalele Point; [it] was within fifteen minutes, *it was flying*. ... So that's just my concern.

I know this is after-the-fact EIS and why we here is because of Superferry, right? And it was because it was sent down by the government saying that "gotta go get Superferry." Aloha.

Laurie Buchanan

Aloha and welcome to the island of Moloka'i. ... My name is Laurie Buchanan. I'm here tonight as just a community member, but I wear many hats on my small island. One of them is as a field technician for Moloka'i-Maui Invasive Species Committee, where I have been employed since 2002. Being a field tech means that I actually go in the field and do work. Within that work, I've also covered thousands of acres for early protection of miconia by air. I have a lot of opportunity to visit the north shore of Moloka'i, where I have seen the Superferry pass by and pass by very closely. It sets off something in my stomach when I see that. When you're in a pristine place and you feel like you've walked seventeen hours to get to a pristine part of Hawai'i, and here comes a helicopter. You've ruined that beauty and that peace. So, the same is with the Superferry and its routes. I am concerned about the routes that it takes. We've seen all the beautiful commercials with Moloka'i as a backdrop. We try to keep it that way for a reason. It's not to be exploited by commercials or by the Superferry.

---

[60] *Holoholo*: cruising.

Part Two

Evolution of a Boondoggle: History and Chronology

Chapter Seven

BEFORE NAWILIWILI: 2001 TO SEPTEMBER 2007

Koohan Paik and Jerry Mander

THIS AND THE FOLLOWING CHAPTER *present a detailed time line of key events, from June 2001 through October 2008, related to the development of the Hawaii Superferry. This chapter covers all events up to and including the August 2007 protests at Nawiliwili Harbor.*

* * *

The interisland ferry alternative did not burst forth from any great popular clamor for it. Nor were the people of Maui, Kauaʻi, or the Big Island —the publics that the project was supposed to benefit—ever offered any meaningful opportunities to shape the scale or range of its operation, or even to indicate whether they wanted it at all. Instead, the Superferry was announced as a fait accompli, a governmental stance that has never changed over seven years.

Many people in Hawaiʻi felt that a ferry service might have been useful if conceived far more modestly, and thoughtfully. As it stands now, the entire design of the ship—its size, capacity, and speed—is grossly out of scale for its stated purpose and would bring specific dangers. In fact, as the following narrative amplifies, it may ultimately serve far different interests.

Our chronology includes the evolution of Hawaii Superferry Corporation and its management, promotion, and financing, from the time of its creation in 2001. We follow it from its inauguration as what at first appeared to be a homegrown ferry project, through its sudden change of ownership to a New York absentee investor normally focused on military contracts, to its later becoming the subject of huge public controversy with potentially serious environmental and military implications.

We also catalog the collusive roles of Hawai'i Governor Linda Lingle, certain state and federal agencies, and U.S. military interests, as well as the Superferry Corporation itself, in circumventing some of the country's and the state's most important environmental laws to speed the project through. This aspect has made the story as much about the perversion of democratic processes and the effects of irresponsible governance as it is about a local environmental battle.

Finally, we cover chronologically the range of protest activity and complex legal challenges that began in earnest in late 2004 and have been growing steadily since—as potentially grave environmental impacts, cultural harm, and official malfeasance become ever more obvious. What is revealed is a still-evolving tale of inspiring resistance in the face of official deception, arrogance, favoritism, lawlessness, and corruption, worthy of any banana republic under colonial rule.

In addition to the overarching issue of the failure of democratic processes throughout this story, other issues that weave their way through the history include, first of all, the potential of extreme environmental damage to the habitats of whales, sea turtles, and other wild species, as well as the less publicized dangers from invasive species, overdevelopment, traffic, and pollution. A second issue is the possibility, even likelihood, of hidden military agendas from some of the key players, in which the Superferry seems clearly to play a role, as well as the related, raging ambitions of the governor as she seeks to be a national player. A third issue is the struggles of communities of Hawai'i citizens to be heard in these debates and to protect their quality of life.

AN IMPORTANT NOTE ON STYLE: The information in the chronology is meant to be as detailed as we were able to present it, so as to serve as a kind of stand-alone history of the project, possibly a separate document in itself. As such, it may repeat some material you have already read in this book, or that appears in later chapters. Readers are encouraged to skip around for information that is most relevant and timely for them.

The full month-by-month story begins here:

JULY 2001

Mallorca to Hawai'i

On a Mediterranean vacation, California Silicon Valley entrepreneur Timothy Dick sees large, high-speed, car-carrying catamaran ferries operating between continental Spain and the island of Mallorca. Later, when vacationing in Hawai'i, Dick learns there is no interisland ferry operating in the islands. Seeing a business opportunity, he determines to bring such catamaran ferries to Hawai'i.

Dick moves to Hawai'i and forms a new company, Hawaii Superferry, Inc. (HSF), headed by John Garibaldi, formerly CFO of Hawaiian Airlines, which went bankrupt under his watch. Also part of the founding team is O'ahu's Terry White, formerly with American Classic Cruise Lines, which also went belly up, despite a $140 million loan guarantee from the U.S. Maritime Administration (MARAD). This was the largest loan guarantee *failure* in MARAD's history. As a result, a policy was created to freeze further loan guarantees of this type. Nonetheless, MARAD would later defy its own internal rules and back yet another controversial $140 million loan guarantee, this time for Superferry. *(See January 2005 entry: "MARAD Loan Guarantee.")* The plan is to build two high-speed, 340-foot catamaran ferries, five stories tall, capable of traveling at 35 knots (40 mph), while carrying up to 866 passengers and 282 vehicles. The two Superferries will do daily runs between O'ahu and the outer islands of Maui, Kaua'i, and Hawai'i (the Big Island).

Lobbying and Financing

HSF begins to lobby extensively for support from Hawai'i's legislators and executive-branch agencies, including the Departments of Transportation (DOT); Agriculture (DOA); and Business, Economic Development, and Tourism (DBEDT); as well as for support from Hawai'i's U.S. congressional delegation, Governor Linda Lingle, and various candidates for the state legislature. Superferry actively seeks financing of an estimated $180 million for the ships' construction and start-up.

Senator Daniel Inouye Brings Strykers to Hawai'i

On July 25, 2001, U.S. Senator Daniel Inouye of Hawai'i, chair of the Senate Appropriations Committee, makes the first of three announcements over the next two years that his committee is approving defense-related initiatives for Hawai'i. He earmarks $731 million for transportation and military programs in his state. Included is about $20 million for ferry facilities and over $37 million for repaving the potholed Saddle Road on the Big Island, partly diverting it to serve the Pohakuloa Training Area, for its planned expansion of 23,000 acres. Also included is nearly $80 million to establish a Stryker Brigade, to be housed at O'ahu's Schofield Barracks until 2009, when it is expected to be transported to Pohakuloa for live war games and training exercises. The brigade consists of approximately 300 heavily armored light tanks that use depleted uranium (DU) munitions—the same vehicles being extensively used in the Iraq War. These announcements alarm some Big Island residents, who fear that trade winds will blow dangerous levels of DU powder to Kona and other leeward communities.

The fact that this earmarked funding includes facilities for Superferry—buried in transportation and treasury program appropriations, together with military appropriations—points to the Superferry's role as a crucial component in the plans to establish the Stryker Brigade in Hawai'i. It is an early hint of future military potential for this supposedly civilian sea vessel.

NOVEMBER 2002

Linda Lingle Elected Governor

"The 'Open for Business' sign is turned on in Hawai'i." These words ring out during the inaugural address of Linda Lingle, the first Republican elected governor of Hawai'i in forty years. Lingle extends special treatment to Superferry, assigning her chief of staff, Bob Awana, to personally consult with HSF to expedite the project.

JUNE 2003

Honolulu Prepares for Superferry

As reported in *Pacific Business News*,[61] Superferry founder Timothy Dick states, "We've been working with the U.S. Maritime Administration (MARAD) for over a year" on an application to achieve a

---

[61] Prabha Natarajan, "Entrepreneurs float 'Superferry' concept," in *Pacific Business News*, June 15, 2003.

loan guarantee from the agency, which could prove important for future financing. "The final application cannot be done until everything else is locked and loaded," says Dick. He goes on to say, "We've been working with Senator Inouye's office as well."

Honolulu's Pier 19 reopens after major renovation, *largely financed with U.S. funds*, despite the fact that no Environmental Impact Statement for it was completed. It is announced that the updated terminal will soon be ready to serve as an operational hub when two new, high-speed Superferries begin their anticipated service.

The catamarans are expected to be built by Austal USA, a U.S. division of an Australian company that opened facilities in Mobile, Alabama, in 1999. Negotiations with Austal are well under way. Austal possesses distinct appeal, having previously manufactured a light, high-speed, aluminum, shallow-water catamaran vessel that had been contracted by the U.S. Navy to function as the *Westpac Express*, carrying troops and materials throughout the Western Pacific region from its base in Japan. But to build any future ships for the United States, federal regulations require a production facility on U.S. soil. A similar rule applies for achieving loan guarantees from MARAD.

(In October, Superferry will announce that it has chosen Austal from among several builders bidding on the contract. The following January, the deal is signed.)

Soon after this, Austal also announces that it will join General Dynamics in a joint effort to win a U.S. Navy contract to build a prototype vessel for the Littoral Combat Ship (LCS) program. This effort would be in competition with Lockheed Martin, with the winner standing to gain a huge military contract a few years hence. The military prototype design will be very similar to the proposed Hawaii Superferry aluminum catamaran shallow-water design that is seen by some as a stalking horse for a larger contract.

SEPTEMBER 2003

First Protests Against Stryker Brigades

Tempers flare at the first of four public meetings the U.S. Army holds on O'ahu to solicit public comment for an Environmental Impact Statement, concerning plans to bring a Stryker Brigade to the island and the prospect of live war games using depleted-uranium ammunition. Seven peace activists are arrested for trespassing, and for carrying protest signs, which had been banned by the Army. Of the 155 people who testify, only four favor the Army's plans.

JANUARY 2004

HSF Signs Agreement with Austal USA to Purchase Two Ferries

Hawaii Superferry formally concludes and signs an agreement with shipbuilder Austal USA to purchase two 340-foot catamaran ferry vessels for delivery during 2006–2008 under what it calls "an exclusive, strategic relationship."

"For many years, I have envisioned "a marine highway" for our islands, so I am pleased with the progress that Hawaii Superferry has made in creating an interisland ferry system that will serve Oʻahu, Kauaʻi, Maui, and the Big Island," says Senator Inouye. "This initiative will complement ongoing efforts to further enhance ferry service in the tri-islands of Maui County. The economic and social benefits of a ferry system will be significant. The ferries will be an additional way to move cargo from one island to another, and tourists and local residents will have an alternative means to island hop to see our many attractions or to visit family and friends," says Inouye.[62]

Surprisingly, Superferry commits to a $180 million contract with Austal, although it still has *no significant funding!* Austal agrees, nonetheless, to proceed and to carry HSF's liability. *Why* would Austal agree to this? Either the plan is recklessly bold or it has some kind of hidden assurances from the likes of Senator Inouye, for whom the ferry is a key component in his agenda to station a brigade of Stryker tanks in the islands, and/or assurances from MARAD that a loan guarantee would work out. Alternatively, the assurances might have come from unnamed investors. In any case, for Austal, the contract enables the company to begin work immediately on modifying the Westpac design toward the larger Superferry format, possibly usable for military contracts that may be in the offing.

---

[62] "Hawaii Superferry inks agreement with Austal," *Marinelog.com*, January 14, 2004.

February 2004

Investors, Local and Global
As of February 2004, only about $3.3 million dollars has been invested in the Superferry Corporation. Of that amount, $1 million comes from Maui Land and Pineapple Company. A few months later, Grove Farm Company of Kaua'i, owned by AOL founder Steve Case, buys 50 percent of Maui Land and Pineapple's investment.

March 2004

State Legislature Passes Resolutions to Accommodate HSF
The Hawai'i State Legislature passes a set of formal resolutions not only to establish an interisland, fast-ferry service but also to encourage three government agencies key to the project's success—the Hawai'i Department of Transportation (DOT), the State Public Utilities Commission (PUC), and the U.S. Maritime Administration (MARAD)—to accommodate the company's needs. A public relations campaign is mounted to get the word out, including opinion polls that "prove" the public's enthusiasm for the project, though the only voices heard in the media thus far are those of the corporation and the governor.

June 2004

Construction Begins in Mobile
In Alabama, construction begins at Austal USA, six months ahead of schedule, on the first of the multilevel catamarans slated for Hawai'i.
Marinelog.com reports on June 4, 2004, that Austal's "decision to commence construction follows the announcement last week that the U.S. Navy has awarded the Austal and General Dynamics team the opportunity to compete with only one other boatbuilder—Lockheed—for the final design contract for the planned Littoral Combat Ship (LCS). Austal says it considers its Superferry contract as an outstanding opportunity to further develop resources at Austal USA in preparation for the anticipated commencement of LCS construction in October 2005." This is yet another hint at future military dimensions of the interlocking project.

Superferry Applies to Public Utilities Commission

On June 22, 2004, Hawaii Superferry, Inc. submits its first application for a Certificate of Public Convenience and Necessity to the Hawai'i PUC to operate the two catamarans between O'ahu and Maui, Kaua'i, and Hawai'i at speeds of up to 35 knots (40 mph).

The PUC application includes this statement: "In Hawai'i, it is anticipated that an entire battalion of 350 Stryker tanks will be able to be transported from O'ahu to their training grounds on the Big Island in four trips at lower cost." This is the first official public citation of a proposed military role for the Superferry, in direct contradiction to continued statements from the company and Governor Lingle that there is no military dimension to the project.

First Hint of John F. Lehman's Involvement

The PUC application also confirms for the first time that negotiations are in process for an additional $55 million investment. The identity of the investor is not revealed publicly until the following year, after all exemptions from environmental review seem to be fixed in place and the investment is finalized. The investor turns out to be John F. Lehman, head of the New York military investment firm J. F. Lehman and Co. and a former top military official in both the Nixon and Reagan administrations.

JULY 2004

Stryker EIS

The commander of the U.S. Army Pacific Command, Lt. General James Campbell, announces that he has completed and approved an Environmental Impact Statement concerning the relocation of the Stryker Brigade to Hawai'i. The Army plans to bring Strykers to O'ahu soon, with eventual deployment to training grounds on the Big Island.

AUGUST 2004

Hawai'i DOT Environmental Assessment

On August 5, the Hawai'i Department of Transportation announces that it has finished an Environmental Assessment (EA) of early "improvements" under way at the Kahului Harbor. *(This EA is required because the harbor improvements use state funds and are on state* lands. *The EA is to determine, in part, whether a much more comprehensive Environmental Impact Statement will be required for a given project.)* Prepared by outside consultants E. K. Noda and Associates, the Environmental Assessment concludes that an EIS would *not* be necessary, since "the proposed improvements will not have significant impact on the environment." The EA fails to make any references at all to the expected uses and environmental impacts, or "secondary impacts," of the harbor once it is retrofitted and used by the Hawaii Superferry Corporation.

NOTE: *The consultants for the Environmental Assessment, E. K. Noda and Associates, were convicted the previous year in the biggest illegal campaign contribution scandal in Hawai'i history. Recipients of the illegal donations were then-Governor Ben Cayetano and his successor, Linda Lingle. These donations came during the same period that Noda and Associates had prepared another highly controversial Environmental Assessment that gave support for the Kahului Airport expansion, which had been bitterly opposed and was eventually blocked by Maui farmers and environmentalists.*

U.S. Transportation Secretary Mineta: More Money for HSF

A week later, U.S. Secretary of Transportation Norman Mineta, an enthusiastic Superferry supporter, joins Governor Lingle and State Transportation Director Rod Haraga on a tour of the future Hawaii Superferry terminal at Honolulu's Pier 19. Secretary Mineta announces that the state will now receive an *additional* $7.46 million *federal* grant for development of ferry landing projects on Maui, as well as Lana'i and Moloka'i. This raises the question whether Lana'i and Moloka'i are also targeted as future business opportunities for Superferry. Questions also arise as to whether this use of federal funds requires Environmental Assessments and Environmental Impact Statements on the *federal* level for these harbor projects, as required by the U.S. National Environmental Policy Act (NEPA).

As secretary of transportation, Mineta is also the head of the U.S. Maritime Administration (MARAD) and may be key in that agency's later behavior in granting loan guarantees to the Superferry, even while he refuses to honor the NEPA and, more specifically, the Endangered Species Act, as we will see. *(See January 2005 entry: "Federal Agencies Protest.")*

GAO Cites Problem with Airlifts of Strykers

In a development that will later become significant, on August 14, the General Accounting Office (GAO) of the U.S. Congress issues a report determining that the Army's medium-weight armored vehicle, the Stryker, weighs far too much to be efficiently transported by Army C-130 cargo aircraft. According to the *Washington Post*, the GAO reports, "The Stryker's average weight of 38,000 pounds—along with other factors such as added equipment and less than ideal flight conditions [during wartime in such places as Iraq]—significantly limits the C-130's flight range and reduces the size of the force that could be deployed." The report indicates that *"alternative" transportation systems should be investigated to transport the 300 Strykers that the Army had in production.* It would not be long before the management and board of the Hawaii Superferry, as well as Austal USA, begin to see a rich opportunity not only in potential government contracts to transport those Stryker vehicles to military bases within the Hawaiian Islands, but also in much larger contracts to transport them and other equipment to war zones and military bases around the globe.

Earthjustice, on Behalf of Native Hawaiians, Sues the Army

On August 17, Earthjustice files a lawsuit in San Francisco Federal District Court on behalf of three Native Hawaiian organizations: 'Ilio'ulaokalani Coalition, Na 'Imi Pono, and Kipuka. The suit, which names Secretary of Defense Donald Rumsfeld and Acting Secretary of the Army Les Brownlee, concerns the Army's planned deployment of Stryker Brigade vehicles on O'ahu, on lands identified as culturally and historically important to Native Hawaiians. The suit charges that the prior Environmental Impact Statement created by the Army *(see July 2004 entry: "Stryker EIS")* had failed to consider alternative locations for the Stryker Brigade that are less culturally and environmentally harmful, thus violating the National Environmental Policy Act.

The suit argues that transporting the 2nd Brigade to Hawai'i would destroy Native Hawaiian cultural sites, including *heiau* (temples), *ahu* (shrines), and burial sites; prevent the exercise of traditional practices; and irreparably harm Hawai'i's fragile and unique native ecosystems, including the endangered plants and animals that depend on them. "Native Hawaiians have a unique spiritual relationship to the 'aina and as a result a kuleana to preserve and protect the natural and cultural resources of Hawai'i for future generations," says 'Ilio'ulaokalani's president, Victoria Holt Takamine. "Transformation will cut us off from these resources, and these sacred sites, which are vital to the perpetuation of the Hawaiian culture," and would further restrict access for Hawaiians trying to carry out traditional practices.

The suit demands that the Army study and consider locations other than Hawai'i for the Strykers.

OCTOBER 2004

Maui Protests

According to the *Maui News*, environmentalists and canoe club paddlers on Maui say that proposed state harbor improvements, especially plans to add dock space and other shipping facilities to accommodate the Superferry at Kahului Harbor, would destroy an important surfing spot, wipe out the harbor's beach, and severely restrict canoeing in the only protected waters on Maui's north shore.

"The most frustrating thing for me is that we talk about the ice [crystal methamphetamine] epidemic, and prevention programs for kids, and on the other hand we're destroying our way of life" and programs that serve kids, said Hawaiian Canoe Club Head Coach Diane Ho, a former county deputy prosecutor.

DOT Secretly Demands Environmental Assessment

Meanwhile, Hawai'i Department of Transportation bureaucrats *privately* inform the Superferry Corporation that a full statewide EA, and possibly an EIS as well, will be required before the ferry can begin interisland service. In an investigative report published more than three years later, the *Honolulu Advertiser*[63] reports that internal DOT memos and correspondence with the Superferry company originally demanded that Superferry would have to be responsible for doing an EA, as well as an Environmental Impact review, for the state's $40 million in harbor improvements. DOT Deputy Director of Harbors Barry Fukunaga writes in an email to

---

[63] Derrick DePledge, "Hawaii, ferry at odds in '04 over environment," in *Honolulu Advertiser*, January 6, 2008.

DOT Director Rod Haraga, "SF [Superferry] has to do one that addresses their operation to include traffic impacts and the like."

Superferry executives reject any prospect of environmental review, complaining that it would take several months to a year or more to complete and would thus prevent them from securing funding. In the *Advertiser* report, CEO John Garibaldi explains, "If there was a 'legal requirement' that Hawaii Superferry had to do an environmental review then that requirement would have to be fulfilled prior to any funding." *At that point, it had not yet been made public that the company's $140 million loan guarantee from MARAD required that there be no EIS.*

DOT executives condemn Superferry management for focusing "on their vessel and business plans (market, financing, business activities), but [they] seem to have done little to look at the infrastructure and pierside requirements. ... Many critical issues have been overlooked or are not adequately addressed." Other documents reveal that the staff is frustrated that HSF does not provide detailed operational plans during the period when the state is being asked to sign off on the project.

(As mentioned, the above exchanges between DOT and HSF would be kept secret for over three years, until the Advertiser *publishes the first of several exposés on Superferry issues [see January 2008 entry: "New Revelations About DOT Demands for EIS"]. What's most surprising in the report is that, of all people, Barry Fukunaga is revealed as the one demanding the EIS most strongly. Soon after, he reverses his position and becomes Superferry's biggest cheerleader for an EA exemption. He is rewarded by Governor Lingle with a promotion to DOT director, and then, in 2007 she appoints him to be her chief of staff. When Lingle and Fukunaga are later asked, during legislative and court hearings, to explain how they made these decisions, both consistently invoke attorney-client privilege and refuse to answer.)*

HSF and the Lingle administration finally do reach a highly cynical agreement in which Superferry agrees to temporarily scale back its request for harbor improvements in order to avoid an EIS. HSF also describes its operations as having four separate components—for Oʻahu, Maui, Kauaʻi, and the Big Island—and asserts that *each* component should be categorized as *minor*, thus exempting each from the environmental law. The plan is designed to get the boat running right away, without the "hindrance" of environmental regulation. The proposed harbor modifications, they assure the company, could be made after the vessel is in operation. *(See Chapter 12 for more on this.)*

A deal is proposed as to which of the needed "harbor improvements" will be pursued: Instead of requiring a notch in the pier at Kahului Harbor, DOT agrees to install a floating barge and boarding ramp. This compromise enables the company to evade its EIS requirement. (The floating barge later proves insufficient against the rough seas at Kahului Harbor, breaking down numerous times and halting Superferry service repeatedly, and eventually requires a costly, taxpayer-funded tugboat to hold it snug against the pier.)

Docking of such a boarding barge would itself normally require a permit from the Army Corps of Engineers, which should also trigger an EA. But Governor Lingle and Hawaii Superferry persuade the Corps not to issue such EA-triggering permits. Environmental attorneys consider this a violation of the law, but to date no suit has been filed.

NOVEMBER 2004

Shipping Companies Protest Superferry
Interisland shipping firms raise concerns to the State Public Utilities Commission that Superferry could decimate their economic viability. But Superferry Corporation has little patience for their competitors' grumbling, claiming once again that "the clock is ticking."[64] HSF says the federal maritime loan guarantee and $55 million in equity financing that it is seeking are both contingent on its being granted the PUC license before the end of year.

This is another in a series of deadline threats used by HSF to manipulate the State of Hawai'i to either ram through a procedure or circumvent the law entirely. Here, the urgent deadline is set as the end of 2004. Later it becomes June 2005, and then June 30, 2007. No evidence is ever given to confirm the actual imperative of any of these dates.

HSF Meets Privately with Maui Opposition
While charging through with its plans, HSF simultaneously takes steps toward mitigating mounting opposition. Ten days before the

---

[64] Prabha Natarajan, "Young Brothers questions Superferry operating plans," in *Pacific Business News*, November 12, 2004.

PUC hearings on Maui, CEO John Garibaldi and Chief Operating Officer Terry White lunch privately with Maui Tomorrow members and other local environmentalists in hopes of ingratiating themselves to community leaders. The Maui people make their sentiments known: Environmental review must be conducted. This opinion is echoed loud and clear at the upcoming PUC hearings on Maui and Kaua'i.

PUC Public Hearings
The PUC and the Hawaii Superferry Corporation conduct public hearings on O'ahu, Maui, Kaua'i, and the Big Island, as the application for certification requires them to do.

At a PUC hearing on Maui on November 17, the community is *livid*, demanding an environmental review *before* Superferry sets sail. The back wall of the auditorium is lined with canoe paddlers holding protest signs, as speaker after speaker volleys criticism at the project. One paddler, Dan Cohen, says he doesn't agree that the ferry would have a limited impact, according to a *Maui News* report: "If they allow the Superferry to come in, it's going to have a significant impact on the recreational users of the harbor. ... For me it's a fight-to-the-death kind of thing."

Eighteen-year-old Jaymie Moniz says there are already too many things, besides the Hawaii Superferry, cutting off Native Hawaiians from access to the natural environment. "It's just not the kind of place Hawai'i should be," she says. While Moniz often flies to O'ahu to visit family and agrees airfare is expensive, she doesn't think that is justification for the Superferry. "Just because it's convenient doesn't cancel out the negative aspects," she says. *(For more testimonies delivered to the Public Utilities Commission, see Chapter 6.)*

December 2004

Governor's Office Pursues Exemption
Superferry executives meet with Governor Lingle's then-Chief of Staff Bob Awana, resulting in the state's launching an aggressive campaign to *exempt* Hawaii Superferry from all environmental review. A DOT staffer's email following the meeting reads: "Decision made: We need to pursue EXEMPTION; and HSF will not provide any ramps on vessel."

Although it is not revealed to the public for nearly four years, the decision to reverse DOT's position and exempt Superferry was not made independently by the Department of Transportation, but instead was a directive from the governor's office.

PUC Grants Certificate
Meeting in secret, the three-member Public Utilities Commission grants HSF a Certificate of Public Convenience and Necessity. The stacks of testimonies opposing the Superferry have no bearing on the PUC's decision, made in time to accommodate HSF's deadline threats.

JANUARY 2005

New Financing
Hawaii Superferry CEO John Garibaldi asks state legislators to grant HSF a *$40 million state loan*. (According to a January 2008 *Honolulu Advertiser* report by Derrick DePledge, Garibaldi also directly asked Governor Lingle to sign a letter—*one that he wrote for her*—supporting the $40 million state loan, and effusively praising the Superferry. The *Advertiser* reproduces the letter Garibaldi wrote and the letter Lingle sent, which, except for small niceties, are identical. This is only one of many incidents over the years showing Lingle in lockstep with the company.)

At about the same time, the Superferry Corporation reports that an additional $60 million has been raised from private investors, though it does not specify who. Years later, the *Honolulu Star-Bulletin* reveals that more than 80 percent of the investment in the HSF came from John F. Lehman.

MARAD Loan Guarantee
In the same month as the above events, the U.S. Maritime Administration, a division of the U.S. Department of Transportation, approves a *federal loan guarantee* for Superferry of $140 million, via a federal program called Title XI of the Merchant Marine Act. *This is the first loan guarantee under Title XI initiated by the Bush administration since it froze such guarantees four years earlier, in 2001.* This guarantee essentially makes taxpayers liable if the company fails. The guarantee had not been included in MARAD's published annual budget. "Pure pork, for the benefit of one company" is how it is

described by Kyle Kajihiro of the American Friends Service Committee, in Honolulu. Not only does MARAD pull a $140 million guarantee out of thin air, but one of its conditions is that there be no EIS! *Questions are immediately raised:* Where did the funding for this unbudgeted item suddenly come from? What is it about environmental review of Superferry that would be so threatening to the U.S. Maritime Administration? Why was this the first project in years to be so blessed? How was this decision authorized? Did it involve cronies of George Bush? Did it come from Transportation Secretary Norman Mineta, a member of Bush's cabinet? Did Senator Inouye have a role, and if so, why? Are these people already, in 2005, promoting military connections? Colossal profits? For whom, and how? What was John F. Lehman's role, if any?

At this point, MARAD indicates no plans to have an Environmental Impact Statement prepared for this loan guarantee, even though an EIS is required by the National Environmental Policy Act of 1974. MARAD's stance never wavers, despite strong challenges from other government agencies. Years later, it is revealed that MARAD made one of the conditions of the loan guarantee that there be no EIS.

Federal Agencies Protest
As with so many aspects of the Superferry story, important facts are often not publicly revealed until years later. In the case of the MARAD loan guarantee, it is not until three years later that the *Honolulu Advertiser*, in an astonishing investigative report, reveals that several federal agencies had quickly and *vigorously protested the MARAD action*, particularly its failure to follow prevailing environmental laws. The executive director of the U.S. Marine Mammal Commission, David Cottingham, wrote to the U.S. National Marine Fisheries Service in January 2005, immediately after the MARAD loan guarantee announcement, to express his concerns over both the environmental impacts of the proposed Superferry and the MARAD agreement to provide the $140 million loan guarantee. *(The Marine Mammal Commission is an independent government agency created to provide oversight of the marine mammal conservation policies and programs that are carried out by federal regulatory agencies.)*

Cottingham complains in his letter that a "Section 7 consultation" under the Endangered Species Act (ESA) has not been conducted by MARAD on the potential effects of the ferry service on humpback whales and monk seals. *(Section 7 of the Endangered Species Act requires federal agencies to consult with the National Marine Fisheries Service if they are proposing an "action" that may affect listed marine species, which include humpback whales. "Action" is defined broadly to include funding, permitting, and other regulatory actions.)*

Cottingham's letter goes on to say that the high-speed vessel's "potential for injury from a disturbance to humpback whales and other species is clear" and that any federal agency taking action on behalf of the Superferry "has an obligation to conduct appropriate environmental analyses [under federal law] because a 'may affect' situation is obvious."[65]

According to the same news report, Chris Yates, director of the Office of Protected Resources for the Pacific Island Region of the National Marine Fisheries Service, sends a *follow-up* letter to MARAD asking whether the maritime agency would be conducting a "Section 7 consultation," as legally required. Yates says this would be necessary, "since we believed there was a threat of ship strikes to protected species." According to Yates, MARAD finally responds five months later, in February 2006, that a consultation was not required since the loan guarantee "did not fund, authorize or carry out an action" that would have triggered an environmental review. It's as if they felt that guaranteeing loans that would *produce* the action did not qualify. In fact, they had made a condition of the loan guarantee that there be no environmental review, a detail they failed to disclose to Yates.

State Senators Demand an EIS

With local environmental opposition quickly growing, a group of Hawai'i state senators introduces a bill *requiring* Hawaii Superferry to prepare an Environmental Impact Statement *before* it begins operations. They do this as it is becoming apparent that state agencies and Governor Lingle are actively seeking to avoid doing any EIS reports at all, under pressure from Hawaii Superferry. Supporters of the Superferry and of Governor Lingle, and House Transportation Committee Chair Joseph Souki (D-Maui), successfully sidetrack the bill.

---

[65] Christie Wilson, "Hawaii Superferry Risk to Whales Raised in 2005," in *Honolulu Advertiser*, October 4, 2007.

This is just one of several Superferry-related bills introduced during the 2005 and 2006 legislative sessions in which Souki uses his status as Transportation Committee chair and also as former Speaker of the House to foil any cautionary efforts, so as to grease the project through. The question arises: Who greased Souki? (*For the answer, see October 2007 entry in Chapter 8: "Illegal Superferry Donations to Lingle."*)

Start-Up Date Announced
The target date for beginning interisland Superferry service is announced: early 2007.

Lingle and Garibaldi Again Flout EIS Law
In the face of public outrage, Superferry CEO John Garibaldi asserts openly for the first time that having to do an EIS would *kill* the project, and that June 30, 2005, is now the drop-dead date by which all government approvals have to be in place; otherwise, the Superferry will leave the islands. He and other members of his staff continue to repeat this threat, up to and *beyond* the shifting drop-dead dates. They assert, again, that investors will pull out if an EIS is required. They also suggest that it is a condition of the MARAD loan guarantee that there be no such environmental review. Critics assume that the real problem is that the Superferry might not pass a properly done EIS. But another possibility arises: that the only large investor, John Lehman, *did* privately insist that there be no EIS, which might delay the ship's entry into service (thereby slowing recovery of his investment) or might defeat the Superferry's purpose as a prototype for military contracts to follow.

FEBRUARY 2005

State DOT Exempts Superferry from Environmental Review
The Hawai'i Department of Transportation formally announces that it accepts the findings of the EA prepared by E. K. Noda and Associates (*see August 2004 entry: "Hawai'i DOT Environmental Assessment"*) that $40 million in state harbor improvements for the Superferry project, now divided among four ports, qualify as "minor," therefore *exempting* Superferry from environmental review.

This, despite the DOT staff's original position in favor of an EIS. Apparently, pressure from above has pushed the project through sans EIS.

Environmentalists Enraged

The DOT announcement causes an uproar on the outer islands, especially on Maui, where environmental groups continue to demand that Superferry undergo a full environmental review. This demand wins support from the Maui County Council, the Hawai'i County Council, and the Kaua'i County Council, as well as from Maui's Mayor Alan Arakawa. Opposition also mounts from shipping companies as well as numerous small business interests.

"Nobody in Maui County voted for an H-4," says Maui County Councilwoman Michelle Anderson, referring to the Hawai'i Superferry's self-described nickname as the state's "interisland highway."

Maui attorney Isaac Hall, representing the Sierra Club, Maui Tomorrow, and the Kahului Harbor Coalition, asserts, "They owe it to the communities of Hawai'i to do an environmental analysis just like everyone else." He says he is astounded that the state could spend $40 million on what has been described as harbor upgrades while exempting the project from a full Environmental Impact Statement, as already required by Hawai'i state law going back to 1974. He indicates that the groups he represents will sue to demand an environmental review.

John Garibaldi of HSF claims, for the umpteenth time, that the $140 million federal loan guarantee would not continue to be available if time had to be taken to perform an environmental review. He declares that other projects will move ahead in priority and the Superferry will have to work its way up from the bottom. "It will be difficult, if not impossible, to put this together again," he says. However, with regard to the $140 million federal loan guarantee in question from the U.S. Maritime Administration, Chris Yates of the National Marine Fisheries Service tells the *Honolulu Advertiser* that "had MARAD decided to consult there would have been ample time to analyze the potential effects long before the expected start of service." *Here again, the state administration and compliant legislators make a mockery of the democratic process, completely ignoring the resolutions passed on Maui, Kaua'i, and Hawai'i to require an EIS. Later, it will also become clear that any EIS that delays getting the boat into the water could negatively affect potential huge military contracts for Austal USA.*

March 2005

MARAD Will Not Do EIS

In response to the continuing pressures from other government agencies, including the Marine Mammal Protection Agency and the National Marine Fisheries Service *(see January 2005 entry: "Federal Agencies Protest")*, MARAD issues an official "record of categorical exclusion determination" indicating that its loan guarantee for Superferry did not require further review under the National Environmental Protection Act. It gives three reasons.

The first reason is that a review would not result "in a change in the effect on the environment." (How they determined this remains unknown. Chris Yates of the National Marine Fisheries Service says that, as far as he knows, MARAD made *no* effort, whether formally or informally, to check with other agencies on any potential effects before it granted the exclusion.)

MARAD gives as its second reason that the precedent set by the State of Hawai'i in granting an exemption is justification for granting the federal "categorical exclusion." Later in the year, MARAD spokeswoman Jean McKeever offers a third reason: that an environmental review of the loan guarantee is not required because her agency is not providing a *direct loan or funding to* Hawaii Superferry. And yet it is clear that the loan guarantee itself does make possible a direct loan and funding, and in fact makes the entire project financially viable.

(Obviously, a fourth possibility is that a force in Washington, perhaps including the military, wants this project to go through rapidly, despite the operable laws, and has so instructed MARAD, the Superferry company, and the governor of Hawai'i, so that everyone can keep their stories straight. This mysterious force may have been ultimately responsible for the condition that the loan guarantee have no environmental review.)

John Lehman Joins HSF—Major Military Investor

On the heels of MARAD's granting a loan guarantee to Superferry and then exempting an EIS, Superferry investor John F. Lehman publicly joins the company hierarchy. Lehman is appointed to chair the Superferry board and confirms that he is investing $58 million equity capital through his private equity firm, J. F. Lehman and Co. *Is it a coincidence that Lehman moves in just as soon as the money is secured by a federal agency and the pesky EIS requirement is circumvented?*

On its Web page, Lehman's firm describes itself as maintaining an "exclusive and consistent focus" on defense, aerospace, and maritime projects. Lehman is uniquely qualified for this specialty because of his Navy Department experience and extensive political and defense contacts, as well as his long advocacy of a robustly muscular militarism, which was responsible for his advocacy of a 600-ship Navy while in office with the Reagan administration. More recently, he has been advocating for aggressive action against Iran, Syria, and North Korea. Given Lehman's extraordinary experience in military matters, HSF is expected to play an instrumental role in various military contracts within Hawai'i and beyond.

Soon after, in April 2004, Lehman tells *Pacific Business News* that the Superferry "will make it easier for soldiers to train when the Stryker Brigade comes to Hawai'i. ... The brigade will be stationed on O'ahu and conduct training exercises on the Big Island." The Superferry will be the ideal means to transport platoons of Stryker vehicles to the outer islands, says Lehman. The article also quotes founder Timothy Dick: "Hawaii Superferry provided the Army with a cost analysis and expects to negotiate a long-term contract."[66]

Maui Environmentalists' Lawsuit Demands an EIS

Maui attorney Isaac Hall, again representing Hawai'i Sierra Club, Maui Tomorrow, and the Kahului Harbor Coalition, files a request before Maui Second Circuit Court Judge Joseph Cardoza for an injunction to prevent the Superferry from using Kahului Harbor before an EIS is completed. The request is filed hurriedly, because the Department of Transportation is expected to enter into an operating agreement with the Superferry within a month and exempt the company from an environmental review.

APRIL 2005

Garibaldi, Lingle Go on the Offensive

Governor Linda Lingle says, "it would not be fair" to require the Superferry to complete an Environmental Impact Statement "when other shipping companies that use State harbors haven't had to undergo the same review. ... I think they should be treated like everybody else." *She doesn't say, however, that many other companies have*

---

[66] "Lehman joins Superferry project," *Pacific Business News*, March 28, 2005.

indeed had to undergo environmental review, and those that haven't had been in business since before the existence of the Environmental Protection Act. Most important, Superferry is exponentially different in scale, speed, and potential environmental and social impacts from any vessel that has ever entered Hawaiian waters. Never before have four jet engines mounted on a single boat plied the Whale Sanctuary. Never before have hundreds of cars been dumped, in one fell swoop, onto the rural outer islands. Comparing the Superferry to normal boats is like comparing a dirigible to a 747 jet.

On her own Web page, Governor Lingle goes on to laud Superferry:

> Aloha. Hawai'i has an ideal opportunity to expand our interisland travel options and reduce [travel] prices. The Superferry will make it easier to visit family and friends on neighbor islands, or enjoy a weekend getaway. Families will be able to drive their cars onto a high-speed catamaran on one island and drive off a few hours later on another. Farmers could economically ship fresh produce between the islands, which ultimately will save us all money at the grocery store. And a high school sports or debate team could board the ferry along with their bus in the morning and compete that afternoon on a different island. *[No mention of Stryker tanks.]*
>
> My Administration has proposed $40 million to upgrade our harbors and piers to accommodate the Superferry and other ocean vessels. The funds would be reimbursed to the State by ferry revenues and docking fees. ... [O]ur residents, visitors and businesses will be well-served by the Superferry. Please ask the Legislature to support the Superferry.[67]

Legislature Okays Lingle's Harbors Project for HSF

Although the state senate votes *against* spending $40 million over the next two years on harbor improvements needed to begin Superferry service, the funds are reinserted into the legislature's final approved 2006 budget during conference-committee deliberations. A total of $20 million is released to the company; the remaining $20 million will be released in 2006, pending further review.

---

[67] http://hawaii.gov/gov/news/radioadd/2005/april-18-2005-superferry

July 2005

Maui Judge Cardoza Rejects Environmental Lawsuit

Maui Judge Joseph Cardoza throws out the lawsuit filed in March by Isaac Hall on behalf of the Sierra Club, Maui Tomorrow, and the Kahului Harbor Coalition, which had demanded a full and lengthy environmental review before ferry service could start. Cardoza rules that the plaintiffs could not demonstrate sufficient harm from Superferry operations to support the plaintiffs' claims. The groups announce they will appeal to the State Supreme Court.

August 2005

Maui Environmentalists Sue in *Federal* Court—Rejected Again

Meanwhile, at the federal level, in response to MARAD's March 15 "categorical exclusion," which argued that the agency did not need to prepare an EIS, Sierra Club, Maui Tomorrow, the Kahului Harbor Coalition, and Friends of Haleakala National Park file a new lawsuit in U.S. District Court, requesting an EIS.

Only one month later, U.S. District Judge Helen Gillmor dismisses the suit. She does not rule on whether the exclusion is proper; she merely maintains that, by law, decisions regarding federal loan guarantees cannot be contested.

October 2005

New Financing for HSF

In Washington, DC, Hawaii Superferry officials sign documents with investors and federal government officials, thus securing more than $237 million of needed financing. Included in this package is $80 million in equity financing from J. F. Lehman and Co., Norwest Equity Partners, Grove Farm Co., Maui Land and Pineapple, and other coinvestors, plus $140 million in senior debt financing from ABN-Amro Bank (guaranteed by the U.S. Maritime Administration, pursuant to Title XI of the Merchant Marine Act of 1936), and $17 million in subordinated notes from shipbuilder Austal USA.

Chris Yates, head of the Office of Protected Resources for the Pacific Island Region of the National Marine Fisheries Service, sends a letter to MARAD asking it to conduct a Section 7 consultation. He says this would be necessary, "since we believed there was a threat of ship strikes to protected species." MARAD never complies with this request.

Austal/General Dynamics Win Bid for LCS
The Austal/General Dynamics partnership team formally announces that it has won its bid to build a *prototype* for the Littoral Combat Ship (LCS) program of the U.S. Navy. The prototype will be in competition with another model being built by Lockheed Martin, for a contract to build fifty-five Littoral Combat Ships, worth upward of $15 billion. *(See Chapters 14 and 15.)*

Constructing the Superferry gives Austal a competitive edge by providing a project in which a thousand-worker force can gain experience building high-speed aluminum vessels, ready to hit the ground running on construction of the combat ship.

The same crew would also continue work on a third component: adapting the Superferry catamaran design to compete for another Navy contract—construction of the Joint High Speed Vessel connector ships. For that contract, Austal again has a leg up, as it has previously supplied a catamaran almost identical to the Superferry for the Navy's "Westpac Express" transport program in the western Pacific. Austal hopes the Superferry design will confirm it as the shining example of naval efficiency in the Pacific theater.

After Austal USA has been at work building the first Superferry for sixteen months without being paid, Hawaii Superferry corporation finally confirms that it will make payment, according to the Austal website. (Presumably, it was worth it to the boatbuilder to wait over a year for its money, since building the Superferry would enable it both to get the boat in the water and prove that the catamaran design was worthy of the Navy contracts, and to get its construction crew competitively up to speed and ready to build military versions of the ship.)

NOVEMBER 2005

Inouye Comes Through, Again
The U.S. Congress gives final passage to a $44 million infrastructure appropriations bill, sponsored by Senator Daniel Inouye of Hawai'i.

The bill contains $7.5 million for Hawai'i and Alaska (home of another Stryker Brigade) to improve ferry infrastructure.

DECEMBER 2005

Lehman's Big Coup at HSF Company — New Plans

By this point, according to the *Honolulu Star-Bulletin*, John Lehman has increased his company's investment in HSF to $71 million, confirming that he is Superferry's largest single investor, by far. He is named chair of the Hawaii Superferry board of directors. Five of the eleven other HSF directors either are employees of J. F. Lehman and Co. or have close business or military affiliations with the firm, thus giving John Lehman effective control of both the Superferry board and the company. *(Chapter 14 offers details on the high-level military backgrounds of the J. F. Lehman and Co. board of directors, many of whom are now also on the Superferry board.)*

So, by the end of 2005, it seems as if Superferry is being groomed to be integrated as much as possible into the military transport system. At every stage of development it has been given unique special treatment, insofar as it did not have to follow the National Environmental Policy Act or similar state laws—nor have any federal or state regulatory agencies had to follow such acts and laws. And it is run by a board also working for one of the country's most well-connected and outspoken right-wing military boosters.

JANUARY 2006

New Lawsuit by Maui Environmental Groups

A new lawsuit in Maui's Second Circuit Court, before Judge Joel August, is filed by attorney Isaac Hall on behalf of plaintiffs Maui Tomorrow, Kahului Harbor Coalition, and Friends of Haleakala National Park. The suit challenges the final Environmental Assessment for $40 million in harbor improvements (sometimes called the 2025 Master Plan), prepared by E. K. Noda and Associates for Kahului Harbor *(see the August 2005 entry)*.

The 2025 Master Plan was presented to the public in 2001, before any plans for Superferry existed. With the advent of the Superferry, the suit asserts that neither were provisions made to control alien species nor was attention paid to the impact of the proposed Hawaii Superferry in Kahului and throughout Hawai'i.

Timothy Dick Lauded by *Honolulu Star-Bulletin*

The *Star-Bulletin* names Timothy Dick, founder of Hawaii Superferry, one of "Ten to Watch in '06." Those who do watch see, later in the year, that Dick is gone from the company, now effectively controlled by Chairman of the Board John F. Lehman.

FEBRUARY 2006

MARAD Says No to Section 7

After five months, MARAD finally responds to the National Marine Fisheries Service's demand for a "Section 7 consultation," saying that such a step is not required since the loan guarantee "did not fund, authorize, or carry out an action" that would have triggered an environmental review (as if *guaranteeing* funds is not effectively the same as *granting* them).

Superferry Says No to Section 10

The Fisheries Service, one of the most responsible agencies in this entire saga, also approaches the Hawaii Superferry about applying voluntarily for a Section 10 "incidental-take" permit. Such a permit would protect the company from prosecution for illegally injuring or killing marine mammals in the event of a collision. But it would also require that the company observe certain precautions against injuring whales and other sea life. And it would authorize the Fisheries Service to make additional rules if Superferry performance turned out to be inadequate. A condition for granting such a permit is that applicants must work with the Fisheries Service to develop a conservation plan specifying actions that would minimize the risk of harm, and to show that there would be no appreciable impact on the survival of species in question.

Hawaii Superferry declines to apply, apparently finding the whale-protection processes too onerous.

MAY 2006

Senators Threaten to Withhold HSF Funds

Some state senators are frustrated about Superferry's lack of transparency and public outreach. Senators Gary Hooser (D-Kaua'i), Shan Tsutsui (D-Maui), and Kalani English (D-Maui) attach a condition to legislation, saying that none of the 2006 budget of $20 million for harbor improvements will be released until the Superferry Corporation and DOT meet with the public on each of the islands where the vessels will dock.

Superferry CEO Denies Military Connection

A joint committee of the state legislature grills John Garibaldi about Hawaii Superferry's intent in the islands. Questions arise about the company's single largest private investor, J. F. Lehman and Co., which has reportedly sunk $71 million into the project at this point. Lehman's involvement has prompted rumors that Superferry's main client will be the U.S. military, and the vessels will be used to transport the equally controversial Stryker Brigade from Oʻahu to the Big Island.

But Garibaldi says no such military arrangements exist. *He clings to this assertion to the day he is demoted, despite the PUC application, which clearly spells out plans to transport the Stryker Brigade, and similar published remarks by Timothy Dick and John Lehman.*

JUNE 2006

DOT Holds Public Meetings—Finds Anger

Because of a legislative requirement resulting from mounting opposition to the Superferry, the company and the state Department of Transportation begin a series of public meetings on the Big Island, Maui, Oʻahu, and Kauaʻi to assuage public anger. (They do not.) At the outset of each meeting, DOT announces that there is no question that Superferry service will shortly begin—it's a done deal—but they would like to "reach out" and answer questions. Clearly, it's not inclusion so much as public relations.

On the Big Island, officials meet a firestorm of hostility from residents, with heated accusations of deception and blatant lying about how the decisions were made at every stage, as well as exclusion of the most affected communities from the approval process. Issues of whale protection, invasive species, and overdevelopment are repeatedly voiced, as well as the need for an EIS.

On Maui, some one hundred mostly angry residents show up. Not a single person speaks in favor of Superferry. "Shame on you," rails Native Hawaiian activist Leslie "Uncle Les" Kuloloio, directing his comments to leaders of both DOT and Superferry. "This is the lousiest damn job I ever did see." Catcalls and derogatory comments blast the state's Deputy Transportation Director Barry Fukunaga as well as Superferry Executive Vice President Terry White *[White had been Chief Operating Officer under Timothy Dick. Following in Dick's footsteps, White later mysteriously vanishes from the company.]* "You should be ashamed of yourselves," Maui flower farmer Lloyd Fischel says to Fukunaga in an impassioned testimony. "For small- and medium-size businesses, this is a disaster. Every business is going to be affected."

Shortly after, Maui County Council Chairman Riki Hokama introduces a resolution calling for HSF to postpone the start of operations at Kahului Harbor until an update of the Harbor Master Plan and an EIS have been completed.

Stryker Brigade Arrives on Oʻahu

Armored Stryker Force Brigade tanks start to arrive on Oʻahu from manufacturer General Dynamics Land Systems.

July 2006

Maui County Joins Environmental Lawsuit

The Maui County Council unanimously adopts Chairman Hokama's resolution asking county attorneys to join a lawsuit against the state Department of Transportation to challenge the adequacy of its environmental review of the planned Kahului Harbor improvements. Hokama states, "Maui County won't tolerate its future being dictated by people who aren't its residents." *With the alliance between environmentalists and Maui County attorneys, the case can no longer be "spun" by HSF as a complaint by a few grumbling tree huggers, but, rather, as one mounted by the elected representatives of all the citizens of Maui. Unfortunately, this resolution carries no legal weight in influencing Superferry's intentions to begin service as quickly as possible, with no environmental review.*

August 2006

Second Maui Judge Rejects New Environmental Lawsuit

Maui Second Circuit Judge Joel August rules against the suit by Sierra Club, Maui Tomorrow, and Kahului Harbor Coalition, which challenged the adequacy of an Environment Assessment for the Kahului Harbor, saying that the plaintiffs "do not have standing to sue" *(see January 2006 entry: "New Lawsuit by Maui Environmental Groups").* The judge later reconsiders and finds that two of the three groups do in fact have standing to sue, on the grounds that *1)* traffic and *2)* recreational use of the harbor have not been adequately considered in the development plans for Kahului Harbor.

Lehman Buys Atlantic Marine Holding Company

In an extraordinary business move, Hawaii Superferry Chairman John Lehman's investment firm purchases Atlantic Marine Holding Company, a 650-acre shipyard in Mobile, Alabama, adjacent to Austal USA.

This potentially positions J. F. Lehman and Co. to be involved in the military's new wide-sweeping plans to beef up the Navy with hundreds of catamaran- and trimaran-style vessels. *(As mentioned in the Introduction, and in greater detail in Chapters 14 and 15, these fast, shallow-water boats are enjoying newfound popularity among military circles because of their ability to move quickly in coastline situations, whether as combat or transport vessels. They are considered important to preparations for any future friction with China or other Pacific Rim challengers.)*

SEPTEMBER 2006

Governor Rejects Kaua'i Petition With 6,000 Signatures

A group of Kaua'i citizens called People for the Preservation of Kaua'i, led by former policeman Rich Hoeppner, announces they will travel to O'ahu to present Governor Lingle with a petition containing 6,000 signatures from Kaua'i, requesting an EIS before the Superferry is allowed to operate. Governor Lingle refuses to see the group, and her staff will not even accept the petition. Hoeppner and the other Kaua'i residents are ushered out, he says, by a "large man in an aloha shirt."

October 2006

Maui Judge Reconsiders Environmental Suit
Maui Second Circuit Judge Joel August shifts gears and announces that he will *reconsider* his ruling of several months earlier against the three Maui environmental groups that had sued on grounds that the state was planning changes at Kahului Harbor *without* doing a required environmental review.

Hawai'i County Council Seeks Delay
On the Big Island of Hawai'i, the County Council calls for a delay in the launch of the HSF until the state and the HSF do more to address concerns about the project's economic, social, and environmental impacts. However, HSF shows no intention of satisfying the demands of Big Island citizens.

Federal Judge Rules for Native Hawaiians vs. Strykers
The U.S. Court of Appeals for the Ninth Circuit, in San Francisco, rules *in favor of* the plaintiffs in a lawsuit filed by Earthjustice on behalf of three Native Hawaiian groups. The court rules that the U.S. Army violated the National Environmental Policy Act when it did not consider all alternatives to its decision to deploy the Stryker Brigade in the Hawaiian Islands, thereby potentially damaging ecosystems as well as traditional Native Hawaiian shrines and cultural areas. It instructs the Army to begin a process of seeking alternatives.

December 2006

Maui Judge Reinstates Environmental Plaintiffs
In Maui District Court, Judge Joel August reverses his previous ruling and now finds that *two* of the three Maui groups seeking to challenge the state's Environmental Assessment on the 2025 Master Plan for Kahului Harbor improvements do, in fact, have standing to sue. The two groups are Maui Tomorrow (concerning traffic) and Kahului Harbor Coalition (concerning the recreational use of the harbor). Judge August tells them to proceed with the lawsuit, now also joined by Maui County.

Judge August also urges the groups to *negotiate with HSF*, because the ferry launch is only months away.

January 2007

Army Starts Stryker Hearings; Outer Islands Propose EIS Bill

In response to the U.S. District Court's order to seek alternative locations for Stryker deployment, the U.S. Army announces that it will begin public hearings at various locations in Hawai'i and elsewhere in the country concerning its deployment of a Stryker Tank Brigade. *(See also August 2004 entry: "Earthjustice, on Behalf of Native Hawaiians, Sues the Army," and October 2006 entry: "Federal Judge Rules for Native Hawaiians vs. Strykers.")* For Superferry, of course, the contract to transport the Strykers may be an excellent launchpad for more extensive military uses.

Four Hawai'i state senators, from the islands of Maui, Kaua'i and Hawai'i, propose a bill to require an Environmental Impact Statement for the Hawaii Superferry.

Alakai Is Launched

The first Hawaii Superferry craft, named the *Alakai* (Hawaiian for "leader"), is launched by Austal USA in Alabama. The christening includes a highly publicized traditional Hawaiian blessing, part of the company's PR campaign to prove how "indigenous" its Alabama plant is. Another example can be found in the first edition of the Superferry Company's onboard magazine, in which one article likens the enormous, high-speed gas guzzler to a traditional, Polynesian outrigger canoe—the very kind they intend to displace at Kahului Harbor.

Shocking Statement from Ex-CEO of Austal

In a January 19, 2007, article in *Pacific Business News*, the former CEO of Austal USA, Alan Lerchbacker, states his concerns about the Hawaii Superferry's having been built on such a large scale: "I just worry about getting enough business [for Superferry] to cover costs because of the sheer size of it." Lerchbacker says he had suggested a 72-meter vessel, only to see the company order the 100-meter model. "They may need 400 to 500 passengers [per trip] to break even," stated Lerchbacker.

Given Lerchbacker's published concerns, the community begins to wonder: Why would a humble interisland service require enough fuel to traverse half the globe? And why was the ferry originally designed with a *fold-out ramp, requiring $40 million in dock modifications, only to have it later be removed from the boat design? One answer is that a fold-out ramp would have triggered the dreaded EIS. (NOTE: Once the Lingle administration later succeeds in overruling the EIS process, the fold-out ramp will be designed back into the second Superferry ship, the Koa, to be operational in 2009. This is obviously to make the vessel acceptable to future military contracts which require such ramps. See June 2008 entry: "Superferry Lobbies for Military Upgrade.")*

FEBRUARY 2007

Kaua'i Public Supports an EIS Bill
On February 9, the Kaua'i County Building spills over with impassioned citizens testifying before a joint state senate committee in support of Senate Bill 1276 requiring an EIS. Most of the crowd wear red shirts with anti-Superferry slogans.

Environmental Council Criticizes EIS Exemption
Senator Gary Hooser urges the State Environmental Council, a citizen board responsible for making Environmental Impact Statement rules, to include on its agenda whether or not to accept the Department of Transportation's exemption of Superferry from environmental review. At a heated February 22 meeting, attorneys from the state Attorney General's office and the Hawaii Superferry Corporation argue that the council has no place making such determinations. The council, however, declares that the DOT in fact erred and votes 9–1 to deny the exemption that DOT granted to Superferry. Also present were Isaac Hall, attorney for the Maui environmentalists, and Senator Hooser, who called the council's decision to take a stand "an act of courage."

Mike Faye, council chair, supports the bill to require an EIS. "It's pretty clear that a project of this magnitude should have had an environmental review," he says. "They chose to pick some narrow things in their exemption list, used it, and didn't look at the whole picture."

This decision has no sway on Governor Lingle's determination to push Superferry into service. Still, it is included as evidence in the Hawai'i Supreme Court appeal, after which the court will rule, in agreement with the council, that the DOT made a mistake in granting exemption from environmental review.

Lehman Says HSF Is "Environmental Poster Child"

On February 15, John Lehman visits Honolulu to meet with company officials and state lawmakers who are trying to require an EIS. Lehman says the company has gone far beyond state and federal requirements in its environmental planning and protection efforts. "We think we're an environmental poster child," he boasts.

MARCH 2007

MARAD Confirms Military Role for HSF

Speaking before the U.S. House of Representatives Subcommittee on Seapower and Expeditionary Forces, Sean Connaughton, administrator of MARAD under the U.S. Department of Transportation, confirms, "The ferries are also militarily useful and [Transportation Command] has expressed an interest in them. The Hawaii Superferry vessels will be offered for enrollment in the Voluntary Intermodal Sealift Agreement, or VISA, program."

Legislature Kills EIS Bill

Hawai'i lawmakers who support the Superferry succeed in killing Senate Bill 1276, which would have forced the state to perform an environmental review of the ferry service's impact on harbors. The bill passes in the Senate but is killed by Transportation Committee Chair Joseph Souki (D-Maui), who refuses to hear the bill in committee.

APRIL 2007

First Sea Trials for Superferry

The front page of the *Honolulu Advertiser* exclaims that the *Alakai* has completed sea trials in the Gulf of Mexico. The article is accompanied by a gorgeous color photo of the ship that resembles a tourist brochure.

MAY 2007

Setback for DOT

In the case in which Maui Tomorrow, the Kahului Harbor Coalition, and the County of Maui join together as plaintiffs charging that the state's EA for the 2025 Master Plan for Kahului Harbor was incomplete, Judge Joel August rules that the Hawai'i Department of

Transportation's Finding of No Significant Impact (FONSI) was insufficient. He states specifically that the examination of traffic issues was inadequate and orders that only two vehicles per minute may exit the Superferry site during debarkation at Kahului Harbor.

June 2007

Superferry Arrives in Honolulu

The brand-new Superferry arrives in Honolulu, via the Panama Canal, just hours after the company begins to book passenger reservations to commence for vogages on September 4.

Huge Lehman Equity Investment

According to the *Honolulu Star-Bulletin*, John Lehman has by this time invested at least $80 million of an estimated $90 million in private financing. So, clearly, if any single investor was really urging "no EIS," as Garibaldi and Lingle have been repeating, it certainly might have been Lehman.

Austal Confirms Big Military Contract for Superferry Design

Austal issues a press release announcing that the U.S. Navy has extended its lease on Austal's "Westpac Express" catamaran—almost exactly the design of the Hawaii Superferry—"for a further period of up to 55 months," to serve as "a support for the U.S. Marine Corps' Third Marine Expeditionary Force in the Western Pacific." This activity involves regional transport of troops, vehicles, and other equipment on the "roll-on/roll-off" vessels, operating in shallow waters along the East Asian coast. The catamaran will continue to be part of the Navy's High Speed Connector service (HSC), under the Navy's Military Sealift Command.

Austal also indicates that the success of the Westpac Express military transport ship positions the company well for the future expansion of the Navy's Joint High Speed Vessel Program (JHSV), which calls for *six more 320-feet-long high-speed vessels using commercial ferry technology*, starting in 2009. Austal states that "JHSVs will play a crucial role as operational maneuver platforms that can rapidly project forces and sustain support of the Global War on Terror (GWOT) and Theater Security Cooperation (TSC)."

(The JHSV Program provides yet another plausible reason for John Lehman to decide to purchase 650 acres adjacent to Austal's plant in Alabama, to help expand its production capacities for Superferry-type vessels. This is in addition to the Littoral Combat Ship venture mentioned in the June 2004 entry: "Construction Begins in Mobile," and the August 2006 entry: "Lehman Buys Atlantic Marine Holding Company." For further information on these programs, see Chapters 14 and 15.)

August 2007

Giant Shocker:
Hawai'i Supreme Court Rules HSF Needs EIS

In a stunning surprise, on August 23 the Hawai'i Supreme Court rules unanimously, 5–0, that the state must conduct an environmental study on its improvements to island harbors for Superferry operations, scheduled to begin on September 4—only twelve days away. The ruling, written by Associate Justice James Duffy, says, in part, "The exemption [to an environmental study] was erroneously granted as the Department of Transportation considered only the physical improvements to Kahului Harbor in isolation, and did not consider the secondary impacts on the environment that may result from the use of the Hawaii Superferry." Attorney Isaac Hall, representing the Sierra Club, Maui Tomorrow, and the Kahului Harbor Coalition, says, "This means the State has to look at a project as a whole, and not just at the isolated parts." The ruling requires the Department of Transportation to reverse its own opinion that no further environmental review was necessary. *(NOTE: This ruling came out, of course, before it was revealed that it was not DOT at all that made the decision for EIS exemption; rather, the decision was made in a private meeting between Governor Lingle's then-Chief of Staff Bob Awana and Superferry executives.) (See January 2008 entry: "Governor's Push for Exemption Exposed." See also October 2004 entry: "DOT Secretly Demands Environmental Assessment," and January 2008 entry: "New Revelations About DOT Demands for EIS." These entries describe the DOT staff's initial position, which actually demanded that Superferry do an environmental review.)*

Almost as surprising as the Supreme Court decision itself was the speed with which the decision was made. Oral arguments were heard in the morning; the decision was made that afternoon.

Fukunaga: Although EIS Required, HSF Can Operate

Almost immediately after the court's unanimous ruling, Barry Fukunaga, now director of the state Department of Transportation, announces that an Environmental Assessment will be conducted as ordered by the State Supreme Court, but that Superferry will be allowed to operate anyway *while* the EA is being prepared, and that it can use Kahului Harbor.

Both citizens and government officials on Kaua'i and Maui are appalled by Fukunaga's disregard for the Supreme Court ruling. Despite the public outrage splashed on the front page of every newspaper in the state, Fukunaga remains steadfast. This is startling, considering that Fukunaga is the same man who initially advised that a statewide environmental review be conducted. He is later rewarded with yet another promotion, to chief of staff for Governor Lingle.

Plaintiffs Seek Temporary Restraining Order

Meanwhile, plaintiffs in the Supreme Court victory make plans (on that Friday) to file the following Monday in Maui court for a Temporary Restraining Order (TRO) to prevent Superferry from operating while the EA is being prepared. They contend the assessment must be completed *before* the Superferry can begin planned operations, scheduled for eight days hence.

Rather than risk being stymied by the Temporary Restraining Order, Superferry prematurely launches ahead of schedule, beginning operations on Sunday, the day *before* the Temporary Restraining Order is to be filed. A last-minute lure offers one-way tickets for passengers and vehicles for only $5 each.

Superferry Blocked by Angry Surfers, Swimmers

Two days later, Sunday, August 26, emerges as a landmark in the history of this struggle. On this day, Superferry defies the Supreme Court and begins operations from Honolulu to both Maui and Kaua'i. The citizens of Kaua'i are galled by the company's relentless pushiness. On Kaua'i, many hundreds of protesters spontaneously line the dock and shout "Go Back!" Swimmers and surfers leap into the waters of Kaua'i's Nawiliwili Harbor, casting their bodies between the ferry and the dock, and keeping the monolithic vessel at bay for more than two hours. Armed Coast Guard and SWAT teams threaten and arrest swimmers and protesters. Superferry passengers and cars eventually disembark on Kaua'i and, without incident, on Maui.

At the Kaua'i protest, a small group of Native Hawaiians successfully defuse any potential violence within the crowd, acting somewhat like New York's Guardian Angels. They are from the Kingdom of Atooi, a native sovereignty group. Some of them wear a black T-shirt, with the word "MARSHAL" emblazoned on it in white block letters. Dayne Aipoalani, a High Chief of Atooi, blocks the front of the ferry gate with his truck, inviting others to join him. He maintains that the Superferry is unauthorized to enter Nawiliwili Harbor, according to Kingdom of Atooi law. Although fellow protesters describe the Atooi activists as "welcoming" and with an "open spirit of aloha," their activity leads to warrants being issued for their arrest.

Kaua'i's Boston Tea Party:
1,500 Protesters on Kaua'i Turn Ferry Away

The die is now cast. The next afternoon, August 27, is even more important in the history of Kaua'i, as about 1,500 protesters show up at Nawiliwili Harbor. Swimmers, surfers, and canoe paddlers jump into the water, playing a dangerous, three-hour cat-and-mouse game with armed Coast Guard boats. Eventually, the waterborne protesters block the boat's entry, forcing it to turn back to O'ahu, amid triumphant cheers. A turning point in consciousness and confidence has been achieved. *(See Chapters 3, 4, and 5.)*

Maui Judge Issues Restraining Order on HSF

That same day—August 27—Maui Judge Cardoza issues a Temporary Restraining Order (TRO), blocking all ferry service between Honolulu and Maui.

Lingle Chastises Demonstrators

Joan Conrow, writing in the *Honolulu Weekly*, quotes Governor Lingle as saying the protesters have given the state "a very bad reputation." State Representative Fred Hemmings (R-Honolulu) says the protests give Hawai'i "a black eye" and reinforce the perception that the islands are a bad place to do business.

Representative Hermina Morita (D-Hanalei) disagrees. "We do far more damage to our business climate when we send out the message you have to rely on political favors to get things approved, and that's what this reeks of."

MARAD Further Supports Military Role for HSF
Sean Connaughton, administrator of the Maritime Administration (MARAD), U.S. Department of Transportation, again affirms that MARAD supports the military importance of the Superferry. He states in a court memorandum that "the military utility of the *Alakai* could be diminished if the vessel is not operated in normal commercial operations. Consequently, the military readiness of the nation could be diminished if the *Alakai* is precluded from sustaining normal commercial operations." *(Is this why MARAD made a condition of its loan guarantee to Superferry that there be no environmental review? Were higher-ups clearing the way for military purposes? Was everyone in on a grand plan?)*

Superferry Postpones Service
Facing the Temporary Restraining Order, the Superferry finally announces that it will postpone all service, "pending outcome of legal proceedings." Many of the passengers and vehicles that traveled during Superferry's two days of service are stranded on Kaua'i and Maui. Most fly back to Honolulu, leaving their cars behind. Eventually Superferry has to ship back cars via normal cargo ships.

Army Confirms Depleted Uranium on Big Island
The U.S. Army confirms the presence of depleted uranium (DU) at the Pohakuloa Training Area on the Big Island, remnants from the use of a formerly classified weapons system called the "Davy Crockett recoilless gun." Between 1962 and 1968, the Army fired about 298 pounds of depleted uranium, now measurable in the soil at both Pohakuloa and Schofield Barracks on O'ahu. Despite the discovery of such tragic environmental news, the Army continues to work toward securing Hawai'i as the home to hundreds of Stryker tanks, which will disperse yet more depleted uranium into the environment.

September 2007

Lingle Admits MARAD's No-EIS Condition

In a letter to Kaua'i State Senator Gary Hooser, Governor Lingle explains that MARAD has put a *condition* of no-EIS on its $140 million loan guarantee to Superferry. This is the first time this fact has ever been admitted in writing. "It is important to remember that the U.S. Maritime Administration," writes the governor, "put as a condition that no EIS would be required" by the State of Hawai'i. (For years, this is what had been orally asserted by John Garibaldi, other Superferry executives, and Lingle herself.) Lingle and Garibaldi also continue to state that an unnamed investor had said that doing an EIS could force Superferry out of Hawai'i. Again, the only investor with the power to do that would be John F. Lehman.

Meanwhile, Superferry's public relations firm, McNeil Wilson Communications of Honolulu, reiterates Lingle's story to Senator Hooser: "We're saying this: If there is an EIS, Superferry is leaving."

Coast Guard Threatens Kaua'i Protesters

On September 3, the U.S. Coast Guard announces that the security zone around Nawiliwili Harbor will be expanded by hundreds of yards to "ensure safety" when Superferry finally returns, and that violators may be fined up to $10,000 and face jail time. High school senior Torri Law says, "The Superferry is not a person. The Superferry is not in danger. Maybe their business is in danger. That's not the Coast Guard's job to protect that." *(See Chapter 4.)*

Kaua'i Environmentalists Sue for Restraining Order

The next day, environmentalists file suit in Kaua'i Circuit Court for an injunction to stop Superferry service to Nawiliwili Harbor. Daniel Hempey, an attorney for Thousand Friends of Kaua'i, says the "request is simply to enforce the Supreme Court judgment."

Two days later, Judge Randal Valenciano throws out the aspects of the lawsuit that deal with the Hawai'i Environmental Policy Act. According to Valenciano, the HEPA requirement for an EIS does not apply because, within 120 days of the DOT's announcement in 2005 that it would not do an environmental assessment, no one from Kaua'i challenged its decision.

Meanwhile, environmentalists on Maui who *did* make the challenge back in 2005, within the 120-day limit, qualify, in Judge Valenciano's eyes, for protection under HEPA. Because of the ongoing work at Kahului Harbor, starting in 2001, the Maui community had been paying close attention to the goings-on at their harbor, whereas few people on Kaua'i had even heard of the Superferry. According to Valenciano, who has been a judge for only two weeks, filing within the time limit enabled Maui environmentalists to qualify for the HEPA, which led to the State Supreme Court ruling requiring an EIS before the Superferry set sail. Valenciano rules that the Supreme Court ruling applies to Maui only, and not also to Kaua'i—a highly contentious interpretation. Hempey and his law partner, Greg Meyers, argue in vain that the Supreme Court ruling requiring an EIS before operation should apply not only to Maui but also to the entire archipelago.

Although most of the case is dismissed, parts of it remain open because of two remaining complaints: that the Superferry is a public nuisance (issues of smoke, dust, sound, odor, and vibration from offloading cars) and that its operation violates the State Constitution.

Morita Demands That Fukunaga Obey Supreme Court

State Representative Hermina Morita (D-Hanalei) sends a letter to Barry Fukunaga, director of the Department of Transportation, with a copy to Governor Lingle, asking him to halt Superferry service to Kaua'i pursuant to the Supreme Court decision of a week earlier, banning service to Maui. Morita is highly critical of DOT and claims it disregarded the law when it approved Superferry operations without an EIS. She highlights that the counties of Kaua'i, Maui, and Hawai'i all demanded an EIS before service would begin. She said the department's avoidance of this legal process "was done for political expediency, not respect for the law."

Morita Files Complaint with Public Utilities Commission

Representative Morita next files an informal complaint with the PUC against the Superferry, alleging that the company had not met all the requirements when the PUC granted its Certificate of Public Convenience and Necessity. One of those requirements, according to Morita, is that Superferry must comply with the Environmental Impact Statement law. The PUC Certificate is needed for any ship to carry passengers in state waters, and was issued in 2004, before the DOT decided not to require an environmental assessment. *(Yet when the PUC issued the original certificate, it passed the buck onto the DOT, specifying that should any environmental review be needed, it would be the DOT's responsibility.)*

Morita asserts that the Superferry is in violation of the PUC's decision because of the Supreme Court's ruling and the decision to do a statewide study. "We have an administration that is so keen on pushing something through they're missing what the courts are saying," says Morita.

Supreme Court Winners Demand EIS *First*
Because of the 5–0 Supreme Court ruling that required an EIS from Superferry, attorney Isaac Hall, on behalf of the three Maui groups that were plaintiffs in the case, officially requests of Judge Cardoza that the Maui Second Circuit Court require Hawaii Superferry to complete an Environmental Assessment (EA) *before* resuming operations.

Contraband Rocks on Superferry
Some nine hundred large rocks, taken from a Maui riverbed, are discovered in three trucks that had been returning to Oʻahu but were stranded on Maui. Displacement of rocks destroys the riparian (riverbank) ecosystem, and is also a serious offense against Hawaiian religious practice. This later becomes a major issue when the legislature considers its bill permitting Superferry to restart operations. *(See Chapter 11.)*

Lingle Pushes for Resumption of HSF
On September 13, Governor Lingle announces that the Superferry will resume service to Kauaʻi on September 26, 2007, *despite* the Supreme Court ruling, the pending litigation in Maui Circuit Court, and fierce unified opposition from Kauaʻi residents.

Lingle Imposes "Emergency" Security Zone Provisions
Later, at a press conference, Governor Lingle, Kauaʻi Mayor Bryan Baptiste (via conference call), State Attorney General Mark Bennett, U.S. Coast Guard Admiral Sally Brice-O'Hara, and State Department of Transportation Director Barry Fukunaga (Lingle dubs the group the "Unified Command") explain that the U.S. Coast Guard

has established a temporary security zone at Nawiliwili Harbor, on Kaua'i. Anyone on the pier or in the water inside the new zone will be subject to arrest and prosecution under Homeland Security Law. State departments of Public Safety and of Land and Natural Resources, the U.S. Attorney's office, the Kaua'i police, and the Kaua'i prosecutor's office are also part of the Unified Command.

Lingle justifies the move by saying that no "lawless" activity by a small group of protesters can be permitted to "obstruct the operations of a legitimate business, intimidate the people who wish to use its services, or put people's lives at risk." *She makes no mention of her own recklessness in rushing the Superferry project into service by circumventing NEPA, HEPA, and even the Hawai'i Supreme Court.* Governor Lingle says, "It's not our desire or preference to arrest or prosecute people, but no one should mistake the restraint that was shown initially as a lack of resolve on our part to make certain that vessel is allowed to travel safely and that we protect public safety overall."

TRO Filed Against Coast Guard

Big Island attorney Lanny Sinkin asks for a Temporary Restraining Order in federal court to block the Coast Guard from setting up a new federal security zone in Nawiliwili Harbor, where the Superferry is expected to return in a few days. Sinkin argues that "they are using a regulation created out of 9/11 for prevention of terrorism, sabotage, subversion. They are taking that kind of law and applying it to nonviolent, peaceful, civil disobedience, and that's exactly what people were afraid of with the [federal] Patriot Act. ... They've used it, basically, to suppress free speech—suppress First Amendment rights—and make it possible for a business to make a profit," Sinkin says in federal court.

The District Court denies the temporary restraining order and rules that none of the plaintiffs has standing. Sinkin immediately files an appeal at the Ninth Circuit Court of Appeals in San Francisco. *(Later, in September 2008, the federal appeals court upholds the U.S. Coast Guard's decision to bar Superferry protesters from Kaua'i's Nawiliwili Harbor.)*

Hearings Begin in Judge Cardoza's Court in Maui

On Maui, Judge Cardoza begins a month of hearings on the case brought by Isaac Hall and a group of environmental plaintiffs, on whether the ferry should resume service to Kahului Harbor *while* an Environmental Assessment is being conducted, or *after*. Cardoza extends his preliminary injunction against Superferry operations while the case proceeds.

Lingle and Other Officials Face 1,500 Upset Kaua'i Residents

On September 20, Governor Linda Lingle makes her historic visit to Kaua'i, flanked by Unified Command members: Coast Guard Rear Admiral Sally Brice-O'Hara, Transportation Director Barry Fukunaga, Interim Land and Natural Resources Director Laura Thielen, Acting Kaua'i Chief of Police Clayton Arinaga, First Deputy Attorney General Lisa Ginoza, and Kaua'i Mayor Bryan Baptiste. The governor's announced purpose for the meeting is to provide details to Kaua'i residents about the new security zone, including the penalties for violating the zone. She states that the question of whether or not Superferry will sail is moot: It *will* sail. The agenda changes course, however, when she is met by 1,500 very upset and angry Kaua'i residents, nearly unanimous in their opposition to the way the project has been pushed without public participation and reaction, and in defiance of the court rulings on the environmental review.

Councilwoman JoAnn Yukimura asks Lingle, "Why is the State not letting the legal process run its course in determining the legality of the Superferry?" Lingle responds, "Superferry has a legal right to come into the harbor. There has been no legal opinion at this point to stop them."

Yukimura later asks, "What, if anything, does the Superferry have to do with national security?" To which Lingle responds, "I don't know of any issue that the Superferry has to do with national security." She is interrupted by a chorus of boos, heckles, and scattered profanities in response to what is now known to clearly be an outrageous, insulting lie. *(For testimonies of many of those at the meeting, see Chapter 4.)*

Lingle's only comments after the Kaua'i meeting are: "I have never experienced the level of rudeness that existed last night." However, the level of intensity and the sheer numbers of the protesters succeed in prompting Superferry to postpone service to Kaua'i indefinitely.

Environmentalists Survive in Kaua'i Court

HSF files a motion to dismiss the entire lawsuit filed by Thousand Friends of Kaua'i. This is in light of Judge Valenciano's recent refusal to recognize Kaua'i's eligibility for HEPA protection that would require an EIS before Superferry could start service. But because two of the five complaints are not HEPA-related—public nuisance and violation of the State Constitution—Valenciano keeps the case open. Thousand Friends withdraws the case anyway, so that it can qualify for an appeal to the State Supreme Court, which *would* consider its HEPA eligibility. *(For more information on legal cases, see Chapter 12.)*

Chapter Eight

AFTER NAWILIWILI: OCTOBER 2007 TO OCTOBER 2008

Koohan Paik and Jerry Mander

WE PICK UP THE STORY IN OCTOBER 2007, *five weeks after the explosive protests at Nawiliwili Harbor, and six weeks after the Hawai'i Supreme Court has ruled that the Superferry may not operate before an Environmental Impact Statement has been completed. Governor Lingle has already defied the Supreme Court ruling by giving the go-ahead for the ferry to sail to Kaua'i. This anticourt position caused profound frustrations on the part of Kaua'i citizens and was the precipitating cause of the uprising at Nawiliwili, which led to the angry public meeting that followed and cancellation of further voyages to Kaua'i. Now begins Governor Lingle's and the Superferry's legal and public relations maneuverings to try to revive their prospects and to overpower the popular opposition as well as the Supreme Court's position.*

OCTOBER 2007

More Threats from Garibaldi
Superferry Company CEO John Garibaldi testifies in Judge Cardoza's court on Maui that the company is losing $650,000 a week while its ship idles in Honolulu Harbor. He says the company cannot afford to remain out of service for the months it will take the state to conduct a court-ordered Environmental Assessment.

Lingle Urges Legislature to Overrule Supreme Court
Governor Lingle announces that if the Maui court does not rule in

favor of Superferry, she will call a Special Legislative Session to create a new bill that will allow Superferry to sail. (The court has been asked to prevent Superferry from operating while a state environmental review is completed.)

Representative Mina Morita (D-Hanalei) responds: "No correction to the law is necessary. If we do go into Special Session, it will be to exempt the Superferry from the law."

Judge Cardoza Concludes Month of Testimony

On October 8, Maui Judge Joseph Cardoza concludes a full month of testimony concerning whether to permit the Superferry to operate while an Environmental Assessment is conducted. During this time, statements from leading oceanic scientists cite the multiple and apparently inevitable impacts on sea mammals from high-speed ferry operations. Greg Kaufman of the Pacific Whale Foundation recommends that the ferry travel farther north than currently planned, away from whale habitats, and at a speed of less than 13 knots, one-third its normal cruising speed of 37 knots (about 43 mph). According to Kaufman, this is the fastest speed possible that would enable the crew to react to whale sightings quickly enough to reduce the risk of serious injury and death to whales. *(For more on whales versus ferries, see Chapters 9 and 10, and Kaufman's PUC hearing testimony in Chapter 6.)*

Other testimonies include worries over the spread of alien species, as well as degradation of Native Hawaiian subsistence fishing, hunting, and gathering grounds.

Testimony from John Garibaldi states that the company will not be able to absorb the financial blow if the vessel is not permitted to operate during the completion of an environmental review. He threatens, again, that the company will have to lease the vessel out elsewhere in order to generate revenue, a reiteration of ultimatums that have been made for years and never acted on.

Attorney Isaac Hall becomes convinced that the real reason the company and Lingle (and MARAD) want to avoid an EIS is that the company could never mitigate the negative impacts that an environmental review would point out.

The State Transportation Department selects the company Belt Collins through a bidding process to conduct its $1 million Environmental Assessment. Kauaʻi's residents are skeptical, since Belt Collins, which specializes in environmental consulting, is linked to the all-too-recent 2006 Kaua'i dam-break disaster in which 400 million gallons of water were unleashed, sweeping seven people, several homes, and a strip of forest down into the sea. Belt Collins was the engineering consultant for the property where the dam was located, and is named in a lawsuit that claims the firm had been "grossly negligent" in correcting dangerous conditions in the dam's structure.

Cardoza Prohibits Superferry Runs While EIS Is Underway

In an October 8 decision, Maui Judge Joseph Cardoza defers to the Supreme Court decision and rules that Superferry cannot sail while an environmental review is being completed—a great victory for those wanting HSF to follow the law. Governor Lingle immediately announces that she will call a Special Legislative Session to craft a bill to allow the vessel to operate while the assessment is being done, essentially overruling the State Supreme Court's unanimous decision. Questions are raised by attorney Isaac Hall, representing Sierra Club, Maui Tomorrow, the Kahului Harbor Coalition, and others, about the constitutionality of any such legislation.

Superferry Layoffs; Lingle Cancellation

John Garibaldi announces that Hawaii Superferry will furlough 249 employees, more than 80 percent of its workforce. This is seen by many as a move to show state legislators how postponing operation is hurting the economy and the people of Hawai'i. *Many of the furloughed laborers are actually part-time workers; they have been restricted by HSF from working more than 20 hours per week, enabling the company to avoid providing benefits. (A few months later, when Superferry goes into dry dock to repair its broken hull, it again lays off the employees but this time does not tell the press. See March 2008 entry: "Superferry Extends Dry-Dock Repairs.")*

Governor Linda Lingle announces that she has canceled a trip to Asia so she can work with state lawmakers on a potential special session to help Hawaii Superferry.

Illegal Superferry Donations to Lingle

Few people are surprised by a *Honolulu Advertiser* story that Hawaii Superferry officials "spent more than $175,000 over three years on lobbying and campaign contributions, including donations to

Governor Lingle and State legislators."⁶⁸ The article quotes campaign finance expert Craig Holman of Public Citizen, a Washington, DC–based consumer advocacy group: "At the least they are trying to buy access, and at worst they are trying to buy influence." Other key recipients of Superferry money include Senator Daniel Akaka (D-Hawai'i), Senator Daniel Inouye (D-Hawai'i), U.S. Representative Neil Abercrombie (D-Hawai'i), House Speaker Calvin Say (D-St. Louis Heights-Wilhelmina Rise, Honolulu), and House Transportation Committee Chairman Representative Joseph Souki (D-Waihe'e-Wailuku), a key figure in the legislature's manipulations in favor of the Superferry. HSF officials, however, say, "there's no connection between the political donations and any legislative efforts pursued by the company." *So, were donations intended only as some kind of public service?* A response from Lingle's office to the *Advertiser* reports: "The Lingle campaign's policy was to refuse contributions from companies that were negotiating for state contracts," says Miriam Hellreich, finance director of the governor's office. She adds that acceptance of the donations was an "error" and that the money would be returned.

In addition, the State Ethics Commission later reveals, in May 2008, that the company's lobbying expenses for 2007 totaled $379,431. This is more than double the amount spent by any other organization in the state during that period.

Governor Lingle Visits Laura Bush

At the invitation of First Lady Laura Bush, Governor Lingle travels to Texas to speak at the National Park Foundation Leadership Summit. The privatization of national parks is the summit's central theme. Lingle tells the audience, "Our responsibility is not just to the land but also to the Native Hawaiian culture. We must preserve it so that future generations of Native Hawaiians and citizens of the world can explore and learn from it."

State Senators Hold Kaua'i Hearing

Kaua'i residents are given less than twenty-four hours' notice to attend an October 21 hearing conducted on three neighbor islands by state senators collecting input for the proposed new legislation

---

⁶⁸ Rick Daysog, "Hawaii ferry spent $175,000 on lobbying," in Honolulu Advertiser, October 14, 2007.

to permit Superferry to operate while an EIS is in preparation. On the very next day, despite the short notice, the high school cafeteria where the meeting is held is filled well beyond capacity by a reported 500 extremely concerned people.

Senators Tour Maui and Hawai'i Island

Next the senators visit Maui and the Big Island. On Maui, residents speak passionately at both afternoon and evening sessions. Many argue that the bill is unconstitutional, because it is transparently aimed at helping a single private business.

On the Big Island of Hawai'i, they are greeted by 400 people, with 180 signed up to testify. Speakers overwhelmingly favor an environmental study *before* the Superferry is allowed to sail. They are angry that Governor Lingle would even consider a "special session" whereby legislators could overrule the Supreme Court. Mayor Harry Kim says, "I strongly support the Superferry ... but if special legislation is passed to operate while the EA/EIS is under preparation, the perception will be that of politics overriding the legal process." County Councilman Angel Pilago says the council has already passed resolutions urging a full Environmental Impact Statement before the ferry is issued permits.

Governor Lingle Announces Special Legislative Session

Lingle assigns October 24 as the date for the extraordinary Special Legislative Session to circumvent the Supreme Court ruling by allowing the Superferry to resume operations while the state does an Environmental Impact Statement. If passed, the bill will nullify a Maui court ruling that bars Superferry from Kahului Harbor while the EIS is being prepared. The bill disingenuously refers to the Superferry as a "large-capacity ferry vessel," as if linguistic trickery will protect the state from being accused of discrimination by favoring a single company.

"The majority of the people across our state want this important transportation option, and I am pleased that we have worked collaboratively to find a way to allow the service to continue while an Environmental Impact Statement is conducted and concerns are addressed," says Lingle, without citing any evidence of public sentiment. Most observers believe that public sentiment on Kaua'i is at least 80 percent opposed and that there is strong majority opposition on Maui, the Big Island, and Moloka'i. O'ahu residents, a majority of the state population, are thought to be mostly in favor of operating *before* the completion of an EIS. "Allowing this transportation alternative to resume," says Lingle, "will also restore the reputation of our state as a fair place to do business."

Kaua'i Senator Demands Investigation of Lingle
State Senator Gary Hooser of Kaua'i joins other lawmakers in seeking an investigation of the Lingle administration's handling of Superferry, including questions about her interactions with HSF and federal agencies. Hooser also asks why the Superferry should get special treatment. "I think that when you start making special exceptions for one business," he says, "then that's a big problem. I have friends in the development business, friends who are contractors, whose projects have been delayed for months if not years because the government is slow. ... They don't get the law fixed for them." In this case, says Hooser, "A huge mistake was made [by exempting Superferry from an EIS]. The Supreme Court says that. And now they want us to fix their mistake."

Hawaiian Sovereignty Activists Arrested
Two members of the Polynesian Kingdom of Atooi, Dayne Aipoalani and Robert Pa, are apprehended at a Kaua'i Planning Commission meeting while they are addressing issues of the disinterment of Native Hawaiian bones by real-estate developers. The two are arrested on charges stemming back to events at Nawiliwili Harbor, August 26 and 27, for obstructing government operations, disorderly conduct, and trespassing. In fact, both Pa and Aipoalani participated in Kingdom of Atooi efforts to keep the protests peaceful. They are additionally charged with impersonating police officers after they present Kingdom of Atooi credentials naming them "marshals for the Kingdom of Atooi."

Draft Bill Named "Act 2"
In Special Session, the governor flippantly dubs the draft bill "Act 2," as if overturning a Supreme Court ruling were a mere trifle. Act 2 proposes that an Environmental Impact Statement finally be done for the $40 million in state harbor improvements and the secondary impacts of ferry service. The EIS is expected to take one or two

years to complete, during which time the Superferry could continue to operate, in defiance of the Supreme Court's unanimous decision. The Superferry must agree to operating conditions imposed in the bill and by the Lingle administration to protect whales and other marine life, prevent the spread of invasive species, and preserve cultural and natural resources. Superferry would be required to apply for an "incidental-take permit" from the National Oceanic and Atmospheric Administration, which would have the power to modify ferry service to protect whales. (The company had earlier refused to do this, but now, because the Kaua'i protests and Supreme Court ruling ambushed their plans, things are different.) Superferry must also bar passengers from carrying unpermitted rocks, soil, sand, and dirt, and must inspect all vehicles. In addition, Lingle is instructed to impose additional conditions, within two weeks, to protect the environment.

Environmentalists Seek Additional Conditions

On Maui, environmentalists led by Maui Tomorrow and the Sierra Club issue a list of twenty-nine "Conditions of Operation" that they demand be included in any new bill granting permission to Superferry to operate before completing an EIS. Most prominent among the conditions are:

- Superferry must operate only in waters over 1,000 fathoms (6,000 feet, a little more than a mile) deep. If at any time it travels in shallower water, it must cut speed to 13 knots (1 knot = 1.15 miles per hour, so 13 knots is about 15 mph).
- Should the boat strike a marine mammal, a written report must be transmitted to the National Oceanic and Atmospheric Association (NOAA) and other agencies.
- HSF must inspect, wash, and dislodge any debris or organic matter underneath vehicles; vacuum all stations and floors of vehicles; refuse the transport of plants and propagative materials; inspect the trunks of all cars; and perform other acts to avoid transport of invasive species.
- The conditions stipulate various agricultural inspections, passenger declarations, restrictions on transport of tents and camping materials, and the like.
- HSF must submit a "risk assessment" based on the first three months' performance, and will adjust its performance accordingly.

- ▼ The agreement applies only to the first Superferry, *Alakai*, and not to any others.
- ▼ Representatives of plaintiff groups shall be designated to verify HSF compliance with all conditions.

House Defeats Environmental Amendments

The state House defeats a proposed amendment to a Hawaii Superferry bill that would have required the ferry to slow down to under 13 knots in shallow waters to protect whales and to wash the undercarriages of vehicles to prevent the spread of invasive species. The amendment, proposed by state Representative Hermina Morita (D-Hanalei), also would have required Superferry, instead of the state, to pay for an Environmental Impact Statement that would be regulated by the state's Public Utilities Commission.

John Garibaldi, the Superferry's president and chief executive officer, reiterates that significantly reducing ferry speeds is unacceptable. The ferry was marketed as a *high-speed* vessel for passengers and vehicles between the islands. At the same time, he adds, amazingly without irony, that Superferry executives are committed to a whale-avoidance policy.

Fukunaga Refuses to Answer Questions

During hearings on the bill to override court decisions, the Senate (and later the House) question Barry Fukunaga, director of the state Department of Transportation, about why the Superferry project was exempted from an Environmental Assessment, as required by state law. Fukunaga asserts "attorney-client privilege" during several questions from lawmakers about the circumstances that led to the decision. *(It will later be exposed in the* Honolulu Advertiser—*on January 6, 2008—that Fukunaga and the DOT had originally told Superferry that it should do an EIS. They later allowed the company to slip out of the demand by altering its operational plans so as not to trigger the EIS. None of this came out during the legislative hearings, however, due to Fukunaga's and Lingle's legal stonewalling.)*

Representative Oshiro Chastises Lingle

During a state House hearing, critics, including Representative Marcus Oshiro (D-Wahiawa, Poamoho), say the Senate bill is forcing the legislature to choose between the environment and the successful operation of a single company, the Superferry. Oshiro, chair of the House Finance Committee, tells Lingle, "You will be taking apart thirty years of law and policy in the State of Hawai'i for this one company."

As Lingle tries to answer, Oshiro interrupts, "Do you realize this is a major policy shift? ... We are asking for special legislation for one project. Do you understand the enormity of what you are asking us to do? ... It seems astounding that one would put so much political capital on the line."

The *Star-Bulletin* reports that after the hearing, Lingle says she is pleased with her one hour of testimony, adding that she thinks Oshiro was just trying to pick a fight. "Marcus Oshiro either has a different point of view or he just wanted to make it political. Clearly, he just wanted to argue with me. He wasn't there to ask me my opinion," Lingle tells reporters.

State Senate Passes Act 2, Overriding the Supreme Court

Despite all the above, on October 29, the state Senate passes Act 2 in a 20–5 vote. All five negative votes are from the outer islands of Kaua'i, Maui, and the Big Island. The senators who voted against the measure were Gary Hooser (D-Kaua'i), Shan Tsutsui (D-Maui), Roz Baker (D-Maui), Kalani English (D-Maui), and Russell Kokubun (D-Big Island).

Before the final vote, state Senator Russell Kokubun, from Hilo, says his objections to the bill are not so much over operating conditions or even the Superferry project. He says he is very disappointed that lawmakers have been put in the position of coming into special session to overrule the courts and help Superferry, after company executives and the Lingle administration turned their noses up at a Senate compromise last session that would have produced results similar to Act 2's.

Kokubun strongly supports an audit of the Lingle administration. "This thing has been bungled from the very beginning," he says.

House Passes Act 2

Two days later, the House votes 39–11 in favor of allowing the ferry to resume service (Act 2, Second Draft), marking the nearly unprecedented speedy passage of a bill flying through unamended.

Yes votes:
Rep. Karen Awana (R-Kalaeloa, Nanakuli)
Rep. Della Au Belatti (D-Tantalus, Makiki)
Rep. Joe Bertram (D-Makena, Kihei)
Rep. Tom Brower (D-Waikiki, Ala Moana)
Rep. Rida Cabanilla (D-Waipahu, Ewa)
Rep. Kirk Caldwell (D-Manoa)
Rep. Jerry Chang (D-Piihonua, Kaumana)
Rep. Corrine Ching (R-Nuuanu, Liliha)
Rep. Pono Chong (D-Maunawili, Kaneohe)
Rep. Cindy Evans (D-Makalawena, Waimea)
Rep. Lynn Finnegan (R-Mapunapuna, Foster Village)
Rep. Josh Green (D-Keauhou, Honokohau)
Rep. Sharon Har (D-Makakilo, Kapolei)
Rep. Bob Herkes (D-Volcano, Kainaliu)
Rep. Ken Ito (D-Heeia, Kaneohe)
Rep. Jon Riki Karamatsu (D-Waipahu, Waikele)
Rep. Marilyn Lee (D-Mililani, Mililani Mauka)
Rep. Sylvia Luke (D-Pacific Heights, Punchbowl)
Rep. Michael Magaoay (D-Schofield, Kahuku)
Rep. Joey Manahan (D-Kalihi, Kapalama)
Rep. Angus McKelvey (D-Olowalu, Kapalua)
Rep. Colleen Meyer (R-Laie, Kahaluu)
Rep. John Mizuno (D-Alewa Heights, Kalihi)
Rep. Bob Nakasone (D-Kahului, Paia)
Rep. Scott Nishimoto (D-Kaimuki, Waikiki)
Rep. Blake Oshiro (D-Aiea, Halawa)
Rep. Kymberly Pine (R-Ewa Beach, Iroquois Point)
Rep. Karl Rhoads (D-Kakaako, Downtown)
Rep. Roland Sagum (D-Niihau, Poipu-Kokee)
Rep. Calvin Say (D-St. Louis Heights, Wilhelmina Rise)
Rep. Joe Souki (D-Waihee, Wailuku)
Rep. K. Mark Takai (D-Newtown, Pearl City)
Rep. Cynthia Thielen (R-Kaneohe, Kailua)
Rep. Clifton Tsuji (D-Hilo, Glenwood)
Rep. Glenn Wakai (D-Moanalua Valley, Salt Lake)
Rep. Gene Ward (R-Kalama Valley, Hawaii Kai)
Rep. Tommy Waters (D-Lanikai, Waimanalo)
Rep. Ryan Yamane (D-Waipahu, Mililani)
Rep. Kyle Yamashita (D-Pukalani, Ulupalakua)

No votes:
   Rep. Lyla Berg (D-Hahaione Valley, Aina Haina)
   Rep. Mele Carroll (D-Lanai, Molokai)
   Rep. Faye Hanohano (D-Pahoa, Kalapana)
   Rep. Hermina Morita (D-Hanalei, Kapaa)
   Rep. Marcus Oshiro (D-Wahiawa, Poamoho)
   Rep. Scott Saiki (D-Moiliili, McCully)
   Rep. Maile Shimabukuro (D-Waianae, Makua)
   Rep. Alex Sonson (D-Pearl City, Waipahu)
   Rep. Dwight Takamine (D-Hawi, Hilo)
   Rep. Roy Takumi (D-Pearl City, Pacific Palisades)
   Rep. James Tokioka (D-Wailua, Koloa)

Excused:
   Rep. Barbara Marumoto (R-Kalani Valley, Diamond Head)

Outer-island citizens respond: "We're going to demonstrate our strength, our determination, and our resolve to protect Hawai'i," says Andrea Noelani Brower, an activist with Malama Kaua'i, a sustainability nonprofit organization. "It's outrageous that our governor and our legislature have the audacity to undermine our thirty-year-old environmental law." Brower adds, "The legislature could have chosen not to be co-conspirators."

Lance Holter, chair of the Maui chapter of the Sierra Club, says, "This is a sad day not only for Hawai'i's sustainability, but for democracy. Not only did the legislature rush through a bill to override the judiciary branch, the legislature allowed the final outcome of the measure to be dictated by the Superferry Corporation."

NOVEMBER 2007

Navy *Postpones* Littoral Combat Ship Program

In a blow to Austal USA and possibly the Superferry company, the U.S. Navy announces a stop-work order on the Littoral Combat Ship program, due to skyrocketing costs. Austal and General Dynamics were jointly designing and building a prototype of a combat transport trimaran, in competition with Lockheed. *(See also Chapter 15.)*

The Navy attempts to require competing contractors to accept a "fixed-price" contract that would leave contractors to cover any cost overruns. This is unacceptable to the competing contractors, and the project has been delayed, at least for the time being. Negotiations continue, however, as does some work on a single prototype for the Littoral contract.

Lingle Signs Act 2

Governor Lingle signs Act 2, overruling the State Supreme Court and allowing the Superferry to operate while an EIS is being prepared. She complies with the new bill by issuing a series of forty watered-down environmental requirements for the operation of the ferry. Declawed conditions include some having to do with screenings of cars and trucks, rules forbidding transport of certain invasive species, and agricultural inspectors on board. *(Environmentalists had recommended that vehicles be inspected by professionals trained in their fields; Lingle instead accommodates HSF by allowing anyone who has received a mere hour and a half of training to screen offloading vehicles for contraband or invasive species. She does not approve the most important condition put forth by environmentalists, which is that the boat must always operate in water at least 1,000 fathoms deep (except near ports) or slow to 13 knots when in shallower water or if whales are sighted. Lingle's rules allow the boats to move into shallow water if passengers are uncomfortable, which they often are. She also leaves it up to Superferry operators to decide the point, a loophole big enough to drive a catamaran through. Worst of all, the new EIS specifically states that no findings related to environmental impacts will be reason to stop the ferry from continuing service.)*

Jeff Mikulina of the Sierra Club states that the conditions do not go nearly far enough. "We respect that the governor has attempted to go beyond the bill to protect the environment and natural resources," Mikulina says, "but the big one—the speed issue—wasn't in there."

Judge Cardoza Lifts Injunction Against Superferry

Due to the new state legislation, Maui's Judge Cardoza lifts his injunction against the Hawaii Superferry, helping to clear the way for the ship to resume sailing to Kahului Harbor.

Lingle says, "Judge Cardoza recognized that the legislature and our administration worked cooperatively, within the boundaries of our State Constitution, to pass a law that preserves an important interisland transportation alternative for the people of Hawai'i."

Some court watchers leaving Cardoza's courtroom were heard to say, "Only the gods can protect us now." *At the time of writing, the case remains on appeal.*

HSF Announces It Will Resume *Before* Completing EA

Moving up the launch date once more, Hawaii Superferry announces it will begin service between the islands of Oʻahu and Maui on December 1, before an Environmental Assessment is complete.

"We appreciate the support we've received from everyone who shares the vision of uniting our islands and families by sea," says Hawaii Superferry President and Chief Executive Officer John Garibaldi. "Hawaii Superferry and its more than 300 employees look forward to a new beginning as we start our voyages between Oʻahu and Maui, a new choice for interisland travel."

Only one "major operational issue" remains, says Garibaldi. It is the ruling of Maui Circuit Judge Joel August, who ordered that only two vehicles per minute can exit the Hawaii Superferry site at Kahului Harbor. At that rate, off-loading a full ferry holding 282 vehicles at the two-car-per-minute rate would take over two hours. *(See Chapter 7, May 2007 entry: "Setback for DOT.")*

Within two weeks, Judge August complies by lifting his prior order.

Barge Breaks Again

The same day Cardoza lifts his injunction, one of the mooring lines at the Superferry docking barge at Kahului Harbor breaks. Apparently, the rocky seas are too much for the barge, built to flimsy specifications as a compromise to enable HSF to avoid conducting an EIS. It is the second time in a month this has happened. As a result, Hawaii Superferry announces it is moving back the relaunch date for service between Maui and Oʻahu, to Thursday, December 6, 2007, five days later than planned.

Garibaldi Does "Outreach" on Kauaʻi

John Garibaldi meets with skeptical community leaders on Kauaʻi for tips on how to proceed with community outreach. Those present include former mayor and councilwoman JoAnn Yukimura, activist Teddy Blake, and journalist Jonathan Jay.

Garibaldi starts out by saying that he has come with no set date for the return of the HSF to Kauaʻi. He says he wants to talk with the community first, but hopes ultimately to bring the boat back to Kaua'i because he believes it will be a good thing for the island. What he fears most is violence at the docks between Coast Guard and protesters, and the resulting unappealing press coverage.

Kaua'i residents tell Garibaldi flatly that his company has huge credibility problems and that the issue is not only Superferry vs. no Superferry, but also following the right process. They say that HSF never took into consideration the wishes and desires of the communities it would be impacting most: those on the outer islands.

Yukimura adds that anti-Superferry sentiment remains extremely strong on Kaua'i. "There has not been a reconciliation of the division or of the issues the community has raised," she says. "If the meetings don't bring about reconciliation, then they are no better than the previous meetings, which were pro forma meetings held to be able to say they had meetings."

DECEMBER 2007

Third Barge Break
Seasonal storms on December 3 cause the Kahului Harbor barge to break for the third time in about a month. Superferry announces it is postponing its relaunch of service from December 6 to December 13.

Third Promotion for Fukunaga
Governor Lingle appoints the former head of the Department of Transportation, Barry Fukunaga, to be her new chief of staff, replacing Bob Awana. Awana resigned in June after he was targeted in an extortion scheme stemming from his secret extramarital relationship with a woman in the Philippines.

Superferry Resumes Service to Maui
On December 13, a show of military force accompanies the Superferry on its first round-trip journey from O'ahu to Maui, after four months of delays. Helicopters and Coast Guard Zodiacs indicate that the Unified Command expects Kaua'i-style opposition. But all Maui dissenters comply with the security zone boundaries and no arrests are made.

Protests take place on O'ahu and also on board the ship, including a banner unfurled off the side of the ship as it reaches Maui.

The banner reiterates the slogan of the State of Hawai'i, inherited from the Kingdom before it: *Ua mau ke ea o ka 'aina i ka pono* (The life of the land is perpetuated in righteousness). Crewmembers quickly stop the dissenters from displaying the banner.

The sea is rough, and most of the 190 passengers on board become very sick.

Maui Tomorrow to Challenge New Law
The nonprofit group Maui Tomorrow announces that it will pursue new legal action challenging the constitutionality of the just-passed state law that allows Superferry to operate before an EA is completed. The announcement is made the day of a Kahului Harbor rally, which attracts 250 protesters.

JANUARY 2008

HSF Announces Doubled Schedule to Maui
The *Maui News* and Kauai'i's *Garden Island* newspaper both carry front-page banner headlines concerning a Superferry announcement that it would now commence a second round-trip each day between Honolulu and Maui. On Maui, the reaction is outrage that this was done with no knowledge by the mayor's office, the harbor officials, or the general public. Maui Mayor Charmaine Tavares says she is "very disappointed that Hawaii Superferry has made this decision without consulting county officials and members of our community. Just weeks ago I received a commitment from Mr. Garibaldi that the company would extend its efforts to work with us, but their announcement comes as a surprise. It continues to be a contentious matter for many in our community." She also expresses concern about the lack of a study on how the ferry will affect traffic. "Now there will be two daily trips, and still no traffic study."

Mayor Tavares forbids county employees from traveling on the Superferry for county-related business.

Environmentalists also point out that a second trip would take place partly after dark, thus making it impossible to sight whales effectively, *a further expression of the Superferry's sense of entitlement.*

People on Kaua'i, as well, are disgusted at the additional service to Maui and its environmental impacts, but are also jubilant. It is clear that Superferry has abandoned, at least for the time being, the idea of Kaua'i service. This is obvious vindication for the fierceness of Kaua'i's opposition, to say nothing of the willingness of hundreds of people to engage in direct and often personally dangerous protests on the docks and in harbor waters. Superferry tells the public that the soonest it can start its Kaua'i operations is 2009, when a second boat is scheduled for delivery, and when Kaua'i's protesters might have simmered down.

New Revelations About DOT Demands *for* EIS

Another blistering investigative report appears in the *Honolulu Advertiser* on January 6. The Advertiser's government writer, Derrick DePledge, reports that in October 2004, the Hawai'i Department of Transportation informed the Superferry company that a *full statewide Environmental Assessment, and possibly an Environmental Impact Statement, would be required before the ferry could begin interisland service.* "Superferry executives resisted," says the article, and "scaled back the project in a calculated attempt to get an exemption from the State's environmental review law, State records show." This Department of Transportation position and the letter that followed had never been made public and were only obtained by the *Advertiser* under the State of Hawai'i "open-records law," the state version of the federal Freedom of Information Act. "Many of the documents released to the *Advertiser*," says the report, were also "given to State Auditor Marion Higa, who is investigating the administration's decision-making on the Superferry at the request of State lawmakers. Higa told State Senators last week that she has encountered roadblocks and questioned the administration's use of attorney-client privilege and executive privilege in withholding documents."

Documents show that "some in the department not only thought Superferry should be responsible for doing an Environmental Assessment but [should] also 'seriously consider doing an environmental review of the State's $40 million' in harbor improvements."[69] Amazingly, these remarks came from Barry Fukunaga, then the deputy director of the Department of Transportation! It was Fukunaga, of course, who later exempted Superferry from doing an EIS. Asked how he made his decisions, under questioning in court

---

[69] Derrick DePledge, "Documents reveal split in DOT over requiring environmental study," in *Honolulu Advertiser*, January 6, 2008.

proceedings, Fukunaga consistently invoked attorney-client privilege in refusing to answer, except for earlier comments he made about how the MARAD demands for no EIS "had nothing to do with the outcome" of no EIS. Governor Lingle has since promoted him to be her chief of staff.

Internal correspondence at DOT, published in the *Advertiser*, indicates that staff analysts at the department felt that an EA for the Superferry was the "right thing to do" and that it would help "address public concerns ... valid concerns that should not be left unanswered." It also conjectured that an EA that answers the outstanding questions might "minimize opposition and gain support."

It was also strongly argued that the EA/EIS *should be statewide*, not limited to the local site (Kahului Harbor) and conditions, as opposed to Judge Valenciano's reasoning in denying Kaua'i environmentalists protection under HEPA. *(See September 2007 entry: "Kaua'i Environmentalists Sue for Restraining Order.")* The document also noted that major construction could require Army Corps of Engineers permits. This permit process would trigger consultation with other federal agencies, such as the National Marine Fisheries Service which had raised concerns that ferry speed and routes could threaten endangered humpback whales and monk seals. *(See January 2005 entry: "Federal Agencies Protest.")*

"A statewide EA should be pursued in response to the concerns raised in the PUC permitting process," said an internal DOT document, referring to the many public comments related to traffic, invasive species, and whale protection. "Ignoring the concerns may trigger a challenge where we may be subject to the courts' schedule and process," it continued—in a prophetic comment.

Despite all this, from 2004 until this *Advertiser* story of 2008, neither the Superferry nor the DOT nor Barry Fukunaga nor Governor Lingle ever informed the public of these recommendations by DOT staff in favor of an EA/EIS before Superferry operation. Nor were DOT's communications directly with Superferry about the process or the needs for EA/EIS compliance made public. In fact, the impression was quite the opposite: that an EA was deemed unnecessary. Whenever questioned for details, both Fukunaga and Lingle have hidden behind questionable invocations of attorney-client confidentiality and executive privilege, another stance all too reminiscent of the Bush administration.

Superferry Backs Off Second Maui Run

A January 15 news release from the Superferry states, "In consideration of Mayor Tavares' concerns, Hawaii Superferry today announced it is postponing its second voyage between Maui and Oʻahu, certainly inconveniencing passengers with reservations. The company anticipates starting the second voyage later this spring." The previously announced start date for the second Maui trip would have been the day following this announcement.

Barge Breaks for Fourth Time in Three Months

On January 17, the state-owned barge used to load and unload vehicles from the catamaran sustains minor damage as a result of large swells within the Kahului Harbor. This is the fourth time in three months that the barge has been damaged by winter conditions. The barge was installed to substitute for harbor modifications that would have been able to properly accommodate the Superferry but would also have required the company to do an EIS.

Large waves and seasick passengers force the Superferry to cancel its round-trip Honolulu–Maui service for two more days.

The day after the barge breaks, DOT files a request for daily tugboat service—at a cost to taxpayers of $350,000 for ten weeks—that will keep the barge snug against the end of the pier during ocean surges and will provide safe loading and unloading of passengers and vehicles.

Governor's Push for Exemption Exposed

In another scathing *Advertiser* exposé (January 27, 2008), it is revealed that a December 2004 meeting between Superferry executives and Bob Awana, Governor Lingle's then-chief of staff, resulted in the state Department of Transportation's aggressive pursuit to exempt Hawaii Superferry from an environmental review. One of the incriminating documents included a DOT staffer's email following the meeting, which read: "Decision made: We need to pursue EXEMPTION; and HSF will not provide any ramps on vessel."

Both Awana and Fukunaga vigorously deny that Awana—representing the governor—played any role in the push for exemption. If Awana played no role, who did? Another representative of the governor? Or was it Governor Lingle herself?

Cracks Found in Rudder
Ominously, inspectors discover cracks on the Superferry rudders.

After studying the circumstances as described in the media, Kauaʻi blogger and retired architect Juan Wilson writes that the mechanisms within the stern of the Superferry comprise several rudders and a braking system. All of these penetrate the large aluminum hull through multiple rods. Each of these steering devices can potentially compromise the integrity of the hull, causing "hot spots" of stress when the ship is twisted, bent, and shocked by a succession of the kind of massive waves that are found throughout the Hawaiian Islands during much of the year. Metal may fatigue, yield, and even fail under such repetitive conditions. From leaks detected at the seams around the rudder post penetrations, Wilson deduces that stress on the posts probably created the cracks and allowed some water to enter the ferry's hull.

Austal Awarded Military Contract
On January 31, the U.S. Navy awards separate contracts to competing companies Austal USA, Bath Iron Works (a subsidiary of General Dynamics), and Bollinger Shipyards Inc. for a fixed price of $3 million apiece to do *preliminary* designs for Joint High Speed Vessel (JHSV) concepts. *(NOTE: This contract is different from Austal USA's other endeavor: vying against Lockheed for the Navy's Littoral Combat Ship contract.)*

"Once delivered, the Joint High Speed Vessel will be a key component of the U.S. military's expeditionary warfare capability," said Rear Admiral Charles Goddard, program executive officer for ships. "This high speed transport will carry soldiers or Marines, with their gear, to harbors that would normally be unusable by conventional maritime assets."

The Navy intends to award one company a Phase Two detail design contract, with construction options, in late 2008. The first ship, an Army vessel, is expected to be delivered in 2011.

FEBRUARY 2008

Superferry in Dry Dock
Superferry announces that the boat is "taking advantage of off-peak travel season to [move] up its annual dry dock for maintenance and

recertification by the U.S. Coast Guard to make permanent repairs related to the vessel's auxiliary rudders, which will enhance passenger comfort. The *Alakai* will be dry-docked beginning February 13 for approximately two weeks ... with service expected to resume March 3."

Contraband on Board

The *Honolulu Advertiser* reports the monthly findings of the Act 2 Temporary Oversight Task Force Committee. During Superferry's first weeks of service, in January, contraband screeners have intercepted coolers containing 'opihi and other marine resources, fishing nets, dozens of dead honeybees, and an uncertified shipment of fifty orchids. Their report also reveals that on thirteen of the twenty-four days of operation, the vessel's captain chose to pass through the Whale Sanctuary south of Moloka'i. Twenty-two whales were sighted and avoided, three of which were approached within a hundred yards. Concerns are raised as to whether any whales were unknowingly struck, and what contraband was *not* intercepted.

New Superferry Calamities: Weak Construction?

On February 13, as the Superferry prepares to enter the dry-dock facility, it runs aground on a sandbar. It is only the first of a series of calamities. A tugboat called to push it off the sandbar punctures a large dent in the side of the aluminum boat, raising discussion over the hull strength. Then, as the boat is being positioned squarely to be placed onto dry-dock blocks, the lines meant to steady the vessel snap, causing the boat to fall hard off the blocks, *further* damaging the ship's hull. One week later, HSF Corporation announces that the ship will be in dry dock until March 25, three weeks longer than originally planned, "to repair damage to the *Alakai's* hull that occurred during the dry-docking process." Controversy grows over the sturdiness of the ship's construction.

Maui Tomorrow Appeals Judge Cardoza's Lifting of Injunction

Maui Tomorrow Executive Director Irene Bowie says the group will soon appeal Judge Cardoza's November 14th ruling upholding the Act 2 special legislation that allows the Superferry to sail without first conducting an EA. Isaac Hall, attorney for Maui Tomorrow, argues that the legislation is designed to benefit a specific business and is therefore unfair, and that by approving Act 2, elected leaders violated their public trust duties under the State Constitution to protect Hawai'i's fragile environment and the traditional and customary rights of Native Hawaiians.

Army Insists Strykers Must Go to Hawai'i
The Army completes its Environmental Impact Statement on the Stryker deployment, supplementing an earlier one that was challenged in 2004 by Native Hawaiian and environmental groups. In the report, the Army states that, despite greater environmental impacts in Hawai'i than in either Alaska or Colorado, stationing the Strykers in Hawai'i is necessary to meet national security requirements.

Garibaldi Denies Military Connection
In a *Honolulu Advertiser* report, Superferry CEO John Garibaldi maintains that there are no plans to use the *Alakai* outside Hawai'i. He also denies that the company has made any deals with the military or is in negotiations to provide service to the military or other state or federal agencies.

Garibaldi has been denying any military connection from the beginning, which is difficult to accept, as the company's chairman is John F. Lehman, who rarely touches projects not related to the military.

Lawyers Appeal Permission for HSF to Operate During EIS Process
On February 29 on Maui, HSF opponents file a notice to appeal Judge Cardoza's post-Act 2 decision to allow the boat to operate *while* (as opposed to *after*) the state prepares an Environmental Assessment of ferry-related Kahului Harbor improvements. The Maui environmentalists contend that Act 2 is unconstitutional because it allows a single business to circumvent Hawai'i's environmental law. An attorney for the plaintiffs, Isaac Hall, says, "Once Hawaii Superferry is out of dry dock and begins to operate, the threat of actual irreparable harm to multiple endangered and protected resources returns."

March 2008

Hawai'i State Auditor Denounces Lingle Stonewalling

Marion Higa, the state auditor, expresses frustration over the governor's negligence in complying with the Superferry audit. When Superferry was allowed to resume operations, Act 2 called for an audit of the administration's February 2005 decision to exempt the project from environmental review. Legislators set a deadline of March 1, 2008, for State Auditor Higa to submit a report, based on documents to be furnished by the Lingle administration. But Higa, unable to meet her deadline because of Lingle's stonewalling, writes to House and Senate leaders, "We have encountered significant delays and a variety of roadblocks in conducting our audit tasks." State Senate Majority Leader Gary Hooser (D-Kaua'i, Ni'ihau) says, "I'm extremely disappointed that the administration is not cooperating fully with the auditor so we can resolve all these questions once and for all."

Nearly 300 Pounds of Depleted Uranium to Be Left in the Ground

An Army study concludes that the 298 pounds of radioactive material found on O'ahu and the Big Island do not pose a threat and so will be left in place. *(See August 2007 entry: "Army Confirms Depleted Uranium on Big Island.")*

Superferry Extends Dry-Dock Repairs

HSF announces that it is extending its dry-dock period through April 22. Terry O'Halloran, the company's director of business development, says that the extra time is needed to finish repairs and that the extension is *not* because of any new problems discovered while the ferry has been in dry dock.

Superferry Layoffs Ignored by Press

Because of the extended time needed to perform the *Alakai's* dry-dock repairs, the Superferry company lays off hundreds of employees, but this time very quietly—a far cry from blaring press reports months earlier, when sobbing Superferry workers and the company blamed environmental lawsuits for their layoffs.

Dispute Over Blame for Ferry Damage

In an interview in the blog *kauaieclectic.blogspot.com*, Dennis Chun, who is Kaua'i's representative on the Superferry Oversight Task Force, speaks with writer Joan Conrow about damages to the boat's hull during dry docking: "When they were taking it to dry dock, a boat ran into it and put a big *puka*[70] in it. Then in dry dock, the keel was all damaged because they blocked it wrong. And because other companies were involved, there's all this litigation going on, guys are suing each other. So that's why they haven't said in public what actually happened, because it's still under investigation, and the Coast Guard is involved in it, too."

Meanwhile, a squabble ensues between Superferry, DOT, and barge-builder Healy Tibbits Builders, Inc., over who will foot the bill for the tugboat that was used to secure the barge, as well as for the barge damages.

Austal Superferry Design Wins Prize; Company Sued for Racism

The Mobile (Alabama) Area Council of Engineers gives Austal USA its Engineering Project of the Year award for building the *Alakai* Superferry—though at that moment it is still in dry dock, fixing damages to an apparently unsturdy hull. According to the organization, the *Alakai* project was recognized for its superiority in engineering technology and the effect it has had on the economy in Mobile, Alabama, home of Austal's shipyard.

A few weeks later, twenty-two African-American employees at Austal USA file suit against the company, charging systematic racism.

Superferry Denounced at Public Hearings on EIS Process

The first of a series of public meetings by Belt Collins, the company awarded the state contract to complete the Environmental Impact Statement—as delineated in Act 2 legislation—is held on the islands of O'ahu, Hawai'i, Maui, Kaua'i, as well as the smaller islands of Lana'i and Moloka'i. Few people show up, except on Kaua'i, where about a hundred people deliver testimonies nearly as fiery as those given the day Governor Lingle came to visit.

Citizens on all islands express disgust at the dishonesty of Hawaii Superferry Corporation and the State of Hawai'i, and at the

---

[70] *Puka*: hole.

company's and the state's unconvincing commitment to the environment, as well as at the drain on their taxes to bail out the apparently still-sinking ship. *(See also Chapter 6.)*

Aloha Airlines Bankrupt

Aloha Airlines goes out of business, opening up markets for interisland passenger and cargo services. Although not involved in interisland service, ATA, another carrier of passengers from the continent to Hawai'i and back, also goes out of business a few days later.

APRIL 2008

Alakai Resumes Service

On April 7, the Superferry finally resumes service after being drydocked for nearly two months for repairs. When the vessel arrives at Kahului Harbor, Maui, one passenger describes the ride as "sick and fast." Another passenger, Kim Lane of Seattle, calls it "one of the most miserable rides I've ever had." The captain, apparently worried about seasick passengers, "gunned it" at top speed during the last half hour of the journey, shortening the trip by thirty minutes. It is unknown definitively if it was through the Whale Sanctuary that the vessel charged at full throttle, but we do know that Act 2 permits the ship to pass through the sanctuary, located on the northwest coast of Maui, in the event of seasick passengers.

Austal Workers Interviewed on Kaua'i Radio Say *Alakai* May Be Unsafe

Kaua'i community radio activists Katy Rose, Jimmy Trujillo, and Jonathan Jay broadcast a live phone interview *(April 10)* with Carolyn Slay, a former Austal USA welder; Wayne Jenkins, a welder currently with the shipbuilder; and labor organizer Swan Cleveland. The three are embroiled in legal disputes against the company over race discrimination and other unfair labor practices. During the interview, the workers disclose damning facts about shoddy workmanship of the *Alakai*. When asked why quality was not controlled in building the ship, Cleveland says, "It seems as though they're casting everything else aside to complete this project for the U.S. Navy, because they want those other 55 warships to be built here in Mobile." *(See Chapter 18.)*

HSF Caught Concealing Lobbying Expenses

Blogger Ian Lind writes a letter to the state Ethics Commission expressing skepticism about the accuracy of Superferry's lobbying expense reports. Further investigation reveals that, in fact, the company spent more than seventeen times the amount disclosed while lobbying for special legislation during 2007. While the company had claimed spending only $21,791.56, it had actually spent a total of $379,431.52—more than double what any other organization spent for lobbying in Hawai'i that year.

State Senate Majority Leader Gary Hooser (D-Kaua'i, Ni'ihau) says the lobbying revelation "reinforces the doubts that have existed for a long time about the Superferry management and their conduct in regard to the Environmental Impact Statement and their community dealings."

Strykers to Remain in Hawai'i

The Army announces its final decision to base a Stryker Brigade at Schofield Barracks on O'ahu and to train the unit at Pohakuloa Training Area on the Big Island. The decision was made despite public concerns that the fleet of DU-firing Stryker vehicles would damage Hawai'i's fragile environment and cultural sites. The choice was made, according to Lt. Gen. Benjamin Mixon, commander of the U.S. Army, Pacific, to send a powerful signal to friends and enemies that the nation is committed to its interests in the Asia–Pacific region.

Superferry Bullied DOT, Says State Audit

Hawai'i State Auditor Marion Higa finally releases her report, in accordance with Special-Session legislation, which requires an examination of the Lingle administration's actions related to Superferry. Higa finds that the company bullied the state Department of Transportation into exempting the company from an EIS requirement, back in 2005. This matches an earlier *Honolulu Advertiser* exposé. *(See January 2008 entries: "New Revelations About DOT Demand for EIS" and "Governor's Push for Exemption Exposed.")* The audit also confirms the extraordinary fact that the Maritime Administration made it a condition of its loan guarantee that there be *no* Environmental Assessment done, despite protests from other government agencies.

Second Run to Maui Announced, a Second Time
After having backed down from scheduling a second Maui trip when the community took offense at not having been consulted, Hawaii Superferry makes the announcement again, this time after a modicum of public relations work. The company publicizes a second run between Oʻahu and Maui, to begin May 9, and hopes ridership will build through the calm summer months. But evening tugboat services on Maui must be paid for by Hawaii Superferry, says the state Department of Transportation. Although the state agrees to pick up the bill of $350,000 for ten weeks of tugboat service for the day sail, it says that HSF must pay for the evening run.

Austal Worker Fired for Speaking Out
On April 22, Wayne Jenkins, a welder at Austal USA, is fired in Alabama for describing on the radio how cracks were appearing in the thin aluminum hull of the *Alakai*, and for revealing that workers were told not to repair them due to time constraints. The live phone interview took place twelve days earlier, on KKCR, Kauaʻi Community Radio. *(See Chapter 18 for a transcript of the interview.)*

Garibaldi Demoted; Tom Fargo Is New Superferry CEO
Superferry CEO John Garibaldi is suddenly demoted and replaced by Admiral Tom Fargo. Fargo is a managing director at J. F. Lehman and Co., and before that was head of the U.S. Pacific Command—in charge of all U.S. military operations in the Pacific—from May 2002 until February 2005, when he retired from Navy service after thirty-five years. Coinciding with this appointment, Lehman infuses HSF with a large, undisclosed sum, to see the company through its next phase, under Fargo's leadership.

Fargo hits the ground running. His first move is to blitz the media with the announcement that Superferry is waiting for a signal from the Kauaʻi community to begin Oʻahu–Kauaʻi service. State Senator Gary Hooser (D-Kauaʻi, Niʻihau) responds that passions on Kauaʻi have cooled somewhat, but the underlying sentiment is unchanged.

Austal Launches Warship
Austal's version of the Littoral Combat Ship (LCS), christened the *Independence*, is launched into the Mobile River in Alabama despite

several small leaks that have to be sealed up. The *Independence*, built by Austal in partnership with General Dynamics, is in direct competition with a ship being built by Lockheed Martin. One of these high-speed, coastal-warfare ships will be chosen as the prototype for the lucrative Navy LCS contract.

June 2008

Lingle Stonewalls; Cites Attorney-Client Privilege

The Lingle administration, again citing attorney-client privilege and executive privilege, refuses to release hundreds of emails and other documents related to its decision to exempt the Hawaii Superferry project from environmental review. The *Honolulu Advertiser* requested the documents, under the state's open-records law.

The documents include emails from late 2004 in which a deputy attorney general assigned to the Superferry project discusses an environmental review. One email, which had been released months earlier, was written from a DOT design engineer to a project consultant, and suggests that *the deputy attorney general was supportive of environmental review*. "Our attorney ... feels that one statewide comprehensive document is necessary that would cover the improvements as well as the cumulative operational impacts," the design engineer wrote.

State Representative Marcus Oshiro (D-Wahiawa) says he sees no justification for the administration to withhold either a legal analysis of whether an exemption was warranted, or discussions about strategy related to an environmental review, based on its claim of attorney-client privilege. He says that since the decision itself has been ruled to be in error by the Supreme Court and is no longer the subject of any Superferry lawsuits, the only reason for the administration's withholding documents is to avoid embarrassment.

Dave Shapiro of the *Honolulu Advertiser* points out that a flaccid legislature is also to blame for having approved $40 million in harbor improvements for the Superferry without a thorough legal review on an EIS.

> The House especially, at a time when Oshiro was majority leader, rejected demands from environmentalists for an EIS—again without any sign that they solicited inde-

pendent legal advice. There was nothing stopping them from asking then the questions they have now about what the attorney general's opinion was. They could have gotten an opinion from their in-house legal staff. Lawmakers' excuses that they followed the administration's lead on legal issues are as weak as members of Congress taking President Bush's word for it that Iraq had weapons of mass destruction without doing their own due diligence.

Superferry Lobbies for Military Upgrade

The *Honolulu Advertiser* reports, on June 18, 2008, that Hawaii Superferry has spent $210,000 in the past year to lobby for federal financial support to install new features on its second high-speed catamaran, which will make it more attractive for *military* use. For more than a year, lobbyists hired by Superferry have been approaching both the U.S. Congress and the U.S. Department of Defense seeking $5 million to help pay for improvements, including an onboard, fold-out vehicle ramp; a water desalination plant; and wastewater treatment facilities right on the ferry.

The requested vehicle ramp would allow the new catamaran to load and unload cars and trucks (and tanks) directly, instead of relying on shore-based ramps and barges that are steered into place as the boat arrives.

According to the *Advertiser* report, the Superferry company hired the prominent law and lobbying firm, Blank Rome LLC, in the summer of 2007 to attempt to apply for the National Defense Features program to cover the cost of adding these *military-ready* facilities to its second Superferry catamaran, named the *Koa*,[71] under construction at the Austal USA shipyard in Mobile. This federal defense subsidy program covers the installation of militarily useful features on commercial ships, provided that the owners agree to make the ships available to the military during emergencies.

The Superferry company may also eventually retrofit the *Alakai* with the vehicle ramp and other facilities, to better suit it for military assignments both here and abroad.

All this lobbying for federal subsidies to build military-friendly features onto the Superferry had been taking place while company officials

---

[71] *Koa*: soldier, warrior, courage.

repeatedly denied any military interests or connections for the ferries, as they have been doing for years. Or perhaps the company, which has yet to break even financially, is planning for a financial escape hatch—such as selling or leasing the boats to the military.

Ironically, as mentioned earlier, the Alakai had originally been designed with a fold-out ramp—but to use it would have required construction accommodations at each harbor, which in turn would have triggered the EIS the company was trying so desperately to avoid. So Hawaii Superferry dropped the ramp from its design to avoid the EIS. Now, however, after the governor and the legislature have successfully manipulated and circumvented the EIS law, the Superferry can build its military-friendly, fold-out ramp as part of its next boat, with impunity.

What's more, if these features are approved, federal tax dollars will pay for them! Then, after the ferries have their military upgrades, if they are ever sold or leased to the military, U.S. taxpayers will have paid for the upgrades and Hawai'i taxpayers will be left holding the bag for the $40 million spent to construct the harbor barges that helped avoid compliance with the Environmental Impact Statement requirements. Such a deal.

Kaua'i journalist Joan Conrow points out in her blog that these subsidies don't begin to include all the taxpayer money that has also been expended on legal fees, a special legislative session, tugboats, an audit, an oversight task force, and harbor security—not to mention undermining the integrity of Hawai'i's courts, inciting a deep emotional rift between the islands, increasing the environmental hazards, and other community traumas this project has visited upon the people of Hawai'i.

July 2008

Hawai'i County Council: No Bombs Until DU Is Gone

On July 2, the Hawai'i County Council takes a stand to ask the U.S. military to halt all B-2 practice bombing, as well as all live firing exercises at Pohakuloa Training Area (PTA), until the depleted uranium there can be found and removed.[72] Although the resolution passes by a wide margin, on an 8-1 vote, the council has no authority over the PTA. Only the Pentagon can halt live-fire exercises and

---

[72] Starting in October 2007, the Air Force's *B-2 Spirit* stealth bomber began regular trips from Guam to drop dummy 2,000-pound bombs, twice a month, at Pohakuloa Training Area on the Big Island. See William Cole, "B-2s drop dummy bombs on Big Island," *Honolulu Advertiser*, October 30, 2007.

order a cleanup. Lawmakers on the Big Island say it is still important to send a message to the Army that Hawai'i County is concerned about the effects of depleted uranium.

August 2008

U.S. Department of Commerce: Cut Ship Speeds in Whale Zones

On August 26, the *New York Times* reports that after many months of fierce arguments between the White House and its own administration's federal fisheries scientists, the U.S. Department of Commerce has proposed new rules for ships traveling within twenty miles of the nation's coast through whale zones along the eastern seaboard, from Florida to New England. The department is proposing that ships be required to cut their speeds to 10 knots (about 12 mph) to avoid the kinds of whale collisions that have seriously endangered the remaining right whales of that region. Only about three hundred right whales now survive. The World Shipping Council was "cool to the speed limits," the *Times* reports, but approved the twenty-mile zone as opposed to the thirty-mile zone that scientists thought was actually necessary. No recommendations have yet been made about Pacific shipping through similar zones of endangered whales and other species.

Oversight Task Force Reveals Shocking Findings

Findings at the August meeting of the Superferry Oversight Task Force alarm Maui residents; in July alone, 205 instances were reported of passengers trying to take from Maui to O'ahu aquatic life such as 'opihi, crustaceans, fish, algae, rocks, and coral. In June and July combined, attempts were made to take a whopping 741 pounds of limu and 654 pounds of nearshore and reef fish from the island. Many of these fish are critical to the health of the endangered reef. Hunters, fishers, and environmentalists on Maui are worried that the island's resources will soon be stripped entirely. *(See box "The Oversight Task Force" for more details.)*

September 2008

Federal Court Rules in Favor of U.S. Coast Guard

The Ninth U.S. Circuit Court of Appeals upholds the U.S. Coast Guard's decision to bar Superferry protesters from Kaua'i's Nawiliwili Harbor. Big Island attorney Lanny Sinkin, who filed the lawsuit, had argued that the Coast Guard was "using a regulation created out of 9/11 for prevention of terrorism, sabotage, subversion ... to suppress free speech—suppress First Amendment rights—and make it possible for a business to make a profit." *Does this mean that the brave citizens of Kaua'i who protest at the harbor should be considered terrorists?*

U.S. Senate Passes Bill Allowing $629 Million for Military Expansion

The Senate approves a defense bill that authorizes spending $629 million in 2009 for military construction and research in Hawai'i. Most of the money would go to building a "brigade complex," two battalion complexes, and infrastructure at Schofield Barracks, in anticipation of the increase of 2,000 troops on O'ahu over the next five years. Also included in the budget are funds for the construction of a drive-in magnetic silencing facility at Pearl Harbor to help submarines maintain their stealth, a new satellite communications operations center, a new radar detection laboratory at the Pacific Missile Range, and a gym. In addition, $21.3 million will go toward continued improvements of the Saddle Road to the Pohakuloa Training Area. *(For more on the U.S. military in Hawai'i, see Chapters 16 and 17.)*

Oversight Task Force Meeting Draws Record Numbers

After the last OTF meeting revealed the high volume of resources being plundered from Maui, the September OTF meeting attracts the largest audience ever, with eighty members of the public in attendance, and more than thirty offering testimony, all demanding stricter oversight of ferry operations.

Maui Mayor Charmaine Tavares writes to the task force that she is "gravely concerned about the impacts that are occurring to Maui's special places and resources." She continues, "Many of the negative impacts we feared and predicted are being realized, despite the fact that Hawaii Superferry has been operating well below its optimal passenger load. ... I am appalled by the reported amount of marine resources that are leaving our island with Superferry passengers."

Particularly alarming is the fact that, as legislated in Act 2, the department of Land and Natural Resources and Department of Agriculture officials will cease inspections in December 2008, to be replaced by Superferry employees who have received a mere one and one-half hours training in inspections. In light of this concern, Tavares says state enforcement officers are needed. "The years of education and training they bring to the operations cannot be replaced by a handful of hours of training that Superferry employees receive."

In response, Superferry official Richard Houck, a retired coast guard admiral, responds that he feels his employees are capable of doing the inspections and that the taking of the ocean resources has been small. He adds that he doesn't think the company should be on the hook for government staffing. "It's not the Superferry that's responsible for reefs being devastated," he says. *(See Chapter 11, and box "The Oversight Task Force" for more details.)*

Linda Lingle Campaigns for McCain-Palin
Governor Lingle is called on by the McCain-Palin campaign to fly to the mainland to speak on behalf of the ticket in six key swing states.

During Presidential Debate,
McCain Cites Littoral Combat Ship Program
During the first presidential debate between John McCain and Barack Obama, McCain describes the severe production problems of the Littoral Combat Ship program of the U.S. Navy *(see Chapter 15)* as a prime example of government mismanagement and waste, mentioning that the cost of the program has skyrocketed to several times higher than originally planned. Presumably, he has been briefed on this matter by his military advisor, John F. Lehman. The roles of Austal USA and the Superferry prototype are not mentioned.

OCTOBER 2008

Hawai'i Supreme Court Accepts Legal Challenge to Act 2
On October 14, the Hawai'i Supreme Court court announces it will hear a challenge from attorneys on the legality of Act 2, the law created by Governor Lingle, passed by the Hawaii legislature, which

had the effect of circumventing the prior *unanimous* Supreme Court ruling that had demanded a full Environmental Impact Statement *before* the Superferry could begin operations. The case is being brought by Maui attorney Isaac Hall on behalf of Maui Tomorrow, the Sierra Club, and the Kahului Harbor Coalition. They charge, among other things, that Act 2 violates the state constitution, as it gives special treatment to a single company. Hall has also argued that Act 2 interfered with a court order, violating the balance of power among the three branches of government, and that elected leaders disregarded their public trust duties under the state constitution to protect Hawai'i's fragile environment and the traditional and customary rights of Native Hawaiians.

Superferry Cancels Big Island Launch; Will Lease Ferry

On October 28, Superferry CEO Thomas Fargo announces that the spring 2009 launch of the company's second ship, the *Koa*, will be delayed by one year, and that service to Maui will also be cut back, due to the advancing economic turndown. In the meantime, according to Fargo, the company will seek short-term opportunities to lease the vessel to another operator outside Hawai'i. He does not specify whether that will be a military contractor or a private enterprise, and there are certainly no guarantees the company will remain in Hawai'i in the long run.

Speculation immediately surfaces that Superferry may not be commercially viable, certainly not in the short run, just as critics had predicted. It is also clearly possible that the Wall Street financial crisis has seriously affected J. F. Lehman and Co., which, like most other major finance companies, needs to quickly convert risky or unproductive assets into immediate cash. So, even after dozens of millions of state and federal dollars have been spent on harbor subsidies to accommodate Hawaii Superferry, and even after Governor Lingle engineered her appalling avoidance of a Supreme Court-ordered Environmental Impact Statement, the company may still turn its back on its local sponsors and seek more profitable fields, military or otherwise. That would leave the people of Hawai'i holding the bag, and $40 million poorer. Meanwhile, in the midst of the economic woes of not only Superferry, but the state of Hawai'i itself, Lingle is off thousands of miles away campaigning for presidential hopeful John McCain.

Part Three

Insider Reports

{ ENVIRONMENT }

Chapter Nine

How Superferry Threatens Life in the Oceans

Hannah Bernard

This is the first of two chapters on the impacts of ocean vessels on whales and other sea creatures. The author, Hannah Bernard, a marine biologist who testified as an expert witness in the Maui Superferry court trial, writes specifically about the high-speed ferry's impacts on the wide diversity of marine life in Hawai'i's waters. In Chapter 10, A Global Problem: Whale Collisions with Fast, Large Boats, Teri Shore *offers examples from around the world of the direct connection between boat speed and whale deaths. [Eds.]*

HUMPBACK WHALES, leatherback sea turtles, hawksbill sea turtles, and the critically endangered Hawaiian monk seals are among the creatures whose habitat is plied daily by the Hawaii Superferry. Other marine life documented in Hawaiian waters include the sperm whale, Blainville's beaked whale, Cuvier's beaked whale, short-finned pirate whale, false killer whale, melon-head whale, pygmy killer whale, bottle-nosed dolphin, roughtooth dolphin, Hawaiian spinner dolphin, spotted dolphin, fin whale, bride's whale, minke whale, right whale, pygmy sperm whale, dwarf sperm whale, Risso's dolphin, Baird's beaked whale, killer whale, and striped dolphin, as well as the whale shark, the green sea turtle, and the manta ray.

The launch of the Superferry and the enabling legislation, in my opinion, palpably *increases* the risk of harm to all these species, many of which are threatened or endangered. Permission to operate the giant, high-speed ferry contradicts the spirit, letter, and intent of the most significant law in Hawai'i: the Environmental Policy Act. This law, which is more comprehensive than the nation's own federal Environmental Policy Act, has been in place since 1974 to protect these and other creatures—more than thirty years before Governor Lingle tailored her own list of operating conditions favoring Superferry. Lingle's list of conditions and protocols, known as Executive Order 07-10, was created with the disingenuous intention of protecting whales, prevent the spread of invasive species, and protect natural and cultural resources. What the new order *actually* does is substitute for more rigorous environmental legislation already in place. It is yet one more example of Superferry and the governor consistently and aggressively seeking to disregard environmental law.

Another egregious instance was Superferry's attempt to circumvent the preparation of an Environmental Impact Statement even before the lawsuits, the Supreme Court and the Circuit Court judgments, and the Special Legislative Session. An EIS would have revealed the many environmental problems associated with the vessel and bound the company to support mitigative measures.

Cetaceans

Ship-whale collisions have not only injured whales, causing shattered jaws and skulls, massive hematomas, sliced-off flukes, and multiple lacerations—they have also harmed and even killed human passengers. Such accidents have occurred off Spain's Canary Islands involving sperm whales and in Hawai'i involving humpbacks.

Already, whales had been struck every year in Hawai'i's waters *without* the Superferry. We know this from firsthand observers' reports and from autopsies of whales after they have stranded themselves. Those that subsequently strand themselves are by far in the minority of all whales hit. The fate of most whale victims of boat collisions goes unreported, because Hawai'i's deep-water channels, high-velocity currents and winds, and narrow beaches significantly lessen the chance of strandings. Given the size and velocity of the high-speed Superferry, it is not a question of *if* whale strikes will occur—but *when*.

From a century of data on ship strikes to whales, we have learned definitively that most severe and lethal injuries to whales are caused by vessels traveling 13 knots (about 15 mph) or more. The Superferry travels between 25 and 37 knots (up to 43 mph), depending on environmental, geographic, biological, and safety conditions outlined in the Executive Order. There are virtually no recorded collisions at speeds below 10 knots. The range in which the risk of collision reaches dangerous levels is between 10 and 13 knots.

In addition to speed, size also kills. Smaller vessels cause fewer injuries and deaths to whales. Most severe and lethal whale injuries are caused by ships greater than or equal to 260 feet in length. The larger the vessel, the greater the likelihood a whale will be killed if struck. Both the speed and the size of the 351-foot Hawaii Superferry are a treacherous threat to marine life, significantly exceeding the range associated with serious and lethal collisions.

In 93 percent of confirmed ship strikes, either the whale was not seen or it surfaced in front of the vessel too quickly to be avoided. Sadly, 80 percent of the confirmed humpback whale strandings that were caused by ship strikes were calves or juveniles—and this statistic is from an area that does *not* include calving grounds, as we have in Hawai'i. Calves are at greater risk to ship strikes, because they spend more time at the surface.[73]

> It was only about twenty-five years ago, after dead calves began washing up on Southern [Atlantic] beaches, that scientists learned that right whales used this area as a nursery, said Barb Zoodsma, right whale recovery program coordinator in the Southeast regional office of the fisheries service, an agency of the National Oceanic and Atmospheric Administration.[74]

From then on, officials began taking precautionary measures to divert ship routes and to slow speeds.

Two of the five whale species most commonly involved in ship collisions worldwide are found in Hawai'i's waters—humpback whales (which are still listed as endangered under the Endangered Species Act of 1973) and sperm whales (which, while not sighted as

---

[73] David W. Laist *et al.*, "Collisions between Ships and Whales," in *Marine Mammal Science* 17, no. 1 (2001): 35–75.

[74] Shaila Dewan, "Even the Whales Have Their Predators: Ships," in *New York Times*, April 12, 2008.

often, are here year round). Both these species were hunted to the brink of extinction in the 1800s and afforded protection only in the 1960s. It has taken nearly forty years for them to reach near-recovery levels. Both are increasing in number, with humpback whales estimated at over 10,000 in the North Pacific.

Executive Order 07-10 suggests that the use of certain technologies, such as radar, night-vision equipment, and bow-mounted cameras, can avoid harm to whales. In fact, it is virtually impossible to prevent collisions through the use of this equipment. The Superferry just goes too fast. In addition, the more sophisticated technology designed to detect whales or other marine life such as side-scanning sonar and active sonar have in themselves proven highly detrimental to marine life. During the 1980s and 1990s, side-scanning sonar was discouraged and then banned on whale-watch boats in Hawai'i because it appeared to cause whales to breach, possibly suggesting that they had been disturbed.

Before the enactment of EO 07-10, governmental agencies and mechanisms were already in place to ensure safety of our marine life. Section 7 Consultation of the Endangered Species Act requires federal agencies to consult with the National Marine Fisheries Service (NMFS) if they are proposing an action that may affect listed marine species, which include humpback whales. Rather than comply with the consultation, Governor Lingle's executive order simply assigns whale observers to the vessel. This is no substitute for the mitigative and regulatory measures that are identified in a consultation with NMFS. She has achieved a *net loss* for species protection and undermined the effectiveness of both state and federal laws.

Sea Turtles

Although whales and dolphins are the obvious marine fauna most likely to be struck and killed by the Hawaii Superferry, because of their need to breathe, rest, and travel at the surface, I am also concerned about the precarious situation of sea-turtle populations, especially the endangered leatherbacks and hawksbills. Satellite and radio telemetry research have documented the presence of at least one hawksbill using the waters of Kahului Bay as foraging habitat for five months of the year. Mitigation measures for leatherbacks and hawksbills have not been addressed at all in EO 07-10. All over the Pacific, fisheries are being prevented from operating, to prevent the deaths of a few individuals from these near-extinct populations, and Lingle's executive order contains no precautionary actions to ensure their continued survival. To the contrary, the order essentially proposes an increase in high-speed vessel traffic! It is preposterous.

Hawaiian Monk Seals

Critically endangered monk seals are declining at the alarming rate of 5 percent a year. Since they are endemic, no other population will replace them should they go extinct. This is, in fact, the paradox of much of Hawai'i's endemic marine life. With such a high rate of unique species (25 percent overall), the loss of these irreplaceable populations would have significant negative effects on the intrinsic and economic value of Hawai'i's reefs.

While the majority of Hawaiian monk seals reside in the Northwestern Hawaiian Islands and are declining, those found in the main Hawaiian Islands are on the increase and are moving between the islands. This metapopulation is being viewed by the National Marine Fisheries Service (NMFS) as extremely important to the success of the entire species. The NMFS knows from its Monk Seal Watch program that several productive females are moving regularly between the northwest and east sides of Maui and Moloka'i. The loss of even one female due to a vessel collision is significant for the future of this species. EO 07-10 contains neither mention of nor mitigation measures for this critically endangered species.

Downed Seabirds

Executive Order 07-10 is also insufficient in addressing the incidence of downed seabirds. Merely monitoring and caring for downed seabirds does not take into account the potential biological impacts to individuals and/or populations that an Environmental Impact Statement, conducted before the ship set sail, would have had. Nor does this provision support the Department of Land and Natural Resources (DLNR) in determining what resources are necessary to effectively handle this type of program.

Four Jet Engines

The Superferry's four jet engines, with their ferocious suction power, will also have a tremendous negative impact on marine life. No studies have dealt with this, but it seems certain these engines will disturb, if not kill, whatever is in their path—from monk seals to turtles to dolphins to many other species. In addition, these jet engines churn up the waters of the small harbor at Kahului, twice a day, violently stirring up sediment, fertilizer, and other runoff, thus causing an increase in algae growth and bloom. With this Osterizer effect, the chemicals settled at the ocean floor are resuspended and swirled around, creating toxic conditions dangerous to swimmers, surfers, paddlers, and marine life.

Indirect Environmental Impacts

In addition to these anticipated *direct* effects of the Hawaii Superferry on the natural world, there will be indirect impacts as well.

It is commonly acknowledged by Hawai'i's citizens, practitioners of Hawaiian gathering and hunting rights, the scientific community, and the Department of Land and Natural Resources that O'ahu's marine resources are more depleted than the resources of the more sparsely populated neighbor islands, with their many rural communities. Members of these communities, which have a longstanding tradition of living through fishing, farming, hunting, and gathering, are very concerned about the potential for rapid depletion and degradation of sensitive marine ecosystems due to the increased ease of access for fishers and hunters coming in on the Superferry.

Between September and November 2007, members of coastal communities testified before the Maui Circuit Court and the legislature about possible threats brought by the Superferry to remote sites essential for subsistence fishing and gathering. These citizens expressed fear that the delicate ecosystems on which rural lifestyles depend would be plundered, both accidentally and intentionally, by users who do not share their allegiance, investment, or sense of ethics regarding the stewardship of these areas. The ability to bring trucks and ice chests from one island increases the likelihood of the spread of alien plants and algae.

This is in direct opposition to the Department of Land and Natural Resources' efforts to support local communities in the management of their resources. DLNR's Division of Conservation and Resource Enforcement (DOCARE) has been working since 2004 with twenty-seven coastal communities. Executive Order 07-10 is woefully inadequate in addressing the overharvesting of natural and cultural resources or the spread of invasive species.

In my opinion, the attitude that the Hawaii Superferry company has demonstrated to date does nothing to bolster confidence that its representatives and employees, on whose judgment much of the enforcement of EO 07-10 resides, are up to the task. They have already demonstrated both their inability to act responsibly and their disregard for the future sustainability of Hawai'i's unique resources. Therefore, Governor Lingle's list of conditions has no real enforcement or oversight components and is largely meaningless. In fact, the governor, the legislature, and the Superferry Corporation have together set a dangerous precedent for *all* businesses in Hawai'i in the way they have flouted the Environmental Policy Act that, until now, has been highly beneficial and effective.

THE LATEST FINDINGS ON VESSEL-WHALE COLLISIONS
Manuel Carrillo and Fabian Ritter

A 2008 scientific paper on the relationship between whale deaths and high-speed ferries corroborates Hannah Bernard's article. Titled Increasing Numbers of Ship Strikes in the Canary Islands: Proposals for Immediate Action to Reduce Risk of Vessel–Whale Collisions, *the report focuses on one main point: simply that "speed kills," as illustrated in the photo on the next page, and in the following excerpts. [Eds.]*

The Canary Islands, known for their extraordinarily high cetacean species diversity, have witnessed a rapid expansion of high-speed ferry traffic during the past few years. At the same time, ship strikes have been increasing. Of 556 dead whales found ashore in the Canary Islands between 1991 and 2007, fifty-nine (10.6 percent) were found to have been caused by collisions with vessels...

Large high-speed craft [like the Hawaii Superferry] have become a major concern, because they travel regularly [at] speeds of up to thirty-five to forty knots, and collisions appear to be increasing.[75] These craft typically incorporate modern hull shapes like wave-piercing catamarans or trimarans which intuitively appear especially dangerous to cetaceans...

Fatality rates and severity of lesions are related to size and speed of vessels. According to Laist *et al.* (2001), 89 percent of accounts where the whale was severely hurt or killed occurred at speeds of fourteen knots or higher. Moreover, most lethal and serious injuries were caused by large ships of 262 feet in length or more. *[The Hawaii Superferry is 351 feet long. Eds.]* Thus, speed appears to be the central factor with regard to collisions. High traveling speed also limits the time frame left to take evasive navigational action. For example, detecting a whale in the ship's path 600 meters away at a speed of forty knots leaves a vessel's captain a reaction time of only thirty seconds before a whale potentially is hit. *[And yet one of HSF's whale-avoidance procedures advises, "If a whale is sighted within 500 meters, change course and/or speed until vessel is at least 500 meters away." Eds.]*

---

[75] M. Weinrich, "A Review of worldwide collisions between whales and fast ferries," in *International Whale Commission Scientific Committee SC/56/BC9*, 2004; and F. Ritter, "A Quantification of Ferry Traffic in the Canary Islands (Spain) and Its Significance for Collisions with Cetaceans," in *International Whale Commission Scientific Committee SC/59/BC7*, 2007.

{ ENVIRONMENT }

Chapter Ten

A Global Problem: Whale Collisions with Fast, Large Boats

Teri Shore

Around the world, ship and ferry strikes are causing the needless and bloody deaths of alarming numbers of whales, many of them young whales and newborn calves. The death toll is likely to rise with the expansion of global shipping, ocean cruising, and fast-ferry systems.

Nearly 80,000 ships weighing more than 100 tons travel the world's oceans—each one easily capable of crushing a whale. In some waterways, vessel collisions account for the demise of between one-third to half of all whales found floating at sea, washed up on beaches, or carried into port on the bow of a ship.

Not long ago, the *Queen Elizabeth II* cruise ship sailed into port in Lisbon, Portugal with a 60-foot fin whale impaled on its bow. Neither the crew nor the passengers were aware that a whale had been run down until the luxury liner arrived in port. The seemingly nonchalant captain told the UK Press Association, "It is one of those things, like running over a cat."

The disturbing image of a fin whale jammed across the bow of the Celebrity cruise ship *Galaxy* as it cruised into Vancouver dominated the front page of the *Vancouver Sun* in June 1999. A blue whale was carried into Narragansett Bay in Rhode Island on the bow of a tanker in March 1998.

This article originally appeared in *Earth Island Journal* 16, no. 3 (Autumn 2001).

In the Canary Islands off northwest Africa, the high-speed passenger ferry system instituted in 1999 has taken a major toll on pilot whales, sperm whales, and dolphins. During the first three months of operation, four whales died from collisions. The impact of one collision was so strong that a ferry passenger was also killed.

Which Whales Are Killed?

Ship strikes pose a serious threat to highly endangered right whales, Western Pacific gray whales and blue whales. When combined with other human-related causes of death, ship strikes could imperil the long-term survival of the more populous humpback and fin whales. This was one of the conclusions of "Collisions Between Ships and Whales," a groundbreaking report published in the January 2001 issue of *Marine Mammal Science*.

A key finding from the report was that the bigger and faster the vessel, the more lethal the collision. A total of 89 percent of lethal or severe injuries were inflicted by fast ferries traveling twelve to thirteen knots, cargo ships traveling above fourteen knots and cruise ships traveling at twenty to twenty-two knots. Most whales swim at three to four knots. When frightened, some whales can swim seven to fourteen knots, while a few can reach more than twenty-six knots.

Fast ferries have reportedly killed or injured whales in Maine, Washington state, British Columbia, Spain, New Caledonia, the Sea of Japan, the English Channel, and the Mediterranean. In France and Italy, more than one in ten whale strandings was attributed to ship strikes, many from speeding ferries. Between France and Corsica, a ferry hits at least one whale per year.

Most whale-ship collisions occur in coastal waters of the continental shelf, areas with high concentrations of whales and vessels. Whales become more vulnerable in these coastal feeding, nursing, calving, and mating grounds. Whales spend more time on the surface in these shallow coastal waters. Sometimes a whale sleeping on the surface gets run over by a ship.

Between 1975 and 1996, 14 percent of whale strandings along the U.S. East Coast were attributed to vessel collision. Each year near Chesapeake Bay, nearly one-third of humpbacks found dead were killed by collisions with ships. Most of the humpback and right whales killed by ships were calves and juveniles.

As many as 50 percent of all right whale deaths are the result of ship strikes. At this rate, ship collisions could drive the 300 remaining northern right whales into extinction by 2020.

[Due to this frightening statistic, in August 2008, the U.S. Department of Commerce proposed new rules for ships traveling within twenty miles of the coast through whale zones along the eastern seaboard, from Florida to New England. The department is proposing that ships be required to cut their speeds to 10 knots (about 12 miles per hour). Eds.]

Preventing Collisions

In 93 percent of ship strikes, ship operators don't see the whales, or see them too late to avoid a collision. In the majority of the remaining cases, the vessel operators saw the whales but did not attempt to avoid them. To address this problem, the National Marine Fisheries Service (NMFS) has instituted aerial surveys and a mandatory ship reporting system in critical right whale habitat off Georgia, Florida, Massachusetts, and Rhode Island.

Aerial surveillance has enabled the NMFS to locate whales and warn approaching ships of their locations. The International Fund for Animal Welfare (IFAW) has installed high-tech acoustic buoys to track right whale migrations in the busy Great South Channel off the northeastern U.S. A ship-collision workshop organized by the IFAW and NMFS in April 2001 released a set of recommendations requiring ships to reduce speed in right whale zones and change course to avoid springtime calving areas.

Vessel operators, ports, and stranding networks should be required to report all whale collisions, so that a more complete database can be developed. Some waters should be declared seasonally or permanently off-limits to ships and ferries to prevent collisions with endangered whales. The most effective means of reducing fatal collisions would be to require that commercial vessels moving in waters frequented by whales slow to ten knots or less.

[ENVIRONMENT]

Chapter Eleven

The Parable of the Rocks: Threats to Hawai'i's Ecosystems

Lance Holter

Most of the public and legal battles about the Superferry have focused on its many potential impacts on the environment, including specific threats to humpback and other whale species and sea-turtle habitats—now that such a huge, high-speed boat is running through whale calving grounds at up to 40 miles per hour. But there are other significant, more subtle threats from wildlife, such as the transport of invasive species, which include destructive insects, or highly ravenous mongoose to Kaua'i, an island currently free of the pest. Lance Holter, director of the Maui chapter of the Sierra Club, which has been a plaintiff in the lawsuits challenging the environmental impact from Superferry's presence, offers this report on the dangers of invasive species. [Eds.]

THE HAWAIIAN ISLANDS are the most isolated major island group on Earth, 2,400 miles from the nearest continent. According to *The Haleakala Visitors Guide* published by the National Park Service, over the 900,000-year geologic history of the islands, "species drifted on the wind, floated on ocean currents, or hitched rides on storm driven birds" at an average of *only one species every 35,000 years*. A period of 900,000 years of isolation and evolution has created unique species and ecosystems found nowhere else on Earth.

Since humans first arrived in Hawai'i, sixty-nine or more species of endemic birds[76] alone have become extinct, and the rate is now rapidly increasing. The U.S. Fish and Wildlife Commission lists 292

---

[76] Endemic species are those found nowhere else in the world.

federally endangered plants and eighty-seven vertebrates and invertebrates, and is considering listing another twenty-four arthropods as endangered or threatened.[77]

The problem is vastly accelerated by the rate at which *invasive species*—insects, plants, and animals—reach the islands on airplanes and ships from distant places and from the other Hawaiian islands. Among them is the mongoose. A weasel-like creature, though not related, the first mongoose were imported to the Big Island from Jamaica in the 19th century as a solution to rats in the sugar fields, and have since ravaged the islands of Oʻahu and Maui. The creature has, however, not yet made it to Kauaʻi or Lanaʻi. There are also the wild pigs, the Varroa bee mite, and fruit flies—which cost Hawaiʻi agriculture more than $300 million in exports per year — and many more.

Hawaiʻi's unique genetic and biological resources require the utmost vigilance for their protection. So, it should have been no surprise when the superintendent of Haleakala National Park, Don Reeser, and the Friends of Haleakala, as well as the Sierra Club, Maui Tomorrow, and the Kahului Harbor Coalition, all expressed outrage at the prospect of a huge, high-speed ferry making daily forays from Oʻahu to Maui, Kauaʻi, and the Big Island, carrying cars, trucks, produce, and *who knows what else* across waters that have been a protective moat until now for thousands of rare species. This is not even to mention the impacts on whales' calving grounds, sea turtles, and other shoreline species. These groups joined in a set of legal actions that demanded that a full Environmental Impact Statement be completed *before* the vessel be allowed to make its voyages, and even if allowed, only under very strict environmental controls. It was a complex case involving evidence of dozens of impacts from invasive species, but, in the end, the unlikely key element in the lawsuit was the surprise discovery of *three truckloads of contraband rocks*.

Turning Point

Environmental groups well understood that the Superferry posed many real environmental dangers, and eventually they prevailed at the level of the Hawaiʻi Supreme Court. But it took the discovery

---

[77] Alan C. Ziegler, "Hawaiian Natural History, Ecology and Evolution," in *U.S. Fish and Wildlife Commission*, 2002.

of yet another endangered natural resource—rocks!—being secretly transported by Superferry from Maui to Oʻahu for the courts and the public to take notice. On August 28, 2007, residents reported to the Maui office of the Department of Land and Natural Resources that three trucks with Oʻahu license plates were loading rocks from the shoreline of Waiheʻe, Maui. These were special lava rocks, called *imu pohaku*, used for traditional earthen *imu*[78] cooking, the ancient method of preparing foods in Polynesian society. These pohaku do not explode when heated in open fires. As innocuous as it may sound, this was the major turning point in public understanding of the issues involved.

It had never occurred to Maui residents that Oʻahu could be out of lava rocks. This incident started people thinking, Hey, if they don't have pohaku on Oʻahu, what else will they come looking for? As one official of the Department of Land and Natural Resources said, "This is the beginning of environmental Armageddon." With that perspective in mind, residents—particularly Maui's rural citizens who subsist on fishing, hunting, and gathering—began to pay attention to Superferry issues.

Three truckloads of rocks might seem harmless enough, when put in the perspective of the possibility that hundreds of vehicles would be coming daily on the Superferry from Oʻahu, with its population of 800,000, to a small island like Maui with 130,000 people, or Kauaʻi with 60,000. When people realized that these visitors might fill their trucks, ice coolers, boats, trailers, and trunks with the outer islands' precious resources, starting with rocks, this became a revelatory, pivotal event that ultimately galvanized Maui residents' understanding of the real potential harm that the Hawaii Superferry could bring to their island home, its environment, and its many limited fragile resources.

Media Frenzy Over the Rocks

Up until the pohaku incident, opposition to the Superferry was largely marginalized as being from a fringe group—environmentalists and activists. The local cultural habit in Hawaiʻi is generally not to speak up and draw attention to yourself; to maintain an accepting, aloha spirit. And anyway, wasn't the Superferry just another

---

[78] *Imu*: pit oven.

boat? This perception changed after the rocks were found, and columnists writing in the Honolulu papers and people on Honolulu TV and talk radio spread the word about the incident. It was reported as a kind of conspiracy, almost too convenient to be true. Had anti-Superferry activists secretly set the whole episode up to gain attention? Locals who had been mainly concerned about overcrowded surfing sites, fishing spots, hunting lands, and camping areas began to speak out. The alarm spread, and the balance of opinion shifted. Newspapers began to cover some of the *real* environmental consequences, as in the *Maui News* of September 12, 2007: "Superferry opponents [are] worried that overcrowded Oʻahu would send over hordes of urbanites to plunder Maui's reefs and forests and crowded surfing breaks and campgrounds." The problems were suddenly palpable. And the incident of the rocks became significant in the court.[79]

The issues and evidence surrounding the truckloads of rocks became so important that two attorneys from the state attorney general's office, joined by the Superferry attorneys, fought for days to keep the evidence out of the courtroom and the hearing. What was at stake would be the finding that the Superferry would—and could—cause real and probable environmental harm, and would undermine the state and Superferry attorneys' efforts to achieve a Finding of No Significant Impact (FONSI). If no FONSI was granted, that would mean an Environmental Impact Statement would be required for the Superferry, as the court eventually ruled. Island residents were appalled that the governor and the state government, which one would think should protect its citizens from harm, were siding with the Superferry against its citizens. Because of the rocks, the plaintiffs prevailed, at least for that moment, until the governor ordered her Special Legislative Session. The case remains in the courts to this day.

THE HIGH TOLL FROM INVASIVE SPECIES

The stakes are high. Environmentally invasive species cost Hawaiʻi $153 million a year to manage, not including the cost of lost agricultural production and native species habitat, as exemplified by the

---

[79] Harry Eagar, "Testimony Limited on SF Rock Incident," in *Maui News*, September 12, 2007.

damage caused by invasive fruit flies. These all pose a serious threat to Hawaiian ecosystems.[80]

The Hawai'i Invasive Species Council (HISC) found that "at least two serious arthropod pests have arrived in Hawai'i every year for the past ten years, including the little fire ant, the Erythrina gall wasp, the Varroa bee mite, the latter a threat to the multimillion-dollar queen bee, honey, and pollinating industry." Hawai'i Bee Keepers' president, Dr. Michael Kliks, believes the Varroa mite will cost Hawai'i agriculture $60 to $120 million over the next ten years should it spread to the other islands. Currently confined to O'ahu, the mite is causing real damage there, but the Superferry could easily spread the pest to Maui and Kaua'i in vehicles and trucks. On November 26, 2007, Dr. Kliks removed a heavily Varroa-mite-infested wild colony from a roof flange just "a stone's throw away" from the Superferry berthing at Honolulu harbor.[81] During one DLNR inspection of vehicles coming from Maui, dozens of bees were found on vehicle radiators, demonstrating the ease with which all species travel on the Superferry. But the real question is: Will Honolulu ferry inspectors be able to keep the mites from Maui-bound voyages?[82]

Already the cute but extremely noisy (90 to 100 decibels) nocturnal coqui tree frogs from Puerto Rico, the forest-smothering South American Miconia, and some 1,200 flowering plants and weeds have established wild populations in Hawai'i, together with nineteen alien mammals and forest-stripping ungulates such as goats, deer, and sheep. And there are also the earth-moving, disease-spreading wild pigs that have arrived in large numbers in Hawai'i.[83] According to the Hawai'i Invasive Species Council, this "silent invasion by insects, disease spreading organisms, snakes, weeds, and other pests [is considered] the single greatest threat to Hawai'i's economy, natural environment, and the health and lifestyle of its people." [84]

---

[80] Christie Wilson, "Fighting Invasive Species in Hawai'i," in *Honolulu Advertiser*, January 14, 2008.

[81] Larry Geller, in *disappearednews.com*, December 4, 2007.

[82] Cheryl Ambrozic, "To Bee or Not to Bee," in *Maui Time Weekly*, May 31, 2007.

[83] Daniel Duane, "The Boar Wars," in *Sierra* Magazine, March/April 2007.

[84] Wilson.

As a result of its isolation, Maui has thus far been spared the invasion from the Varroa mite, the glassy-winged sharpshooter, and the nasty stinging little fire ant. Allowing the Superferry to run without completing its EIS is illegal and irresponsible. At a minimum, we must first develop interdiction and inspection programs for vehicles and farm products, as well as rules and protocol for visiting recreationalists and resource collectors.

Many people feel that the entire process that has allowed Superferry to operate is in violation of the Federal Endangered Species Act of 1973 and leaves citizens only "the right to sue," as people have done, for environmental justice. When the three truckloads of over 900 pohaku made it through inspections and into the boarding area, this alone was proof that the Superferry's promises to be environmentally conscientious were vacant words. If it had not been for Judge Cardoza's finding in favor of the plaintiffs, granting an injunction to stop the untimely and ill-conceived Superferry voyages, we might never have heard the stories that the pohaku would eventually tell—that the natural world of Hawai'i is more seriously threatened than previously thought.

The Oversight Task Force
Koohan Paik

An Oversight Task Force was established for the Hawaii Superferry as part of Act 2, the statute rushed into law to allow the Superferry to operate concurrently with conducting the Environmental Assessment. The temporary job of the thirteen-member team of specialists is to examine the impact of ferry operations on the community, the environment, and the harbors, and other infrastructures, and then to report those findings to the legislature, which is completing its final report before disbanding in 2009.

Like the related executive order (EO 07-10), signed by Governor Lingle to establish operating conditions intended to protect whales, prevent the spread of invasive species, and protect natural and cultural resources, the formation of the task force *gives the appearance* of caring for the environment. But if HSF or Governor Lingle really cared about the environment, they could have simply followed the existing environmental law rather than circumvent it. However, that would not have accommodated Hawaii Superferry Corporation's business goals.

The task force's most alarming finding from only eight round-trip sailings during February (the ship was in dry-dock for the rest of spring) was the sighting of an average of thirty-one whales per day! During whale season (January 1 to April 30), seas are at their roughest, so the catamaran's captain chose to slice through the calmer waters of the National Humpback Whale Sanctuary, south of Moloka'i. One of the conditions of Executive Order 07-10 was that the *Alakai* must steer clear of the sanctuary during these months, *unless sea conditions compromise passenger comfort*. That might look good on paper, but the fact that the months of the roughest seas are also the months of the densest whale populations in the sanctuary shows how meaningless this executive order is, and how potentially fatal for the whales. Essentially, the ship can travel anywhere it pleases, anytime.

This was not lost on the people of Moloka'i. At a public hearing in March 2008, conducted as part of the Act 2 sham EIS, citizens were infuriated at the frequency—and the speed—with which they had already witnessed the boat pass through the Whale Sanctuary, a place Molokaʻi's people hold dear to their hearts. One woman expressed bitter disgust that, of all the available scenery on the Alakai's route, HSF chose for its slick advertisements the image of the boat passing through the beloved sanctuary, essentially commodifying a sacred site that is supposed to be off-limits anyway. During January 2008, in over half of the twenty-four one-way trips from Honolulu to Maui, the ship cruised right through the whale sanctuary—during the season when mother whales are known to nurse their young. One whale specialist likened Superferry's route through the Whale Sanctuary to gunning a hot rod through a playground.

Equally alarming were the findings during the summer: In August alone, the state Conservation and Resources Enforcement Division and agriculture inspectors reported finding on vehicles leaving Maui 109 pounds of ʻopihi, 412 pounds of reef fish, sand, rock, and coral—materials specifically prohibited on the Superferry—as well as two gill nets, devices barred from Maui waters. Irene Bowie, executive director for Maui Tomorrow, expressed her alarm, explaining the importance of reef fish: "Fish such as *uhu* are important not only for the health of the reef but also in the creation of sand for our disappearing beaches. The people of Maui treasure our cultural and natural resources and greater effort must be made to stop this plunder. ... How long will these natural resources remain for our community and what studies have been done to examine the situation?"

In addition, a hundred dead honeybees or bee parts had been found earlier in the year in engine compartments, on grilles, and elsewhere in vehicles. Honeybee parts coming from Oʻahu could be carrying the dreaded Varroa mite, still unknown on Maui. The Varroa mite is a threat to the state's multimillion-dollar honey, queen bee, and pollination industry and is a designated invasive-species priority.

To add insult to injury, the Oversight Task Force is scheduled to conclude in December 2008, at which time inspections will no longer be carried out by the departments of Agriculture and of Land and Natural Resources, but instead by ferry workers who have received *only one and a half hours' training*. Needless to say, Maui residents are justifiably worried about the fate of their island's natural resources and ecological health.

{ LAW }

Chapter Twelve

SUMMARY REPORT ON THE LEGAL CASES INVOLVING SUPERFERRY

Daniel Hempey

In April 2005, the State of Hawai'i determined that it would spend $40 million on harbor improvements on state lands to facilitate the Hawaii Superferry's docking needs. But, in negotiations with the HSF, the Department of Transportation permitted the company to argue that the harbor improvements should be considered as four smaller separate projects, on O'ahu, Maui, Kaua'i, and the Big Island. This allowed the company to make the case that each was too "minor" to be subject to Environmental Assessment. The DOT was then able to assert that no EA was necessary. So in February 2005, DOT indicated that these individual harbor improvements would have no significant environmental impact. Environmentalists responded with five lawsuits—two on Maui, one in Honolulu, and one on Kaua'i. An additional case was filed in federal court, in Honolulu, relating to the state's abuse of the new "security zone" at Nawiliwili Harbor.

Daniel Hempey, lead attorney in the Kaua'i case, which demanded that an EA be conducted before Superferry could operate, gives a blow-by-blow account of the five legal cases involving the company. [Eds.]

IN 1974, THE LANDMARK Hawai'i Environmental Protection Act (HEPA) mandated that any project that uses state or county lands or funds must undergo an Environmental Assessment (EA) before the project can begin to operate.

Hawai'i Revised Statutes, Chapter 343-1, adopted in 1974, spells out the purpose of HEPA:

The legislature finds that the quality of humanity's environment is critical to humanity's well being, that humanity's activities have broad and profound effects upon the interrelations of all components of the environment, and that an environmental review process will integrate the review of environmental concerns with existing planning processes of the State and counties and alert decision makers to significant environmental effects which may result from the implementation of certain actions. The legislature further finds that the process of reviewing environmental effects is desirable because environmental consciousness is enhanced, cooperation and coordination are encouraged, and public participation during the review process benefits all parties involved and society as a whole.

An EA can be avoided under HEPA only if there is a legitimate "finding of no significant impact" (FONSI). If, however, a project that uses state land or funds does have significant environmental impacts, the law requires that those impacts be identified and mitigated. This is detailed in the Hawai'i Revised Statutes, Chapter 343. An analogous law at the federal level is called the National Environmental Policy Act (NEPA).

Since the birth of environmental legislation, industrialists have been designing ways to avoid compliance. Hawaii Superferry Corporation spent more than $300,000 lobbying the governor, the Hawai'i Department of Transportation (DOT), and the state legislature, all of which have been supporting Hawaii Superferry since its inception.

After consulting with Hawaii Superferry, DOT classified the improvements needed at four harbors statewide on state land for the Superferry to be able to dock as separate projects. Then, in February 2005, DOT found that these individual harbor improvements would be minor and would have no significant environmental impact (a FONSI, despite the fact that these "minor" improvements ended up costing the state $40 million dollars and that the Superferry would be slicing through endangered humpback whales' calving areas). Had the project been assessed statewide, as a whole, the impact would likely have been deemed "significant." And regarding these as smaller, separate projects created bureaucratic hoops, and thus expense, for anyone who might want to challenge the exemption.

In 2008, an audit by the State of Hawaiʻi, ordered and conducted by the state legislature, revealed that Hawaii Superferry had influenced DOT by saying that any environmental-law requirement would be a "deal-breaker," a charge HSF continued to make in many contexts. The audit also found that DOT was not a "neutral party," as is required by law for determining the need for environmental review, and concluded that the orders to exempt actually came from the Office of the Governor.

In 1997 in *Kahana Sunset Owners Ass'n. v. County of Maui*, the Hawaiʻi Supreme Court found that segmenting a project into small component parts in order to evade environmental review violates the purpose of the environmental protection laws, stating that "a group of actions proposed by an agency or an applicant shall be treated as a single action when: *1)* The component actions are phases or increments of a larger total undertaking; [or] *2)* An individual project is a necessary precedent for a larger project."

In Sierra Club v. DOT, 115 Haw. 299 (2007), the Hawaiʻi Supreme Court found that, "The proposed action must be described in its entirety and cannot be broken up into component parts which, if each is taken separately, may have minimal impact on the environment. Segmenting a project in this incremental way to avoid the preparation of an environmental impact statement is against the law."

The fact that the DOT used *four separate FONSI exemption letters*, one for each harbor, to exempt the project from having to perform an EA demonstrates that a single project was broken into component parts to avoid environmental review. The four harbor exemption letters were nearly identical and all were signed by Barry Fukunaga (deputy director of DOT at the time, and since promoted to be Governor Lingle's chief of staff) on February 23, 2005. The only meaningful difference in the four letters was the description of the details of the layout at each harbor.

Brief Overview of Legal Cases

The chronology of legal challenges related to the Hawaii Superferry Corporation begins with a lawsuit filed on Maui by Isaac Hall, attorney for the Sierra Club, Maui Tomorrow, and Kahului Harbor Coalition, on March 21, 2005, just a month after the FONSI. This filing, *Sierra Club v. DOT*, challenged "certain exemptions issued by DOT as of February 23, 2005, for Harbor Improvements." The plaintiffs claimed that an EA should be required before the Superferry project could commence. On July 12, 2005, Maui Circuit Court Judge Joseph Cardoza dismissed the case. The plaintiffs appealed to the Hawai'i Supreme Court.

Another lawsuit was filed by Hall in U.S. District Court in August 2005 by the three Maui groups—Sierra Club, Maui Tomorrow, and Kahului Harbor Coalition—along with Friends of Haleakala National Park, challenging a federal exemption from an EIS by the U.S. Maritime Administration (MARAD), the agency that provided the Superferry with a $140 million loan guarantee. The case was dismissed the following month by the federal court, clearing the way for the Superferry Corporation to move forward on financing.

In January 2006, Hall filed yet another lawsuit, this time on behalf of Maui Tomorrow, Kahului Harbor Coalition, and Friends of Haleakala National Park, which challenged the adequacy of development plans for Kahului Harbor on Maui, including concerns over traffic and invasive species. This case came before the Second Circuit Court, which initially, in August 2006, ruled against the groups, on the grounds that they did not have standing to sue. But, in December 2006, the court partially reversed its decision and ruled that two of the three groups *did* have standing to proceed with the lawsuit (Maui Tomorrow had standing regarding traffic; and Kahului Harbor Coalition for recreational use of the harbor). The same court later ordered the DOT to implement traffic mitigation, prohibiting the Superferry from unloading more than one car every two minutes.

Supreme Court Intervenes

Just days before the Superferry was to set sail, on August 23, 2007, the Hawai'i Supreme Court issued a 5–0 ruling that Superferry must conduct an Environmental Assessment before it begins operation. This was the ruling that came out of the appeal of Judge Cardoza's dismissal of *Sierra Club v. DOT*. The Supreme Court concluded that the "DOT did not consider whether its facilitation of the Hawaii Superferry project will probably have minimal or no significant impacts, both primary and secondary on the environment." Secondary impacts, such as potential harm to endangered whales, effect on other sea life, spread of invasive species, increases in traffic and crime on the outer islands, economic impact, all of which should have been studied and mitigated, were not even considered when DOT issued its FONSI. In a defiant response to the Supreme Court's ruling, and with no apology to the environment, Hawaii Superferry Corporation, with the full support of the DOT, accelerated the previously scheduled date to begin service from Honolulu to Maui and Kaua'i.

Just a few days later, on August 26, 2007, the *Alakai* vessel bore down upon Nawiliwili Harbor on Kaua'i. Turtles and an endangered monk seal were seen in the harbor when the vessel arrived. When the DOT permitted the ship to dock at the state-owned harbor—without having completed the Environmental Assessment ordered by the Supreme Court only days earlier—thousands of protestors shouted that the DOT was breaking the law as determined by the Hawai'i Supreme Court.

Meanwhile, DOT, headed by Barry Fukunaga, interpreted the Supreme Court's ruling as applying only to Maui. It claimed that the Superferry could legally sail to Kaua'i, even though the court had just ordered that the project should have been considered as a whole.

On Monday, August 27, 2007, the Maui Circuit Court followed the Supreme Court's order by issuing a Temporary Restraining Order, enjoining the HSF from commencing operations on Maui until a preliminary injunction could be heard.

That very same day, Superferry attempted to enter Nawiliwili Harbor a second time and dock on state land. A gathering of even more citizens than the night before barred the boat from entering the harbor, sending it back to Honolulu.

Soon after these events, Nawiliwili Harbor was declared a federal "security zone" by the Coast Guard. A new federal lawsuit, *Wong v. Bush*, was promptly filed, alleging the state's abuse of "security zone" enforcement rules. Attorney Lanny Sinkin argued that the security zone rule violated Administrative Procedures Act, and that the security zone regulation, meant to prevent sabotage, terrorism, and subversion, was being illegally used to suppress First Amendment rights of Kaua'i protesters and to protect a private business. A key argument in Sinkin's filing was that the continued operation of HSF after the Supreme Court decision on August 23, 2007, was illegal. Therefore, he argued, everything done to further such operation, including instituting the security zone, constituted acts in furtherance of a conspiracy to violate the law.

The U.S. District Court in Honolulu denied the Temporary Restraining Order and ruled that none of the plaintiffs had standing. Sinkin immediately filed an appeal at the Ninth Circuit Court of Appeals in San Francisco.[85]

NEW APPEALS

As noted, on August 31, 2007, the Supreme Court issued an opinion, in *Sierra Club v. DOT*, ordering that a full EIS was required before sailing. While that opinion did not specifically forbid the Superferry from sailing to harbors other than on Maui, it made it clear that the Superferry was a *statewide* project, implying that the required Environmental Assessment should apply to the project in its entirety, as it impacts the state as a whole. Meanwhile, DOT and Hawaii Superferry announced that the Superferry would commence Oʻahu–Kauaʻi operations on September 26, 2007, *despite* the ruling and public sentiment on Kauaʻi.

On September 4, 2007, the environmental group Thousand Friends of Kauaʻi (with the support of People for the Preservation of Kauaʻi) filed a suit to stop the Superferry from using Kauaʻi's Harbor until it had completed the EA, as the State Supreme Court had ruled. DOT and HSF argued that the *Sierra Club v. DOT* decision only affected Kahului Harbor. The attorney general (representing DOT) and Superferry lawyers argued that the entire case was "time-barred" in that people on Kauaʻi did not file suit to challenge the exemption for their island back in 2005 when the state-funded harbor improvements were first announced. Because of this failure to file a separate lawsuit on Kauaʻi two years earlier, the state and Superferry filed motions to dismiss the Kauaʻi lawsuit. The state and HSF took the position that the Supreme Court had invalidated an EA exemption for Kahului Harbor alone, and citizens from other islands who wanted environmental justice under the Supreme Court ruling were just too late. In the eyes of the DOT and the Lingle administration, the other islands "missed the boat" by two years.

---

[85] *On September 8, 2008, the appeals court upheld the U.S. Coast Guard's decision to bar Superferry protesters from Nawiliwili Harbor. (See Chapter 8, September 2008 entry.) [Eds.]*

On September 20, 2007, Governor Linda Lingle made her controversial visit to Kauaʻi. There, residents would not accept her stern declarations that the Superferry would be returning to Kauaʻi. Instead, Kauaʻi people broke into a loud mantra of "EIS!...EIS!...EIS!"

On the same date, the Kauaʻi Court dismissed three of Thousand Friends' claims, holding that they had missed the 2005 deadline to file a complaint under the Environmental Protection Act, but also leaving two claims alive, including one based directly on the state's constitutional right to enforce environmental law. The intensity of the governor's visit and the prospect of continued litigation on Kauaʻi were likely reasons the Hawaii Superferry Corporation announced the next day that it would suspend service to Kauaʻi, indefinitely.

Special Session: Act 2

Shortly thereafter, on October 23, 2007, Governor Lingle hurriedly called for a Special Session of the legislature, ostensibly to accommodate HSF's race for time to qualify for federal and private investment (which turned out to be partially false—no federal investment was involved with this deadline, and private investors had let pass similar prior threats of deadline). In just one week, compliant legislators passed a bill, dubbed "Act 2," effectively allowing the Superferry to run while a redefined environmental review was being conducted.

Act 2 changed the very purpose of HEPA just to accommodate the Superferry Corporation. Until November 1, 2007 (the day Act 2 took effect), HEPA had been based on the fact that EA studies were "critical to humanity's well being...and that an environmental review process" was necessary to "alert decision makers to significant environmental effects which may result from the implementation of certain actions." Act 2's stated purpose is to "facilitate the establishment of interisland ferry service and, at the same time, protect Hawaiʻi's fragile environment by clarifying that neither the preparation of an environmental assessment, nor a finding of no significant impact, nor acceptance of an environmental impact statement shall be a condition precedent to, or otherwise be required prior to... operation of a large capacity ferry vessel company."

Once Act 2 passed, the state attorney general's office and HSF filed motions in Maui Circuit Court to lift the injunction that had blocked Superferry from Kahului Harbor. Within 10 days, Judge Cardoza lifted the court injunction, enabling HSF to relaunch operations.

Article XI, Section 5 of the Hawai'i Constitution states that the legislative power over "lands owned by or under the control of the State and its political subdivisions shall be exercised only by general laws."[86] On February 29, 2008, the Maui opponents asked the Maui Circuit Court to declare Act 2 unconstitutional, claiming that the Act violated the Hawai'i Constitution, because it was not a "general law" but was aimed at helping a single business.

After the passing of Act 2, Judge August on Maui reversed his earlier decision and rescinded his 2006 order to regulate flow of traffic from the Superferry.

On November 13, 2007, Thousand Friends of Kaua'i appealed the partial dismissal of their case. The appeal argued that the state and Hawaii Superferry Corporation had manipulated the statewide Superferry project into a piecemeal series of smaller projects, with the ultimate goal of avoiding environmental review as required by law. Therefore, argued the environmentalists, the court should enjoin Superferry operation on Kaua'i until the DOT complies with environmental law. Superferry and DOT claim that this appeal is moot, since it is based on environmental law as written before it was trumped by Act 2 legislation. But Act 2 may be declared unconstitutional (via the Sierra Club case), thus restoring the Hawai'i Environmental Protection Act to what it was before the Superferry, DOT, and the governor rewrote it.

Both Maui and Kaua'i appeals, including a decision as to the constitutionality of Act 2, are pending in the Hawai'i appeals courts at the time of this writing.

NOTE: *On October 14, 2008, the Hawai'i Supreme Court announced it was accepting the legal challenge to the constitutionality of Act 2. A ruling is anticipated by early 2009. [Eds.]*

---

[86] *The term "general laws" means that each law must apply in general, rather to any specific project. [Eds.]*

{ LAW }

Chapter Thirteen

FLOOR REMARKS ON ACT 2

Senator Gary Hooser

SIERRA CLUB V. DOT *challenged the legality of Superferry operating without an Environmental Assessment. The case was dismissed in Maui Circuit Court, but was later appealed to the Hawai'i Supreme Court, which ruled unanimously in favor of the plaintiffs that an EA, and probably an EIS, must be conducted before the ship sails. Governor Lingle responded quickly by calling a special session of the legislature, with the express purpose of enacting "SB1, SD1," a new environmental law, applicable only to high-speed ferry vessels. She was summoning the state's lawmakers to assemble in order to pass special legislation favoring a single private company, Hawaii Superferry. Two days before the vote was taken, Senator Gary Hooser, of Kaua'i, delivered the following speech on the senate floor.*

Lingle's compliant senate voted 20–5 in favor of Act 2; fourteen of the senators voted "aye with reservations." Senator Hooser was one of the five senators, all of whom were from outer islands, who voted "no." [Eds.]

OCTOBER 29, 2007

Madam President, I rise in opposition to SB1, SD1.

I speak today in opposition to SB1 not as the Senate Majority Leader but simply as the senator who represents District Seven and the people of Kaua'i and Ni'ihau.

And Madam President, I will say upfront and directly: I know full well that people in my district as well as people throughout the state are divided on this issue. Some believe strongly that it is right, fair, and just that we amend the law as is being proposed today, and others believe equally as strongly that to do what is being proposed is wrong, terribly unjust, and are appalled that we are even considering the bill now before us.

There has been much talk over these past few weeks about how the majority of the people in our state want the Superferry. I do not doubt one bit that this is true, and I also believe that if done properly, an interisland ferry system can be good for Hawai'i. But I also believe that most people would not be so eager to offer their support if they knew it had the potential to irreparably harm our environment, as was the conclusion of Maui Judge Cardoza. But this question was not asked in the polls that were conducted.

Neither was the question asked: Do you believe the Hawaii Superferry should comply with all state and federal laws? If it was asked, I suspect an overwhelming majority would say yes. But yet the Superferry is here today asking us to change the law, just for them.

And this is one of the most fundamental points upon which my opposition is based. We are here today to change the law to benefit one particular business, which as we all know, is the Hawaii Superferry. Yes, the bill does not name a specific business but only refers to "a large capacity ferry vessel." But the entire reason we are here today in this Special Session, in my singular and humble opinion, is to save the Hawaii Superferry.

I respect that position; however, I personally believe that it is not okay, and in fact believe that the legislation before us clearly violates, at the very minimum, both the spirit and the intent of our State Constitution. Some will argue, I am sure, that this is an extraordinary situation that demands extraordinary measures, and I respect that view, but I just cannot support it.

As most of you know, I was an early supporter of the Hawaii Superferry. In 2004 it seemed like a great idea, and I signed and supported, like most in the room, a resolution to that effect. I was told by proponents at the time that the service would provide a low-cost, interisland transportation alternative to our residents, that it was environmentally friendly, and it would be a boon to our economy, so I said, "Yes, sounds good to me. Let's expedite the permits and get this thing going." Needless to say, I was not aware that they were going to ask the State to provide $40 million in harbor improvements nor was I aware that they intended to bypass the environmental review process. *Expedite* means hurry up the paper shuffling; it does not mean cut corners, bypass protections, or make an end run around the law. And certainly *expedite* does not mean "exempt."

For the record, I still believe that expanding interisland travel options, including an interisland ferry operation, is probably a good idea, but it needs to be done right, and it needs to follow the law, not make the law. Perhaps if the Hawaii Superferry was just an unwitting victim of an inept decision by state government, I might feel differently. Perhaps if the "mistaken exemption" which created this whole ungodly mess was simply an inadvertent error that no one could have possibly anticipated, perhaps the entire community might feel differently. But as we all know, this is not the case.

The Hawaii Superferry operation is controlled by very wealthy and extremely politically connected individuals. The primary principal is the former Secretary of the Navy, Mr. John Lehman, who served under President Ronald Reagan, is a close friend of Henry Kissinger, an appointee to the 9/11 Commission, and is closely associated with the top of the top in military and national-security circles of influence. Mr. Lehman's investment group has placed approximately $80 million into this venture, and they can easily afford the best lawyers in town—perhaps the best lawyers in the world. So, no, the Hawaii Superferry is not an unwitting, naïve, and innocent victim in this situation.

The Hawaii Superferry, the DOT, and the Lingle administration have known this outcome was a possibility since day one. And they have worked hand-in-glove since day one to push this project through. The political process according to public records began in 2003 when the Superferry operators began briefing the Lingle administration and various community groups.

According to recent testimony, Bob Awana, the former chief of staff to Governor Lingle, was personally involved in consulting on the process and helped draft the operating agreement between Hawaii Superferry and the state. So how much money does it require for a project to be able to negotiate directly with the governor's office?

In 2004, the PUC began extensive public hearings, with strong public sentiment pointing out the need for an environmental review. HSF management and the DOT had to have known at this point that the lack of an EA or EIS would likely pose a problem. But rather than slowing down and doing it right, they chose to plow ahead.

In 2005, the Kaua'i County Council, the Hawai'i County Council, and the Maui County Council all passed resolutions calling for the requirement of an Environmental Impact Statement. The DOT and the Hawaii Superferry adamantly opposed each of these resolutions.

In 2005, Senate Bill 1785, also demanding an EIS be conducted, was introduced and passed out of the Senate Energy and Environment Committee but was defeated in the Transportation Committee after intense opposition from both the State DOT and the Hawaii Superferry. If the state and the Hawaii Superferry would have conceded the issue in 2004 or even 2005, the EIS would likely have been completed by now and the Superferry service would be well underway. But, as we all know, they did not and chose instead to keep their heads down and just push on through, in spite of growing community and legislative opposition to their position.

The lawsuits started in 2005, and though the Maui court denied the plaintiff's case, both the Hawaii Superferry and the DOT were well aware that the matter was being appealed to the Hawai'i Supreme Court.

During the 2005 and 2006 legislative sessions, further attempts were made in the Senate via budget provisos to force the owners of the HSF to be more forthcoming in their dealings with the neighbor-island communities, who were expressing increasing concern about potential impacts.

In 2006, a community group, People for the Preservation of Kaua'i, attempted to present Governor Lingle with a petition containing some 6,000 signatures requesting an EIS, and the governor's office refused to even receive the petition.

Again, if the Hawaii Superferry and the DOT had at this point decided to just do things the right way, all of this mess that we find ourselves in today could have been avoided.

Then, in February 2007, the Environmental Council, a group of citizen volunteers appointed by the governor and responsible for offering input and advice on the environmental review process—again, these are volunteers appointed by the governor whose job it is to offer input and advice on environmental review matters, including the exemption process—issued a nine-votes-to-one decision that stated in no uncertain terms that the DOT had made a mistake when granting the environmental review exemption. Once again, both the state's own attorneys and the Superferry attorneys fought hard in opposition.

For three years running, many state legislators, county councils and private citizens attempted to convince the DOT and the Hawaii Superferry to undergo an EIS process. Finally, during the 2007 legislative session, we in the Senate passed SB1276SD2, a compromise solution that would have required an EIS while allowing the HSF to operate. Once again, arm and arm and in lockstep, the DOT and the HSF vehemently opposed this requirement, thumbed their noses at the Senate, and refused the offer of compromise.

While some might suggest that the language of SB1276 needed further clarification, one thing that was very clear and was made in numerous public statements by numerous people including myself right here on the floor of the Senate—what was eminently clear was the *intent*. Obviously as is routine in the legislature, language corrections and amendments, if needed, could have easily been made in the House. Once again, if the DOT and the HSF had accepted our compromise, we would not be where we are today. All along the way, the state administration and the Hawaii Superferry have fought and resisted the requirement for proper environmental review of this project. They have been together, locked together, arm in arm, like two peas in a pod, every single step of the way.

So, no. The Hawaii Superferry is not an innocent and unwitting victim deserving of special dispensation in the form of a special session and this pending legislative bailout. They are highly influential, sophisticated, and very wealthy business operators who knowingly and willingly worked closely with the Lingle administration in an effort to avoid, at all costs it seems, to avoid and circumvent the proper and legally required environmental review process.

The Hawai'i Supreme Court ruled unanimously, 5 to 0, that the DOT erred and should not have exempted the project. The Hawaii Superferry knew full well what they were doing, they took a calculated risk, and on August 23 they rolled the dice and lost. Blaming the protesters for this debacle and attempting to fault those in the community who believe in protecting the environment is nothing short of pathetic. No doubt we will hear repeated here today the mantra of how this is all the result of "a small vocal minority." That mantra, my friends, is simply *shibai*.[87]

---

[87] *Shibai*: Hawaiian pidgin English for lies, usually used in a political context. [Eds.]

For the record, it was the egregious mistake made by the DOT and confirmed by a decision of the Hawai'i Supreme Court which ultimately led to the stop of the Hawaii Superferry—not some mythical and all-powerful "small, vocal minority group." The truth is much simpler than that: The Lingle administration, working hand in glove with the Hawaii Superferry owners, made a bad decision and have been called on it by the highest court in our state.

In addition to being unwilling to support special-interest legislation on principle, I also believe, given the history of this particular situation, a bail-out of this nature is totally unwarranted, and, quite frankly, they don't deserve it.

Again, for those who believe this is the only way we can fix this sorry state of affairs, I respect your opinion; I do not question your integrity, your principles, nor your intent, but I do disagree. I believe that good people, people of goodwill and intelligence, can agree to disagree. I believe that good people can look at the same set of facts and circumstances and come to different conclusions.

However, in my heart, I also believe that in this particular situation we are poised on the edge of making a grave error. If passed, this legislation, in my singular and humble opinion, has the potential to seriously undermine our existing environmental laws and establishes a new standard that is sure to encourage other businesses to follow. Worst of all is the message this decision sends to those in our community who believe that playing by the rules is important. What do we tell those folks on Maui who fought so hard in court, against overwhelming odds and the tremendous combined legal resources provided by the state and the Hawaii Superferry? What do we tell those in my district whose community and political awareness has been incredibly galvanized by this issue? What do we tell our youth, young adults in their twenties and thirties who, up until now, most would have considered disenfranchised young adults who, up until this point, have had little faith in government, until, that is, the Hawai'i Supreme Court ruled in their favor, proving to them, at least for a little while, anyway, that the fix was not in, and that the system did in fact work? What do we tell those folks who played by the rules, fought against overwhelming odds, finally were awarded a victory, and then we come along and change the rules and yank that victory away before the ink is even dry on the paper it was written on?

Yes, technically it is true that the court judgment stopping the HSF from sailing to Maui does not apply to Kaua'i and there is no legal impediment at this time preventing the HSF from going to Nawiliwili—tomorrow, if they like. But to most in my community, this legal technicality does not dampen nor detract from the truth. And the truth is that the DOT should not have granted the exemption and the Hawaii Superferry should not have been allowed to sail prior to conducting the required environmental review.

So what now? It is inevitable that this bill or some version of it will pass and the Hawaii Superferry will sail soon once again without the EIS but, yes, with some conditions that should help, and I thank my colleagues for the significant effort it took to amend this legislation.

This issue has drained our spirit and divided our community. It is time now for all of us to move on. Before I close, I have two requests to make: one of my community and one of the Hawaii Superferry.

I am asking those in my community and on Maui and elsewhere: those who may be outraged at the legislative action that is taken this week, please know that I share your outrage, your anger and your disappointment. I agree, the system has let us down. But I ask you to please, please take a deep breath and think about the future before acting in haste. Jumping in the water, putting yourself and your friends in physical danger, risking arrest—it is just not worth it. Protest and boycott if you must, but please do so peacefully and within the bounds of the law. Better yet, I urge you to focus your positive energy and join with others of like mind to help change and improve the system.

To the owners of the Hawaii Superferry, I ask that you also help heal the rifts and calm the tempers by participating in and embracing a community-centered *ho'oponopono*[88] process of conflict resolution, prior to launching service. I urge you to accept the assistance and participation of an independent third-party facilitator who might gather community leaders together for positive collaborative dialogue, without the presence of government. Put off your launch date for now and work instead to help mend the wounds that have been created in our communities and around our state.

Madam President, colleagues, and friends, I thank you for your indulgence in allowing me extended time to share with you my

---

[88] *Ho'oponopono*: : Hawaiian protocol to achieve truth and reconciliation.

deepest thoughts on this issue, which has taken so much from each and every one of us. As you know already, my vote will be NO, but as I hope you also understand, I do respect and honor your decision and your vote, whatever it may be on this issue.

Thank you.

{ MILITARIZATION }

Chapter Fourteen

U.S. Navy: The New Role for Fast, Shallow-Water Vessels

Joan Conrow

As an experiment, in 2001, the Navy leased a catamaran from Austal, builder of the Superferry, to function as its Westpac Express, *shuttling cargo and troops between Okinawa and South Korea. It was a huge success. From that point on, a new paradigm for twenty-first-century naval warfare has dominated military discourse: Produce hundreds of small, fast ships whose design has already been tested in the civilian arena. In other words, build more ships for less money. Hawaii Superferry just happened to be the kind of civilian vessel that fit the bill perfectly, and the timing couldn't have been better for the company to play an instrumental role in the upcoming Navy buildup.*

In this chapter, Joan Conrow writes about the profitable military potential for Hawaii Superferry. [Eds.]

AFTER EXHAUSTIVELY RESEARCHING the relationship between Superferry Corporation and the U.S. military and interviewing a wide variety of sources, I am now convinced that Hawaii Superferry was not created to provide the islands with an alternative form of transportation, as is claimed by the company and Governor Lingle, but essentially to build and test a military prototype vessel at very little risk to investors.

I'm not just speaking about ferrying the Stryker Brigade when it comes to Hawai'i, either. That's the small stuff. What's really at stake here are U.S. Navy contracts for building the Joint High Speed Vessel (JHSV) and Littoral Combat Ship (LCS), contracts potentially worth billions.

My suspicions were corroborated by a source from my days as a journalist in San Diego, who told me that Austal USA is also looking to sell the Superferry design to foreign navies.

U.S. Navy Planning

In a series of blog postings, I outlined the Navy's push to quickly build up its fleet with these lighter, faster, more versatile craft, as well as the budgetary challenges it is facing in meeting that goal. In response to new "enemies" like China, the Navy is seeking vessels that are smaller, faster, and more versatile than traditional warships and able to operate in both deep and littoral (nearshore) waters. Four-star Admiral Gary Roughead, chief of U.S. Naval Operations, told Congress in December 2007 that the Navy is now building up its forces to be ready to challenge a future military threat from China. Admiral Roughead was asked by Congressman Duncan Hunter (R-CA), during a House Armed Services Committee hearing, what steps were being taken by the Navy to address China's large-scale naval buildup and whether China's overall military buildup had prompted planning for more submarines, more missiles, and more aircraft.

Admiral Roughead said, "Yes sir. ... We look at the capabilities that navies have that are evolving, China being one of them. ... And that has driven our advancements in certain capabilities, whether it be in anti-submarine warfare, ballistic missile defense, the command-and-control capabilities that we need on our ships as we operate as a global Navy."

The admiral said that one example is the Navy's Littoral Combat Ship being built for fighting near coastlines but also "capable of running and providing enhanced [antisubmarine warfare] capability to our more traditional battle formations, our expeditionary strike groups and carrier strike groups." The new ship is "for anti-submarine warfare, mine warfare, and anti-surface warfare capability in areas where we see the threat evolving," he said, "to include China."[89]

Several types of craft are now emerging from this urgent push to develop new ships and to drastically expand the Pacific fleet to meet perceived new threats. One is the Littoral Combat Ship, men-

---

[89] Bill Gertz, "Inside the Ring," in *Washington Times*, December 14, 2007.

tioned above. Two prototypes of the LCS are now under construction; one of them is being built by Austal USA, which also built Hawaii Superferry's *Alakai*. Austal is partnering with General Dynamics on this project, in direct competition with Lockheed Martin. The eventual prize in this contest would be a contract to build fifty-five vessels, worth a total of approximately $30 billion.

Another craft in the works is the Joint High Speed Vessel, which is intended to serve the Navy, Army, and Marine Corps. The JHSVs are designed to move equipment and troops at high speed in a variety of conditions. According to *Defense Industry Daily*, "The JHSV will not be a combatant vessel. Its construction will be similar to high-speed commercial ferries used around the world, and the design will include a flight deck and an off-load ramp which can be lowered on a pier or quay wall—allowing vehicles to quickly drive off the ship."[90]

The article continues, "JHSV's shallow draft will allow it access to small austere ports common in developing countries. This makes the JHSV an extremely flexible asset ideal for three types of missions: support of relief operations in small or damaged ports as a flexible logistics support vessel for the Joint Commander or as the key enabler for rapid transport of a Marine Light Armored Reconnaissance Company or an Army Stryker unit."

The Navy, which is leading the program, released an RFP (Request for Proposal) for the JHSV contract in 2007. The contractor selected in 2008 will build all eight JHSVs, and Austal USA seems to have an excellent chance to win it. The Navy is looking to pay $150 million for the lead ship, and $130 million each for the other seven. Five will go to the Army, and the Navy will operate three for itself and the Marine Corps.

J. F. Lehman and Co.

John Lehman, chairman of Hawaii Superferry and former Navy secretary under Ronald Reagan, has championed the rapid buildup of the Navy fleet—in fact, this has been a major push of his since his days as Navy secretary.

---

[90] "JHSV Fast Catamaran Transport Program Moves Forward" in *defenseindustrydaily.com*, July 31, 2008.

From the beginning of Lehman's involvement in the Superferry, it seemed odd to me that his firm, J. F. Lehman and Co., which invests primarily in marine and aerospace defense projects, would suddenly go into passenger transport service in such a big way, investing upward of $80 million equity capital in the Superferry project.

I also found it interesting that, according to the Superferry website, four of the ten members of the HSF board of directors have strong ties to the Navy and defense industries. They include Lehman, who was secretary of the Navy for six years under Reagan, as well as Tig Krekel, vice chairman of J. F. Lehman and Co. and the former president and chief executive officer of Hughes Space and Communications and past president of Boeing Satellite Systems. Krekel is a graduate of the U.S. Naval Academy and spent five years as a naval officer, including service as an aide in the office of the Chief of Naval Operations.

Director George A. Sawyer, a founding partner of J. F. Lehman and Co., is former assistant secretary of the Navy, Shipbuilding & Logistics. He was also a submarine engineer officer in the U.S. Navy and is a member of the American Society of Naval Engineers and the Society of Naval Architects and Marine Engineers.

Director John W. "Bill" Shirley is the former program manager of the U.S. Department of Energy, Naval Reactors Division, Seawolf and Virginia Class Submarines. He has thirty-four years of experience in senior positions at the Navy Division of Naval Reactors. Shirley now works as a private consultant, giving preference to J. F. Lehman and Co.

Two of the remaining six directors of Hawaii Superferry Corporation—C. Alexander Harman and Louis N. Mintz—are employed by J. F. Lehman and Co.

It's also telling that, in spring 2008, Admiral William Fargo, former commander of U.S. military operations in the Pacific, was appointed CEO of Hawaii Superferry, thus rounding out an exceedingly impressive, well-connected, military rogues' gallery at the helm of an otherwise innocuous little civilian interisland ferry operation. This eminent group might qualify as a shadow U.S. Navy Department. One might wonder if all that brass is required to run a local ferry business? If not, then why are they all here?

Who Benefits?

Another question making the rounds is whether J. F. Lehman and Co. stands to gain financially from any of these Navy contracts because of its involvement with HSF. If so, how? One can only speculate. J. F. Lehman and Co. has made acquisitions that could support both JHSV and LCS construction contracts. These include Elgar Electronics, which manufactures electrical power test and measurement equipment for military and commercial uses, and Atlantic Inertial Systems, a leading-niche supplier of highly engineered guidance, stabilization, and navigation products and systems for aircraft, weapons, and land systems applications.

Most notable, however, is that J. F. Lehman and Co. also recently bought Atlantic Marine Holding Co., a leading provider of repair, overhaul, and maintenance services for commercial seagoing vessels and U.S. Navy ships, which is located *adjacent* to the Austal USA shipyard in Mobile, Alabama. The company also owns and operates another shipyard in Mobile, as well as one in Jacksonville, Florida, where it leases a third facility at the Naval Station Mayport. Should Austal actually receive a large Navy contract, as may be imminent, Atlantic Marine might be in an ideal position to collaborate in various production tasks.

As for the issue of whether the Hawaii Superferry has military intentions, this has been openly argued since its inception. Military roles (such as transporting Strykers) were acknowledged by the Superferry as early as 2004, in its PUC application for a Certificate of Public Convenience and Necessity. A March 2005 article in *Pacific Business News* quoted HSF's original chairman, Timothy Dick, as saying, "Hawaii Superferry provided the Army with a cost analysis and expects to negotiate a long-term contract." The same article indicated that "with Lehman's expertise, the Superferry plans to operate a Westpac Express, essentially to carry military equipment and ferry vehicles from O'ahu to the Big Island on a daily basis."

The article continues, "This logistical plan will make it easier for soldiers to train when the Stryker Brigade comes to Hawai'i. The Brigade will be stationed on O'ahu and conduct training exercises on the Big Island," Lehman said. "The Superferry is strong enough to take Stryker vehicles," he said.

Despite these indications, the Superferry has officially continued to distance itself from the appearance of military intentions. When I asked Terry O'Halloran, director of business development for the Hawaii Superferry, about this in late 2007, he said, "Absolutely false. Boy, that's a good one."

O'Halloran did acknowledge that John Lehman had discussed using the vessel to transport the Strykers, and initially felt the military "could be a good potential market. Subsequently, we have learned our primary market is our local residents and businesses. We're not in any discussion with the military about a contract to move personnel," he said.

He did add, "We welcome the military use of HSF just like they currently use Young Brothers and Aloha [now defunct] and Hawaiian Airlines to move personnel between the islands."

O'Halloran also said the Superferry—the largest aluminum ship ever built in the United States, whose construction was documented by *National Geographic*—is no different from other fast ferries around the world.

"The idea that this vessel is unique or has some kind of military connection is absolutely false," he said. And yet, months later, on June 18, 2008, a *Honolulu Advertiser* story by Derrick DePledge revealed that at the time that O'Halloran made his assertions, the Superferry company had already applied for a federal defense subsidy program that would cover the cost of installing militarily useful features on its second ship. The article went on to say that Superferry was also considering retrofitting the *Alakai* with such features.

In addition, Austal USA's own website contains this nugget: "U.S. Navy and Army representatives have toured *Alakai* throughout its construction as part of the ongoing evaluation of potential Joint High Speed Vessel platforms. The JHSV will provide a transformational capability supporting the global war on terrorism, major combat operations, and emerging operational concepts, including the Army Future Force and Seabasing."

Meanwhile, the Navy is moving ahead this year to award a contract to build eight JHSVs and plans to award an LCS contract in 2010. The LCS program is already behind schedule, and the Navy is at least three years behind its fleet-building goals. *(See also Chapter 15.)*

The LCS program is also way over budget. This has prompted some to question whether the Sea Fighter, which has the strong support of Representative Duncan Hunter of San Diego, former chair of the House Armed Services Committee and now its ranking Republican, might be proposed as a cheaper substitute. Navy officials already have said it could be outfitted with electronics and weaponry.

But the Sea Fighter has demonstrated some fishtailing and other performance problems, and Nichols Brothers, the Washington state firm that built the vessel, shut down last November.

So, here comes the Superferry, which not only is very similar in design and specifications to the Sea Fighter, but also is proving itself by running at high speeds day after day, weather and harbor surges permitting, in some of the nation's roughest waters.

As one source told me: "In an accelerated procurement environment, it would give [Congressional appropriations] committees great comfort [to be] granting money for something up and running."

Superferry Design Still in the Running

On January 31, 2008, the Navy announced that it had awarded preliminary Joint High Speed Vessel design contracts worth $3 million each to Austal USA (which designed and built the Superferry, and also the Westpac Express), Bollinger Shipyards, and Bath Iron Works (a subsidiary of General Dynamics, the manufacturer of the Stryker tank and the partner *with* Austal in the bid for the LCS). Austal USA is now in the unique position of being able to scrutinize the performance and cost of *two* Superferries it designed and constructed, in developing its final proposal for the JHSV design.

In April 2008, Austal announced that it had also been awarded $33.7 million from the Navy to develop a 100-acre expansion of its shipyard, which would allow it to produce three aluminum boats each year.

The company also stated that it is "confident of its ability to deliver a low-risk JHSV platform to the U.S. Navy and Army" because it's the only U.S. shipyard with a track record of building high-speed aluminum vessels over 325 feet in length.

What's at stake? The JHSV contract alone is valued at more than $1 billion, and additional sales could be possible to navies around the world. As for any benefits for J. F. Lehman and Company and the Hawaii Superferry Corporation itself, only time will tell.

Let's not close this discussion without mentioning the role of Governor Linda Lingle, who made it all possible. She expended tremendous political capital to convince legislators to pass a law overturning a Hawai'i Supreme Court ruling, which effectively ensured that the Superferry would be running in time for the JHSV contract award. Perhaps she thought such a favor might hold the prospect of substantial campaign backing if she decides to run for the U.S. Senate or pursue a lucrative position in private industry. Time will tell about that, as well.

Is Superferry for Civilians? Studying the Numbers

Koohan Paik

The Hawaii Superferry promotes itself as *ecofriendly* and serving the people of Hawai'i. But exactly how true are these claims? Let's do the numbers, starting with the ecofriendly part.

To go the distance from O'ahu to Kaua'i, the *Alakai* needs about 6,000 gallons of marine diesel oil. And to travel the same distance by jet? According to researcher/blogger Brad Parsons, a Hawaiian Airlines jet traveling the same distance requires only 400 gallons of jet fuel—one-fifteenth of the fuel burned by the *Alakai*! Not only that, but the fuel burned by the jet is far cleaner than the marine diesel consumed by the *Alakai*.

On the other hand, the *Alakai* can transport up to 866 passengers, while an interisland jet holds only 123 people. So wouldn't the ship come out ahead, in terms of per-person fuel consumption?

Unfortunately, no. The jet still comes out ahead. The ferry carries seven times as many people, but uses fifteen times as much fuel.

In other words, Hawaiian Airlines is at least twice as fuel-efficient for moving people interisland as is Hawaii Superferry (and it's six times faster: thirty minutes instead of three hours). And that's assuming a full load for both.

One can't help wondering why a more fuel-efficient design wasn't implemented for the Superferry, especially in light of skyrocketing fuel costs. From a profit standpoint alone, how could those who run Hawaii Superferry have ever thought they could possibly break even?

Brad Parsons has calculated that the Superferry may be cheaper per passenger-mile on shorter distances because of the higher costs for the jet to take off. For example, the *Alakai* is more cost-effective on one-way routes of one to two hours or distances of thirty to seventy-five miles per revenue-generating load. However, a profit is unlikely to be generated once the ride exceeds two hours or seventy-five miles, due to the voracious diesel fuel consumption of the Superferry's four jet engines.

HSF's planned one-way route distances range from about 105 miles to 160 miles, three hours in duration. In other words, according to Parsons, Superferry can't make a profit with its interisland routes—and this was probably evident to the ferry owners even before they started operations.

Even Alan Lerchbacker, the former CEO of Austal USA, the builder of the *Alakai*, questioned the ferry's gas-guzzling design. In a 2007 report in *Pacific Business News*, Lerchbacker commented, "I just worry about them getting enough business to cover costs because of the sheer size of it." Lerchbacker said he had suggested a smaller, 236-foot vessel, only to see the company order the 351-foot model. "For a smoother ride on the ocean, that ferry will have to go over thirty-five knots, and it costs a lot of money on fuel to go that fast," he said.

So why did Hawaii Superferry's investors do it? Why did HSF push ahead a design for a superlarge, superfast, turbocharged ferry, knowing full well that such a design would undercut profitability by consuming more fuel than a jet? Furthermore, did the company really need a gas tank that held 56,800 gallons of fuel for interisland service? That is the size of tank that would be used by a vessel far from its fuel supplies. These were the kinds of questions that first tipped off people to the military connection.

The answer to all these questions might be that, from the beginning, the company had something else in mind besides trying to make a modest living hopping the short distances between the Hawaiian Islands. The gas-guzzling configuration of four diesel jet engines may have been excessive for transporting passengers, even a maximum load, but that herculean power would be needed if the goal were to speedily move a load of *nineteen-ton* Stryker tanks through the water. Increasingly, it seemed that what really matters for Hawaii Superferry is military contracts, whose possibilities range from transporting Stryker tanks interisland, to providing the jumbo aluminum-hull design as a prototype for Navy warships, to providing advanced shipyard training and experience for workers who will be building naval vessels.

As Wayne Jenkins, a welder at Austal USA, said, "We had a conference with Bob Browning, who is the CEO. They said we're trying to build [the *Alakai*] to a spec where if they needed them, that it could carry so many tanks, personnel to wherever they have to be. But they *have* talked about trying to use the ferries for U.S. military."

If Superferry's goal had been mainly to serve the community, the company would have followed the advice of former Austal CEO Alan Lerchbacker and ordered a smaller ship that would have used less fuel, thereby substantially increasing its chances for profitability. It seems as though its goals had little to do with being green or interisland ferry profitability. Maybe it's just about building a warship.

There may be nothing wrong with building a warship. But there is something very wrong for a private company to manipulate Hawai'i lawmakers and taxpayers into footing the bill for building harbor adaptations under the pretense that the ship's purpose is to benefit the community. And there *is* something terribly wrong when the governor of the State of Hawai'i runs interference and does all she can do to give HSF its way, including spending more money on legal fees, on a special legislative session, on tugboats, on an audit, on an Oversight Task Force, and on harbor security—not to mention perverting laws already in place to protect Hawai'i's fragile ecosystems, undermining the integrity of Hawai'i's courts, inciting a deep emotional rift between the islands' people, and bringing all the other associated social and political grief that has come with this project.

[MILITARIZATION]

Chapter Fifteen

How Not to Build a Navy Ship

Philip Taubman

This essay reports on the Navy's catastrophic efforts to complete construction on a prototype light, maneuverable, high-speed transport, and also a combat ship. The boats are intended to offset the supposed advantage of China's fleet of light, fast vessels that have begun operating in coastal situations in Asia and the Pacific. The U.S. versions were to be adaptations of already in-use civilian, high-speed ferries, such as the Hawaii Superferry. Austal USA (builder and creditor of the Superferry) is partnering with General Dynamics to compete against Lockheed for a potentially enormous contract to build at least fifty-five of these vessels. Apparently, the emphasis on quickly completing an operational prototype led to corners being cut, shoddy work, and cost overruns by both contractors, as this article documents, though its primary focus is on the Lockheed team. The same effort helps explain why the idea of an Environmental Impact Statement, which would delay getting the boat in the water, has been such an anathema to Hawaii Superferry.

As we go to press, the Navy has not yet picked a winner to the Littoral Combat Ship competition. If the General Dynamics–Austal design is chosen, the speculation is that it could also mean lucrative contracts for the shipyard adjacent to Austal USA, recently purchased by J. F. Lehman and Co., and possibly also for Lehman's other military technology companies. [Eds.]

A PROJECT HERALDED as the dawning of an innovative, low-cost era in Navy shipbuilding has turned into a case study of how not to

---

This article originally appeared in the *New York Times*, April 25, 2008, under the title, "Lesson on How Not to Build a Navy Ship." Copyright © The New York Times, 2008. All rights reserved. Reprinted by permission.

build a combat ship. The bill for the ship, being built by Lockheed Martin, has soared to $531 million, more than double the original, and by some calculations could be $100 million more. With an alternate General Dynamics-Austal USA prototype similarly struggling at an Alabama shipyard, the Navy last year temporarily suspended the entire program. *[NOTE: The program has since been revived. Eds.]*

The program's tribulations speak to what military experts say are profound shortcomings in the Pentagon's acquisitions system. Even as spending on new projects has risen to its highest point since the Reagan years, being over budget and behind schedule have become the norm: a recent Government Accountability Office audit found that ninety-five projects—warships, helicopters, and satellites—were delayed 21 months on average and cost 26 percent more than initially projected, a bill of $295 billion.

In a narrow sense, the troubled birth of the coastal ships was rooted in the Navy's misbegotten faith in a feat of maritime alchemy: building a hardened warship by adapting the design of a high-speed commercial ferry. As Representative Gene Taylor, the Mississippi Democrat who leads the House Armed Services Subcommittee on Seapower and Expeditionary Forces, put it, "Thinking these ships could be built to commercial specs was a dumb move."

Behind the numbers in the Accountability Office study, experts say, is a dynamic of mutually re-enforcing deficiencies: ever-changing Pentagon design requirements; unrealistic cost estimates and production schedules abetted by companies eager to win contracts, and a fondness for commercial technologies that often, as with the ferry concept, prove unsuitable for specialized military projects.

At the same time, a policy of letting contractors take the lead in managing weapons programs has coincided with an acute shortage of government engineers trained to oversee these increasingly complex enterprises.

The coastal ships—called *littoral combat ships*—are especially important to the Navy, which has struggled to retain a central role in American military operations after the Cold War. In part, they are a response to the Navy's own September 11th moment, which came in October 2000, when two terrorists in a bomb-laden rubber dinghy rammed the destroyer Cole, killing 17 sailors and wounding 39 more.

An examination of the littoral combat ships by the *New York Times*, including interviews with many of the principal Navy and industry officials involved, found that the project was hobbled from the outset by the Navy's zeal to build the ships as fast and inexpensively as possible and the contractors' desire—driven by competitive pressures —to stay on schedule, even as the ferry designs proved impractical and construction problems multiplied.

In their haste to get the ships into the water, the Navy and contractors redesigned and built them at the same time—akin to building an office tower while reworking the blueprints. To meet its deadline, Lockheed abandoned the normal sequence of shipbuilding steps: instead of largely finishing sections and then assembling the ship, much of the work was left to be done after the ship was welded together. That slowed construction and vastly drove up costs.

"It's not good to be building as you're designing," said Vice Admiral Paul E. Sullivan, commander of the Navy branch that supervises shipbuilding.

A Lockheed executive vice president, Christopher E. Kubasik, said, "We have acknowledged all along our shared responsibility for challenges encountered in the design and construction of the littoral combat ship, which are similar to those typically experienced with first-in-class vessels, including the competing LCS design." Mr. Kubasik said the company was working toward "realistic cost goals for subsequent ships." General Dynamics declined to comment.

Despite the problems, the Navy secretary, Donald C. Winter, and other top Navy officials say they remain committed to building 55 of the ships, once a steady, fixed-price production run can be assured. Even at about $500 million apiece, Navy officials add, the coastal ships would be a bargain compared with most Navy combat vessels.

Still, throughout the military-industrial world, the program is seen as a cautionary tale, especially for a Navy whose 30-year shipbuilding strategy calls for building scores of warships—including aircraft carriers, destroyers and submarines—to bolster an aging fleet.

"The littoral combat ship is an imaginative answer to emerging military requirements, but it has the most fouled-up acquisition strategy I have ever seen in a major military program," said Loren Thompson, a military analyst at the Lexington Institute, a policy research center.

A New Mantra

Traditionally the Navy had disdained small combat ships as a major component of the fleet. But strategists came to fear that the David and Goliath phenomenon underlined by the attack on the Cole, what they call "asymmetric warfare," would only grow in the years ahead.

"We needed to figure out how to asymmetric the asymmetric guys," recalled Admiral Vern Clark, who championed the ships as chief of naval operations from 2000 to 2005.

To Navy planners, a ship designed for coastal combat could neutralize hostile submarines, surface warships, mines and terrorist speedboats, clearing the way for other combat ships to operate in offshore waters and support combat ashore. The Navy first publicly declared its intention to build the ship on November 1, 2001. In those days, the Pentagon's defining procurement mantra was "Faster, Better, Cheaper." From the first, the coastal ships' defining characteristic was speed.

The first model was to be delivered no more than six years after conceptual planning began, half the normal time. Construction was to take two years, instead of the usual four or five.

The Navy also wanted ships that could travel fast, better than forty knots. And they needed to be easily outfitted with different weapons and surveillance systems. A removable package of mine-sweeping equipment, for instance, could be replaced with a package of special-operations gear used by a Seal team. Each ship would carry an uncommonly small crew, about forty sailors. Compared with a $2 billion destroyer or a $7 billion to $9 billion aircraft carrier, the new ships would be produced at the cut rate of $220 million apiece, not including weapons packages. In short, the accelerated, cost-conscious acquisition plan—promoted as a new shipbuilding paradigm to help the Navy rebuild the fleet—appeared to be exactly the kind of transformational thinking that Defense Secretary Donald Rumsfeld and his top civilian aides favored as they moved into the Pentagon in 2001. It was quickly approved.

A Plan, Then It Changes

Another idea that had taken hold was that the Pentagon should break free from cumbersome, gold-plated acquisition programs by taking advantage of commercially available technologies. With that in mind, Lockheed and General Dynamics proposed different high-speed ferry models as the template, and in 2004, the Navy selected the two companies to compete for the business. The model for the Freedom was a ferry built in Italy. An Australian ferry was the model for the General Dynamics prototype, named Independence.

[EDITOR'S NOTE: *The "Australian ferry" referred to above was built by Austal Corporation, whose U.S. division, Austal USA, manufactured the Hawaii Superferry as nearly an exact copy. Austal USA has now partnered with General Dynamics to adapt the boat for the potential U.S. Navy contract.*]

Lockheed had virtually no shipbuilding experience. But in keeping with a Pentagon policy that called for letting big military contractors run complex projects with minimal government supervision, the Navy made the companies primarily responsible for all phases of development—from concept studies to detailed design and construction.

In theory, the contractors' business and technological acumen would save taxpayer dollars. But the Navy agreed to reimburse the companies for cost overruns rather than setting a fixed price, leaving little incentive to hold down costs.

To compensate for its lack of experience, Lockheed joined with the naval architecture firm of Gibbs & Cox and two shipyards, Marinette Marine, and Bollinger in Louisiana.

The Lockheed proposal called for a steel single-hull ship 378 feet long and 57 feet wide. It would have a spacious flight deck and space for two helicopters, a stern ramp and side door near the waterline for launching and recovering small boats, and large interior compartments that could be quickly reconfigured for different weapons systems. But as Lockheed and the Navy were completing contract negotiations in 2004, the rules changed drastically. Commercial ferry standards, the Navy determined, would not do.

The underlying principle behind the decision, Admiral Sullivan said, was that the new ships had to be able to "hang tough in a storm and take some battle damage and still survive long enough" for the crew to be rescued.

A military expert said the Navy had badly miscalculated.

"They were eager to take advantage of commercial practices and the lower cost of buying off the shelf, but they did a lousy job of understanding the war-fighting requirements," said the military expert, who asked not be named because he was involved with the program. "It was like, 'You mean you want to put wheels on that car?' "

Admiral Gary Roughead, the current chief of naval operations, said: "We had thought that the commercial variant would not be that far away from what we needed. I'll tell you, that was underestimated."

At the same time, the Navy realized the time had come to modernize its shipbuilding code. The resulting Naval Vessel Rules in many ways trumped the idea that the new ships could draw extensively on commercial ferry designs.

The new rules called for a water-mist fire extinguishing system instead of the commercial sprinkler system normally found on a ferry, forcing the shipyard to order new pipes, high-pressure nozzles and other equipment. Other revised requirements included heavy-duty power cables and reinforced crew compartments.

Ultimately, there were nearly 600 significant engineering changes affecting nearly all parts of the ship, according to the Navy.

The Navy and Lockheed agree that the Navy described the new rules as they were being developed, and that it increased the budget to accommodate some design changes. Even so, both parties acknowledge they badly underestimated the consequences.

"Once the rules were issued, it took us a year to fully understand how they would impact the project," said Craig R. Quigley, a Lockheed spokesman.

By then, early 2005, the ship was already under construction at Marinette.

The Setbacks Begin

Building a ship requires precision sequencing, as sections are built and outfitted in large manufacturing halls, then moved to a towering building where they are welded together to create a ship.

This system allows workers ample space, light and access to heavy construction tools as they build each section, called a ship module, and outfit it with pipes, cables, insulation and other equipment, and apply coats of paint.

Getting the modules as complete as possible before assembly is critical because it becomes far more difficult to work in the cramped quarters of a ship. Marinette's general manager, Richard T. McCreary, said it costs roughly six times more to outfit a module aboard a ship than standing free.

Normally, the Marinette yard prefers to get modules 85 percent to 90 percent completed before they are transported to the ship erection building. In the case of the Freedom, with its repeated design alterations, better than half of the 39 sections fell well short of that goal.

The risks seemed obvious, yet neither the Navy nor the shipyard was willing to reconsider the timetable.

Rear Admiral Charles S. Hamilton II, one of the Navy officers with lead responsibility for the project, said he had given Navy officials several opportunities to slow down the project.

"The clear signal from all quarters was, 'Hamilton, I want that ship in the water, and I want it out there now,' " he recalled in an interview.

Admiral Hamilton left the Navy last year. He now works at Booz Allen Hamilton, the consulting firm.

At Lockheed, executives say they feared that slowing down construction would put them at a disadvantage in their battle to win the contract over the General Dynamics-Austal team.

Yet if the project was troubled, the Navy's oversight at Marinette was less than robust. Because of staffing reductions, the Navy office responsible for supervising shipbuilding initially dispatched no one full time to Wisconsin. Even after a team arrived, it failed to appreciate the severity of problems.

"We had very junior people on site," Admiral Sullivan said.

Construction was also hampered by steel shortages: the lower levels of the hull required the same low-alloy steel the Pentagon was buying to strengthen the armor on Humvees in Iraq.

The most wrenching setback came in autumn 2005, when a key gear for the propulsion system was cut incorrectly, forcing a twenty-seven-week delay in ship construction. Rick Kennedy, a spokesman for G.E. Aviation, the General Electric division that produced the gear, said a machinist had misread a drawing; G.E. absorbed the additional cost.

Shipbuilders usually start with the engine space, which contains the most machinery, then build around it. Because of the gear problem, Mr. McCreary said, "We did just the opposite."

Joe North, who manages the project for Lockheed, said in an interview at the shipyard that he initially thought the yard could work around the problems, that design work would eventually catch up with construction.

Looking back, Mr. North said, "it was death by a thousand cuts."

'It Got Oversold'

With work nearly finished and the Menominee River ice gone, Lockheed plans to take the Freedom to sea trials in Lake Michigan this spring and hopes to deliver it to the Navy late this year.

The competing General Dynamics ship, an aluminum trimaran considerably bigger than the Lockheed model, is to be launched on Saturday, April 26, 2008, in Alabama [at the shipyard of Austal USA, the builder]. Even though the General Dynamics team had more time to digest the Navy's design changes before starting construction, its ship ran into many of the same problems and delays as Lockheed's. The price tag also more than doubled.

Last year, the Navy temporarily put the entire program on hold when it terminated contracts for more ships because it could not reach agreement with the two companies on a fixed price.

While the financial gap was not great, Navy and industry officials said, the Navy, hammered by Congress for its handling of the project, wanted to demonstrate its determination to hold down the price for future ships. Congress has set a spending cap of $460 million per ship, excluding weapons packages.

Once the Navy evaluates the two prototypes, it can select one or order a mixed fleet. While it could opt for a different approach, military experts say that seems unlikely, given the need for the new ships and the money and effort already expended.

The Navy recently restarted the program, inviting the two companies to submit fixed-price proposals for three additional ships. Lockheed, still hoping to win the entire prize, said the problems encountered with the Freedom would not be repeated, now that the company has a finished design.

"It will be great, the next time around," said Mr. North, the program manager. "Lead ships are truly hard."

Navy and industry officials say blame for the program's rocky early history has to be shared.

"It's easy to lay all the blame at the foot of the government, and the Navy was naive, but the companies bear some of the responsibility," said a senior industry official who asked not to be identified because of his involvement in the project. "They were playing the game to get the contract, not owning up about all the issues until well into the game, hoping to make some recovery downstream."

Mr. McCreary, the Marinette general manager, said that while the shipyard might not have fully mastered the Navy's accounting system, it had given the Navy frequent progress reports showing problems mounting.

Mr. Winter, the Navy secretary, complained that the Navy bureaucracy had failed to alert him to rising costs. The Pentagon, he said, was bedazzled by the idea of saving money and time with commercial technologies.

"It got oversold," he said. "The concept was just abused."

He lamented the Pentagon's eroding expertise in systems engineering—managing complex new projects to ensure that goals are achievable and affordable—and faulted the notion that industry could best manage ambitious development projects.

"Quite frankly, industry is not good at doing this," he said.

Recently, Mr. Winter said, he instituted new procedures to ensure tighter supervision of all shipbuilding projects. He says he is confident that the coastal-ships program will produce a fleet of fine, affordable vessels. But as he contemplates the Navy's long-range rebuilding plans, he says he stands behind a scorching critique that he delivered at a convention in Washington last year:

"If we do not figure out how to establish credibility in our shipbuilding programs and plans, and restore confidence in our ability to deliver on our commitments, we cannot expect Congress or the nation to provide us with the resources we so urgently need."

{ MILITARIZATION }

Chapter Sixteen

Stealing Hawaiian Lands for the War Machine

Haunani-Kay Trask

This is the first of two chapters on the historic advance of U.S. militarization of Hawai'i and the Pacific, a process that has been going on for a century and is now picking up speed. The author, Native Hawaiian scholar Haunani-Kay Trask, discusses how militarization impacts indigenous land rights and culture. In the next chapter, Kyle Kajihiro, program director for the Hawai'i branch of the American Friends Service Committee, covers similar ground, as well as the social, environmental, and economic consequences of the ubiquitous military presence in Hawai'i. [Eds.]

> "The worst outcrop of herd life is the military system, which I abhor. This plague-spot of civilization ought to be abolished with all possible speed."—Albert Einstein

IF THE REMARKABLE humanist and scientific genius Albert Einstein were alive today, his abhorrence of the military would galvanize him to resist its latest predations in the Hawaiian Islands. Using the pretext of defending America against terrorist attacks, this new militarization portends increased land takings, Army and Air Force buildup, and massive construction, including roads and harbor extensions. Euphemistically called a *transformation* in military documents, it is nothing less than the largest military land grab since World War II. And a land grab with the approval of the majority of our state's pro-military congressional delegation, particularly Senator Daniel Inouye.

Beginning in the 1980s, with the proclaimed end of the Cold War, the so-called "peace dividend" resulted in the U.S. military's reluctantly downsizing its historically dominant presence in Hawai'i. It also returned some of the land it had been occupying.

But in recent years the Pentagon has reversed direction. Since 1998, under the cover of what is euphemistically called "friendly condemnation," it grabbed some 10,000 acres of land on O'ahu (an area more than twelve times the size of Waikiki). In terms of percentage of land controlled by the military, O'ahu is on par with Guam, Okinawa, and other colonial military outposts.

It is on the Big Island, however, that the greatest land theft in half a century is taking place under the guise of the Army's claim that it needs 98,840 acres of "contiguous land" in order to carry out maneuvers. That is an area larger than the entire island of Lana'i. Although the military already controls 109,000 contiguous acres at the Big Island's Pohakuloa Training Area (PTA) along the Saddle Road, it contends that all but 19,148 acres of this land is unsuitable. That means it will require at least an additional 80,000 or so acres.[91]

While the all-purpose alarm of *national security* serves as the usual excuse for these land takings, increased militarization of everyday life threatens Native cultural practices, endangered species, and the environmental health and continuity of all Hawai'i communities.

THE BAYONET CONSTITUTION

As early as the 1880s, President James A. Garfield's secretary of state, James Blaine, argued that Hawai'i was key to American dominion of the Pacific. And in the Reciprocity Treaty of 1887, King Kalakaua was forced to cede Pearl River Lagoon to the United States in exchange for duty-free sugar. The treaty was a result of the aptly named Bayonet Constitution, forced on Kalakaua by American merchants and politicians. In 1893, when Queen Lili'uokalani was overthrown by haole sugar planters, American troops provided the necessary iron fist to ensure planter success. Once Hawai'i was annexed in 1898—*against strong Native protest*—

---

[91] See the *U.S. Army Land Use Requirement Study*, 1997. Also see *Environmental Assessments for Land Acquisitions at Pohakuloa Training Area, and at the Kahuku Training Area*, Department of the Army.

politicians in Washington began planning global American military strategy.[92]

Because of its unique mid-Pacific location, Hawai'i has always been central to American hegemony in the vast Far East. The latest military *transformation* is but a twenty-first-century version of that domination.

Today, the military controls over 5 percent of all the land in the Hawaiian Island chain.[93] If, and when, its long-term plans for Pohakuloa are accomplished, it will have increased its control of Hawai'i land by almost 50 percent in one fell swoop.

In the past, most of the military acreage carved out of Hawai'i has been Native Hawaiian land, including stolen ("ceded") lands from the Kingdom and from the Hawaiian *ali'i*[94] land trusts. At least 22 percent of O'ahu lands are militarized, while the Defensive Sea Areas range from Kane'ohe Bay to Kaua'i. According to the 2004 *U.S. Pacific Command Handbook*, the military occupies one hundred sixty-one installations throughout the islands. All told, military personnel and dependents account for 17 percent of the state's population.

Even before its newly planned expansion, the Pohakuloa Training Area was the largest military training area in Hawai'i and the largest live-fire training facility in the Pacific. Most of that immense area is ceded land that, by the Army's own estimate, contains twenty-seven endangered species of plants and animals, fifty historical sites, and over 1,000 archeological features. As reported by the *Honolulu Advertiser* on July 9, 2002, Pohakuloa has the highest concentration of endangered species of any Army installation in the world.

But none of this matters, since bombing and artillery training continue unabated. The military, of course, has never cared much about the environment. They simply file their Environmental Impact Statements and take the heat at routine public hearings. Now, however, the Army has stolen another 23,000 acres at Pohakuloa for the training of thousands more soldiers, despite the inevitable impacts on the natural biota.[95]

---

[92] Haunani-Kay Trask, *From a Native Daughter: Colonialism and Sovereignty in Hawai'i* (Honolulu: University of Hawai'i Press, 1999), 2–20.

[93] Larry Jones, "The U.S. War Machine in Hawaii," in *worldcantwait.net*, November 25, 2007.

[94] *Ali'i*: nobility.

[95] Kyle Kajihiro, "No Peace in Paradise," in *Haleakala Times*, May 8, 2007.

Among the projects under way that involve a large increase in the 15,000 to 20,000 soldiers who already train at Pohakuloa are the following: antiarmor live-fire and tracking ranges that include nearly thirty targets, control towers, tracking and service roads, loading docks, latrines, eating areas, training camp sites, and maintenance yards. Entire plant and animal species, along with numerous historic sites, will simply be wiped out.

The road from the Pohakuloa Training Area to Kawaihae Harbor was recently asphalted to accommodate hundreds of Stryker armored vehicles. The Strykers, as well as over 500 trucks and Humvees, will be shuttled back and forth from Oʻahu on a high-speed ferry (most likely, the Superferry), which will dock at Kawaihae. The Army has acknowledged impacts to cultural and natural resources, air and noise quality, and general intrusion into the life and tranquility of the surrounding communities. But that's it. An acknowledgment. No changes, no withdrawals.[96]

The Strykers—the model of tank that is central to the military transformation—will train on Oʻahu, as well. Preparations for the Stryker Brigade Combat Team include twenty-eight construction projects to upgrade training, maintenance, and housing facilities for 800 additional soldiers plus their dependents. One reporter called it "the biggest Army construction project in Hawaiʻi since World War II."[97]

In terms of overall military posture, Bush administration cold warriors support first-strike nuclear capability, quick response, mobile ground forces, and a kind of Dr. Strangelove fascination with high-tech training simulations for the eventual use of high-tech weapons.

On Oʻahu, at the new Information Systems Facility at Schofield, for example, the Army has recently built a 38,000-square-foot, multistory building as "the critical central hub that provide[s] connectivity to support essential constructive, virtual and real information systems." This facility is in addition to the brand-new, 90,000-square-foot, state-of-the-art Mission Support Training Facility housing "war-fighting simulations training and digital classroom training" for all the military services. In other words, while

---

[96] William Cole, "Big Island residents worry about Army expansion," in *Honolulu Advertiser*, July 9, 2002.
[97] Kajihiro.

the military waits for real blood-and-guts combat, they can practice killing by video games.[98]

Other Oʻahu support projects include the recent widening of a twenty-three-mile road between the Helemano Military Reservation and the Kahuku Training Area, to support military vehicle traffic exclusively.[99]

None of us who live in Hawaiʻi will be able to escape this increased military activity—more troops, vehicles, jets, ships, and families. Beyond rabid patriotism, local support of the military, including that given by the major political parties, turns on its role as the state's second-largest industry, just behind that other economic parasite, mass-based corporate tourism. Generating nearly $5 billion of the state's gross product, the military is the golden goose so honored by the state's politicians. And that goose gets fatter by the day.

As guardian of empire, of the far reach of the United States into the Pacific and Asia, the military is becoming the major power in Hawaiʻi. During times of war, including the misnamed War on Terror, the military is particularly despotic. Just how despotic is evident in the Army transformation proposal.

The New World Order

Social scientists and economists have predicted for years the eventual dominance of only one superpower: the United States. The collapse of the Soviet Union, unification of the European states, and the convenient excuse of the War on Terror have enabled the American government to coerce both its allies and its citizens into a frightening kind of conformity. That conformity will be guaranteed by an enlarged police state for domestic purposes and a globalized military for maintaining what Bush Jr.'s father called the New World Order.

At the close of World War II, the U.S. Army issued "Orientation Fact Sheet 64," dealing with the future threat of fascism. "Fascism always camouflages its plans and purposes," the report said, adding that "any fascist attempt made to gain power in America would not

---

[98] List of Proposed Projects to Support Transformation of 2nd Brigade, 25th Infantry Division (L), Hawaiʻi, 1–2.
[99] Ibid., 3.

use the exact Hitler pattern. It would work under the guise of 'super-patriotism' and 'super-Americanism.'"

Within a few years of that warning, the rise of McCarthyism proved its accuracy. Like President Dwight Eisenhower cautioning Americans about the rise of the "military-industrial complex," even the Army can sometimes get things right. And the warning of "Orientation Fact Sheet 64" is as relevant today as it was during the witch hunts of the 1950s.

What Needs to Be Done

More public interventions are necessary, especially in Hawai'i. We must organize against militarization and the proposed fiscal year 2009 U.S. military budget of $713.1 billion—the largest military budget in the world, greater than the total military budgets of the rest of the world's nations combined. We must not allow the process to be closed, overtaken by bureaucrats and politicians. Above all, we must not be cowed into accepting, into going along in the name of patriotism—what Einstein called "heroism on demand" and which he believed would result in "senseless violence."

The greatest need for public discussion is at a time when governments move to abridge our human rights and thereby degrade our humanity. Those of us who oppose militarism must connect with groups in other parts of the world, not only in our own backyard. This includes people on Okinawa, in Europe and Canada, in the South Pacific, in the Philippines, and beyond.

Here, in Hawai'i, we need to link the new peace movement with the fight for Hawaiian sovereignty and its core value of Malama 'Aina, nourishing the land. It is the Hawaiian people whose sovereignty was extinguished by the American military in the nineteenth century. And it is that same military that threatens the safety of the world in the twenty-first century.

Now is the time to speak out and resist. And keep on resisting.

Depleted Uranium on Hawai'i Island
Koohan Paik

The Pohakuloa [Military] Training Area (PTA) is acknowledged by U.S. Army Lieutenant Colonel Dennis Owen to be located in an area that is habitat for the highest concentration of endangered species of any U.S. Army installation in the world. In addition, it is home to more than 150 historically important archeological sites. And it is about thirty miles *upwind* from the resorts, golf courses, and population centers of South Kona, on the Big Island.

Despite these facts, Air Force B-2 bombers fly every month from Guam to drop six 2,000-pound inert bombs on these ecologically important lands. Over seven million live rounds of ammunition are fired annually in live exercises here. PTA is also where a brigade of light Stryker tanks—the same as are used in Iraq—conduct live-fire practice. The means of transporting these Stryker tanks back and forth between O'ahu and the Big Island will soon be the Hawaii Superferry, as part of its long-planned, growing military engagement. The ammunition used by these tanks, and in the exercises at Pohakuloa, are *depleted uranium* shells.

Big Island residents are concerned that the bombing and the live-fire training could be deadly for the endangered species, and for themselves. There are great worries that trade winds are sweeping airborne particles of this toxic DU from the mountains to the coastal resorts of South Kona. Residents fear that their communities, wildlife, air, land, and water are being irreversibly contaminated.

In July 2008, the Big Island County Council passed a resolution, 8–1, to ask the Army to halt all B-2 practice bombing and all live firing exercises at Pohakuloa Training Area until the depleted uranium there can be found and removed. Although the County Council has no jurisdiction over controlling these war games, lawmakers nonetheless felt it was important to send a message to the Army that Hawai'i County is concerned about the effects of depleted uranium.

Gabriel Bissell, who said his sister's leukemia, now in remission, was caused by exposure to pulverized depleted uranium, testified, "If just one breath of this radioactive material is inhaled, that person is in serious danger of becoming ill."

Depleted uranium is attractive to military contractors because it is so cheap, often offered for free by the government. But there is nothing "depleted" about it. Misnamed, depleted uranium is actually what remains after enriched uranium (U-235), which is very dense and used for nuclear weapons and nuclear reactors, is separated from natural uranium. This is called an enrichment process. The radioactive byproduct is called uranium 238 (U-238), or *depleted* uranium. DU emits primarily alpha radiation, and its half-life is thought to be about the age of the Earth, or 4.5 billion years.

DU is approximately 2.5 times denser than iron and 1.7 times denser than lead, so the extremely dense DU shells easily penetrate steel armor and burn on impact. Firing the shells releases microscopic, radioactive, and toxic dust particles of uranium oxide that travel with the wind and can be inhaled or ingested. It also spreads contamination by seeping into the land and water.

According to the Uranium Medical Research Center, the long-term effects of uranium contamination are cancers and other radiation-related illnesses, including chronic fatigue syndrome, joint and muscle pain, neurological and/or nerve damage, infections, lung and kidney damage, vision problems, autoimmune deficiencies, and severe skin conditions. Other problems include miscarriages, maternal mortality, and genetic birth defects.

The full extent of radiation contamination at PTA and areas downwind is still unknown due to incomplete testing, poor military recordkeeping, and the vast size of PTA. However, the U.S. Army Garrison did confirm, on August 20, 2007, "the presence of depleted uranium (DU) in the impact area at the U.S. Army Garrison, Pohakuloa."

In addition to the live-fire Stryker training, the possibility of the monthly bombing kicking up the DU already settled in the soil is a grave concern to many Big Island residents. To assuage public worry, in March 2008, the Army moved the bombing range to areas with no history of DU firing practice.

Still, the Army has conducted no tests to determine the extent to which DU travels to other parts of the Big Island.

{ MILITARIZATION }

Chapter Seventeen

NO PEACE IN PARADISE: THE MILITARY PRESENCE IN THE HAWAIIAN ISLANDS

Kyle Kajihiro

KANAKA MAOLI[101] activist Kaleikoa Kaeo described the U.S. military in Hawai'i as a monstrous *he'e* (octopus), its head represented by the Pacific Command Headquarters; its eyes and ears the mountaintop telescopes, radar facilities, and underwater sensors; and its brain and nervous system the supercomputers and fiber optic networks that crisscross the islands. The tentacles of the he'e stretch from the west coast of North America to the east coast of Africa, from Alaska to Antarctica.

Today the enormity of the U.S. military presence in Hawai'i is staggering. According to the Department of Defense, the combined military branches in 2004 have 161 military installations in Hawai'i. The military controls 236,303 acres in Hawai'i, or 5.7 percent of the total land area. On O'ahu, the most densely populated island, the military controls 85,718 acres out of 382,148 acres, or 22.4 percent of the island. The military also controls vast stretches of ocean, including Defensive Sea Areas in Kane'ohe Bay, from Pearl Harbor to Koko Head, and off the west shore of Kaua'i. The entire Hawaiian archipelago is surrounded by 210,000 square miles of ocean military operating areas and 58,599 square miles of military special-use airspace.

This article, in a slightly different form, first appeared in the *Haleakala Times*, May 8, 2007. Reprinted by permission of the author.

[101] *Kanaka Maoli*: Native Hawaiian. Literally, "true man."

Including the 116,000 retired military personnel living in Hawai'i, the military population totals 217,030, or 17 percent of Hawai'i's total population. According to the 2000 U.S. Census, Hawai'i has the largest percent of its population in the military among the states.

Taking Land

The military land grab is a major source of conflict in Hawai'i. In 1898, the U.S. seized nearly 1.8 million acres of government and crown lands of the Kingdom of Hawai'i. These so-called *ceded lands* are held in a quasitrust status by the federal government and the state. In 1959, when the United States approved Hawai'i's admission as a state, the military retained control of approximately 180,000 acres of the ceded lands, while the rest reverted to the state as trustee. Approximately 30,000 acres of the land returned to the state were simultaneously leased back to the military for sixty-five years. In most cases, the rent paid by the military was a token one dollar for the term of the lease. Today, more than 112,173 acres, or roughly 54 percent of military-controlled land in Hawai'i, consists of the former government and crown lands of the Hawaiian nation. During World War II, other private parcels of land were seized by the federal government to further its war aims.

Threats to the Cultural Survival of the Kanaka Maoli

The displacement of Kanaka Maoli from their ancestral lands has resulted in the loss of subsistence and cultural resources. The cultural conflict over 'aina (land) goes much deeper than a simple matter of property rights or land use. There is a fundamental contradiction between Kanaka Maoli and Western worldviews about the environment itself. In Kanaka Maoli cosmology, the 'aina is the ancestor of the people, the physical manifestation of the union between the gods Papahanaumoku ("Papa who gives birth to islands"), the earth mother, and Wakea, or the sky-father. As a living ancestor, the 'aina cannot be owned, sold, or defiled. By severing the genealogical ties between Kanaka Maoli and their 'aina, and by disrupting their ability to practice and transmit their culture to future generations, the military seizure of land continues to have profound impacts on the cultural survival of Kanaka Maoli. Military destruction of land is a form of violence against the people themselves.

Forced cultural assimilation of Kanaka Maoli has contributed to cultural disintegration. Statistics illustrate the legacy of this occupation: Kanaka Maoli have the highest rates of homelessness, poverty, disease, and crime in Hawai'i. They have the lowest educational achievement and life expectancy in Hawai'i. Kanaka Maoli make up 36.5 percent of persons incarcerated for felony charges (while comprising less than 20 percent of the population). In the century since the U.S. occupation began, the flood of settlers stripped Kanaka Maoli of their self-determination. The scenario resembles the population crises of other occupied nations like Tibet, East Timor, and Palestine. A combination of economic, cultural, and political pressures has pushed nearly one-third of Kanaka Maoli into diaspora.

By generating population transfer of U.S. nationals to Hawai'i, the military has also had a profound impact on Hawai'i's culture and political demographics. Between 1900 and 1950, migration to the Hawaiian Islands from the continental United States and its territories totaled 293,379. The current military-connected population of 17 percent, including dependents and veterans, has nearly eclipsed the Kanaka Maoli population of 239,655 or 19 percent of the total population.

Environmental Contamination

The U.S. military is arguably the largest industrial polluter in Hawai'i. The 2004 Defense Environmental Restoration Program report to Congress listed 798 military contamination sites at 108 installations in Hawai'i, 96 of which were contaminated with unexploded ordnance. Seven of the military contamination sites were considered Superfund sites. According to the Navy, the Pearl Harbor Naval Complex alone contains approximately 749 contaminated sites and is treated as a giant Superfund site. Even these numbers are low, because they do not include contaminated sites that have not yet been listed for cleanup responses. Military installations made up five of the top ten polluters in Hawai'i responsible for releasing persistent, bioaccumulative, and toxic (PBT) chemicals, which include lead, dioxins, mercury, and polycyclic aromatic compounds. Military contamination hazards include unexploded ordnance; various types of fuels and petroleum products; organic solvents, such as perchloroethylene and trichloroethylene; dioxins and PCB; explosives and propellants such as RDX, TNT, HMX, and perchlorate; heavy metals such as lead and mercury; napalm chemical weapons; and radioactive waste from nuclear-powered ships.

Cobalt-60, a radioactive waste product from nuclear-powered ships, has been found in sediment at Pearl Harbor. Between 1964 and 1978, some 4,843,000 gallons of low-level, radioactive waste were discharged into Pearl Harbor. A total of 2,189 steel drums containing radioactive waste were dumped into an ocean disposal area fifty-five miles from Hawai'i. The military recently disclosed that from 1941 to 1972 it had dumped more than 8,000 tons of chemical munitions, including blistering agents mustard gas and lewisite, in the shallow seas off O'ahu island.

Fishers have been burned when they accidentally raised this toxic catch. For many years, the military denied ever using depleted uranium in Hawai'i. However, in January 2006, activists forced the Army to admit the presence of depleted uranium contamination on O'ahu. Military contamination sites are concentrated in and pose the greatest threat to communities housing Kanaka Maoli, immigrant Asian and Pacific Islanders, and other low-income groups. Many Asians and Pacific Islanders subsist on fish and shellfish from Pearl Harbor's contaminated waters. The Wai'anae district, where a third of the land is occupied by military installations, has the largest concentration of Kanaka Maoli and some of the worst health, economic, and social statistics in Hawai'i. In the late 1980s, powerful Navy radio transmitters in Lualualei Valley were suspected to be the cause of a childhood leukemia cluster in the nearby Hawaiian Homestead.

Prostitution

As with other military base towns, prostitution in Hawai'i is fueled by the large military presence. During World War II, the military regulated prostitution in designated red-light districts. In recent years, prostitution has become more decentralized. A proliferation of strip clubs, massage parlors, escort services, and hostess bars, as well as street prostitution, caters to military, tourist, and local customers. One former prostitute estimated that in the Honolulu downtown area at least 60 percent of those seeking prostitutes were from the military, and in Wahiawa, near Schofield Barracks, she estimated that the percentage jumped to 70 to 80 percent. She recounted how she was strangled by a military client until she hit him and escaped. According to an agency that helps prostitutes get out of commercial sexual exploitation (CSE), Hawai'i is particularly susceptible to CSE and the trafficking of women and children due to the large tourism industry and military presence.

Threats to Native Ecosystems and Endangered Species

Hawai'i is considered the endangered species capital of the world. Because of its geographic isolation, unique species and ecosystems evolved in Hawai'i over millions of years. More than 1,100 species, which represents around 82 percent of all native species in Hawai'i, are endemic to the islands. Military training activities threaten native ecosystems with fires, erosion, the alteration of habitats, and the introduction of alien species. Makua Valley, for instance, where the military has conducted live-fire training for more than seventy years, is home to over forty endangered species. More than 270 military fires over the last ten years have destroyed most of Makua's dryland forests except for the highest ridgelines.

Militarization of Youth

Hawai'i has historically had a high rate of military recruitment. In 2006, Hawai'i ranked 13th among states in the number of Army recruits per 1,000 youth. Military recruiters have targeted low-income communities of color where youths lack educational and career opportunities and are especially vulnerable to the economic enticements offered by recruiters. Military recruiters now have unprecedented access to students through the military recruiter access provisions and student personal information disclosure requirements of the federal No Child Left Behind Act. Furthermore, the Pentagon has hired private data-mining companies to compile a database on students. In Hawai'i, the militarization of youth through Reserve Officer Training Corps (ROTC) programs, the proliferation of military imagery in popular culture, and aggressive recruitment practices have also functioned to accelerate the assimilation and Americanization of local populations. In the 1920s, Commanding General Charles Summerall of the Army Hawaiian Department created Hawai'i's second ROTC unit at McKinley High School, which was, at the time, nicknamed "Little Tokyo" for its predominantly Japanese student body. Summerall wrote, "There is no better way of securing the loyalty of such people than to incorporate them in our military forces."

Economic Dependency

Hawai'i's extreme dependency on military spending has distorted the social, environmental, and cultural priorities of policymakers, a condition some liken to an addiction. Since September 11, 2001, U.S. military spending in Hawai'i has increased even further, and, as a result, military expenditures—the second largest industry in Hawai'i behind tourism—reached $4.5 billion in 2003, a 13 percent increase over the previous year. In 2003, Hawai'i ranked second in the United States, with $2,566 in per-capita defense spending, behind only Virginia, home of the Pentagon, where the U.S. Department of Defense is headquartered. The high rate of federal spending in Hawai'i has boosted industries, like construction, that have been detrimental to the preservation of cultural sites and natural resources. Housing subsidies for military personnel are indexed to market values, which tends to inflate the cost of housing, thus exacerbating homelessness. Military personnel in Hawai'i do not pay state income taxes. So the costs of their public services are subsidized by local residents. This adds particular strains on the public school system, which depends on state general funds. Federal Impact Aid, which is supposed to offset the cost of providing services for military families, covers only one-tenth of the actual cost of educating military children.

Past Resistance to Militarization in Hawai'i

Kaho'olawe: Measuring approximately 128,800 acres, Kaho'olawe is the smallest of the eight major islands in the Hawaiian archipelago. The island is sacred to Kanaka Maoli as an embodiment of the sea god Kanaloa. Kaho'olawe was also key to Polynesian navigation and settlement of Hawai'i. Kaho'olawe contains some of the richest cultural sites in Hawai'i.

Originally part of the government lands of the Hawaiian Kingdom, the U.S. Navy seized the entire island for target practice on December 8, 1941. In 1976, the Protect Kaho'olawe 'Ohana movement launched the first of several rescue landings on Kaho'olawe to protest the bombing. After years of direct action, demonstrations, and lawsuits, President George H. W. Bush stopped the bombing in 1990. A sum of $400 million was appropriated for the cleanup of unexploded ordnance and the restoration of the cultural sites and native ecosystems, but the Navy failed to clean up the island to its stated goals. Instead, only one-tenth of the island is now safe for human use. The movement to protect Kaho'olawe was seminal to the Hawaiian cultural renaissance, the emergence of the contemporary Hawaiian sovereignty movement, and other demilitarization struggles.

Makua Valley: The Kaho'olawe movement helped to inspire resistance to the Army in Makua Valley on the west end of O'ahu. The name *makua* means "parents." It is believed to be one of the places where Papa and Wakea came together to create life on Earth. Makua has been used as a military training area since 1929. In 1942, the remaining residents of Makua were forcibly evicted by the military. Their homes and a church were used as targets. All types of munitions have been fired and disposed of in Makua. As a result the valley is littered with unexploded ordnance and toxic chemicals. The rich cultural sites and native forest have been destroyed or seriously damaged. Since the 1970s, Kanaka Maoli have fought for the cleanup and return of Makua Valley. The struggle continues today as the Army pushes for expanded training in Makua.

Halawa Valley/H-3 Freeway: The H-3 Freeway project was conceived in 1963 as a defense highway to connect the Marine Corps base in Kane'ohe with Pearl Harbor. When activists successfully asserted cultural and historic preservation laws to block the freeway from passing through Moanalua Valley, the project was rerouted through Halawa Valley. Despite initial successes at challenging the new route, activists were trumped by Senator Daniel Inouye, who introduced legislation that exempted the H-3 project from applicable environmental laws. The Halawa Coalition, led by Kanaka Maoli women, occupied the Hale-o-Papa Heiau, a women's temple in the path of the freeway, from April 1992 until their arrest in August of that year. Hale-o-Papa was saved, but other sacred sites were destroyed. After a thirty-seven-year struggle, the H-3 was completed at a cost of $1.3 billion, or $80 million a mile, the most expensive roadway ever built.

Nohili/Pacific Missile Range Facility: In the early 1990s, a coalition of Native Hawaiian and environmental organizations mobilized to block the Army Strategic Target System (STARS) missile launches at the Pacific Missile Range Facility (PMRF) on Kauaʻi. At issue were Kanaka Maoli burial sites in the sand dunes of Nohili, endangered species, and contamination and accidents from the missiles. Thirty-five protesters were arrested for civil disobedience during the first two missile launches. Although President Bill Clinton defunded the STARS program in 1996, new threats emerged as PMRF's capabilities were expanded and as work on missile defense programs later accelerated under President George W. Bush. Post–September 11 security measures have blocked cultural, subsistence, and recreational access to beaches at Nohili and have sparked new activism. The Navy is expanding ocean training maneuvers and intensifying its use of sonar, which would be extremely dangerous to marine mammals.

Waikane Valley: Located in windward Oʻahu, Waikane Valley contains many Kanaka Maoli sacred sites and traditional agricultural production. During World War II, the military leased 1,061 acres in Waikane and adjoining Waiʻahole for maneuver and live-fire training until 1976. The Kamaka family, which owned 187 acres of the most heavily impacted areas, asked the Marines to clean up the unexploded ordnance as stipulated in the original lease. Instead, the Marine Corps condemned the parcel, over the objections of the Kamaka family. In 2003, the Marine Corps announced plans to conduct "jungle warfare" training in Waikane as part of its war on terrorism in the southern Philippines. This triggered strong protest from the community. In a public meeting held in March 2003, the community demanded that the Marine Corps clean up and return the Kamaka family lands in Waikane. Another important development was the solidarity from Filipinos/Kanaka Maoli youth protest against a Marine Corps amphibious landing at Bellows Air Force Base in Waimanalo. Many of those living in Hawai'i challenged U.S. intervention in the Philippines as well as the training in Waikane. The Marines eventually cancelled their plans for training in Waikane, citing safety concerns, but they have not cleaned up the unexploded ordnance.

Pohakuloa: Located on the island of Hawai'i, Pohakuloa is a vast plain of lava fields and native dryland forest situated on the saddle between three sacred mountains: Mauna Kea, Mauna Loa, and Hualalai. Established in 1956, the Pohakuloa Training Area (PTA) encompasses 116,341 acres, of which 84,815 acres are ceded lands.

PTA is the largest U.S. military training outside of the continental United States. Although thousands of cultural sites have been identified within the PTA, the range is used for all types of live-fire training. PTA is the home to twenty-one endangered plant and animal species. With the recent expansion of the training area by 23,000 acres, Pohakuloa has again become a focus of resistance.

Current Military Expansion Threats

The U.S. strategic rivalry with China, hostility toward North Korea, the second-front war on terrorism in Southeast Asia, and the realignment of U.S. military forces and bases in East Asia have all created added pressures to militarize Hawai'i.

Stryker Brigade

The Army has recently stationed a Stryker Brigade Combat Team (SBCT) in Hawai'i, comprising 328 Stryker vehicles, 800 additional soldiers and their dependents, and 28 construction projects to upgrade training, maintenance, and housing facilities. One reporter called it "the biggest Army construction project in Hawai'i since World War II."

Strykers are twenty-ton, light-armored combat vehicles designed for rapid deployment and suppression of urban unrest. They are stationed in Hawai'i, along with a new squadron of C-17 cargo aircraft and new high-speed attack ships to provide transport for the brigade.

The Army has recently seized an additional 25,000 acres of land—1,400 acres in central and northern Oʻahu and 23,000 acres adjacent to the Pohakuloa Training Area on Hawaiʻi Island. The extent of the Strykers' impact will stretch the entire length of the North Shore of Oʻahu. On Hawaiʻi Island, the Stryker trail would go from the port at Kawaihae on the western flank of Mauna Kea to the Pohakuloa Training Area. Hawaii Superferry will likely be the transport vehicle for the Strykers between Oʻahu and the Big Island.

Despite the discovery of numerous hazardous chemicals from live-fire training, proposed munitions use in Hawaiʻi would increase by 25 percent. The Army's own studies concluded that cultural sites will be destroyed and that there will be serious impacts due to fire, erosion, and other environmental damage.

The adequacy of the Stryker Brigade Environmental Impact Statement (EIS) was challenged in court by three Kanaka Maoli organizations. An appeals court ruled that the Army violated the National Environmental Policy Act by failing to consider reasonable alternatives to the Stryker Brigade in Hawaiʻi. While this procedural victory temporarily delayed construction on Stryker Brigade projects in Hawaiʻi and forced the Army to study alternative sites in Alaska and Colorado in a supplemental EIS, the Army hastily prepared a second EIS and in April 2008 issued its decision to proceed with stationing of the SBCT in Hawaiʻi.

Navy University Affiliated Research Center

The University of Hawaiʻi (UH) administration wants to establish a Navy University Affiliated Research Center (UARC) at UH. The proposed center would conduct Navy weapons-related research, including development and testing of various components of the "Star Wars" missile defense program and other advanced military research programs. This would have harmful impacts on Mauna Kea and Haleakala, where astronomy and astrophysics research is conducted, and on the sand dunes of Nohili and the oceans off the north shore of Kauaʻi, where missile launches as well as undersea warfare and sonar experiments are conducted. A coalition of students, faculty, and community members launched a series of actions to protest the UARC, which culminated in a week-long occupation of the UH president's office demanding cancellation of the UARC. The UH administration has continued to pursue the UARC, but contract negotiations have been delayed due to the continued protests. In 2008, the UH board of regents voted to approve a UARC contract over strong student and faculty objections.

Strategic Defense Initiative

Hawai'i has been used to test a number of missile defense programs, including the Ground-Based Midcourse Defense, the Aegis Missile Defense, and Theater High-Altitude Area Defense programs. U.S. officials have continuously demonized North Korea as an *axis of evil* country that poses a threat to Hawai'i, to generate fear and justify the expansion of these missile defense programs.

Facilities for the Strategic Defense Initiative (SDI)—popularly known as the Star Wars Defense—span the island chain: the Pacific Missile Range Facility in Nohili; radar tracking stations at Koke'e, Makaha Ridge, and Ka'ena Point; the Air Force Optical Tracking Station on Haleakala; and the supercomputer in Kihei, Maui. Lasers are tested on Haleakala. Target missiles are launched from Kaua'i.

Aircraft Carrier Strike Group

One of the largest militarization threats facing Hawai'i is the proposal to homeport an aircraft carrier strike group in either Hawai'i or Guam. A carrier strike group would include a nuclear-powered aircraft carrier, a cruiser, two destroyers, an attack submarine, and a fast combat-support ship and aircraft. In addition to the 3,000 officers and crew of the carrier, the air wing alone would bring 2,600 persons. Overall, the carrier strike group could increase Hawai'i's population by as many as 20,000 military personnel and family members. Because Pearl Harbor is not large enough to homeport an aircraft carrier, major dredging and construction would be required, causing adverse environmental impacts. Due to the insufficient air base facilities to house the fighter air wing, politicians have offered to turn back to the military the recently closed and transferred Barber's Point Naval Air Station. The final decision will be made in the near future.

Ku'e:[105] Current Resistance to Militarization

DMZ-Hawai'i/Aloha 'Aina is a network of organizations and individuals working to demilitarize and reverse the negative impacts of the enormous military presence in Hawai'i. The network was conceived at the Rethinking Militarism in Hawai'i Conference in 2000, organized by American Friends Service Committee, which brought together activists representing various movements and communities in Hawai'i, as well as international resource people. The DMZ-Hawai'i/Aloha 'Aina network united environmental, peace, antinuclear, women's, religious, and Kanaka Maoli sovereignty and independence groups for the common purpose of demilitarization.

The acronym *DMZ* stands for Demilitarized Zone, a term reclaimed from its usual military context. Aloha 'Aina expresses the core Kanaka Maoli value of love for the land, and places Hawaiian cultural and political struggle at the center of this diverse grouping.

The main campaigns of DMZ-Hawai'i/Aloha 'Aina are: opposing the Stryker Brigade, opposing the Navy UARC at the University of Hawai'i, and supporting the struggle for the cleanup and return of Makua Valley. Actions have included pickets, marches, civil disobedience, lawsuits, and Kanaka Maoli cultural forms of resistance.

---

[105] *Ku'e*: resistance.

[MILITARIZATION]

Chapter Eighteen

Radio Interview with Austal Workers

Katy Rose, Jimmy Trujillo, and Jonathan Jay

ON APRIL 10, 2008, *Kaua'i Community Radio (KKCR) conducted a live phone interview with employees of Austal USA, the builder of the* Alakai, *in Mobile, Alabama. During the course of the interview with Swan Cleveland (a union organizer), Carolyn Slay (a former Austal worker), and Wayne Jenkins (a current Austal worker), Jenkins, a welder at Austal, echoes the point of Chapter 15, "How Not to Build a Navy Ship." He states that in Austal's rush to compete for a big Navy contract, the shipbuilder is compromising quality in workmanship. At the time of the interview, Jenkins was working on the second Superferry vessel (he had been on leave for the building of the* Alakai, *the first Superferry). The interview, from which these excerpts were taken, was conducted by Katy Rose, Jimmy Trujillo, and Jonathan Jay. [Eds.]*

KKCR: *What can you tell us about the* Alakai's *construction and the recent damage to the hull that was repaired?*

WAYNE JENKINS: I am a first-class welder at Austal. And I had problems with how some of the welds were being done on the boat, so I mentioned it to a supervisor and they told me that the welds didn't have to look that good because everything was getting covered up with insulation. When you stop welding aluminum, it would leave a little crack. Instead of people taking the time and cutting that little crack out and straightening it up, they would clean over the top to cover that crack up. So that crack is always going to be there. It's gonna continue cracking.

There's a lot I've seen personally, where they've let second-class people weld x-ray butts that are not certified. I've seen fitters who are not certified to weld at all, weld x-ray butts. I've mentioned something about it, but there was nothing ever done about it.

KKCR: *Do you think that that could have led to any of the structural failures or some of the damages that occurred to the Alakai that occurred while it was in transit between Maui and Oʻahu?*

JENKINS: In my opinion, I think it led to every bit of it, because they've got people welding stuff who are not properly trained, and it's caused a lot of problems. The sister ship is going to have just as much if not more problems than the ship y'all have over there right now… *[Jenkins later describes an "x-ray butt":]* Two pieces of plate welded together. What they do is, it's just like x-raying your bones in your body. They take your film and they see all the way through the weld. If there's any kind of impurities or "hull trash," this shows up; it's just like a crack in your bone.

They covered up the little hairline crack. Well, the hairline crack, in stress—the boat's under a lot of stress in the water—that little crack will crack all the way through.

KKCR: *Does this pose a safety problem for passengers and crew?*

JENKINS: Yes, ma'am. It causes a lot of life-threatening situations, in the right place. Like the boat that just got worked on over there, I heard cracked, and they drove it for a week. And they took it and poured concrete down there to stop the crack, the leaking of the water. If it cracked enough, it'd sink the ship and everybody on it. It can lose lives.

KKCR: *So let me clarify this. You're [saying] the* Alakai, *the Hawaii Superferry, was in service for a week with a cracked hull. Is that what you're saying?*

JENKINS: Yes, ma'am. That's what we were told over here. They poured concrete down there to stop the leak and run it for a week before people went over there and worked on it.

KKCR: *And that was because the Coast Guard, during one of their inspections, noticed that the cracks were not just staying the same size but were growing and became irreparable. And concrete patching—it just wasn't going to work?*

JENKINS: No, concrete patching, all it does, it gets into where the crack is, and it'll stop the water, but the initial crack will keep going. The concrete does not stop it; it just keeps the water from coming in—to a certain point. And then, when the crack gets bigger, then the concrete's not there to fill it up, so it's going to continue bringing in water.

KKCR: *Why are they trying to cut corners? Why are they leaning on employees? Why are they treating people unfairly? They're not making any friends doing that and they're not making a quality boat, either. So, what's the benefit?*

SWAN CLEVELAND: For them, I feel like their biggest benefit right now is the U.S. Navy ship that they're working on. It seems as though they're casting everything else aside to complete this project for the U.S. Navy, because they want those other fifty-five warships to be built here in Mobile. *(NOTE: Cleveland is speaking of the Littoral Combat Ship, or LCS. Austal has teamed with General Dynamics and is competing against Lockheed to produce the winning LCS prototype design.)*

KKCR: *That's the big contract that they're looking for.*

CLEVELAND: That's correct.

KKCR: *How much money are we talking about there, with fifty-five warships?*

CLEVELAND: Well, initially, it was supposed to have been a cost of about $233 million per ship. That cost has risen now on this prototype that they're building now to over $500 million. So they're trying to cut every corner they can.

KKCR: *Have either of you heard about military use for the Superferry? Was there talk of it being a military prototype, or do you recall any Navy visits during construction, or anything along those lines?*

JENKINS: Yes, ma'am. We had a conference with Bob Browning, who is the CEO. They said we're trying to build it to a spec where if they needed them, that it could carry so many tanks, personnel to wherever they have to be. But they *have* talked about trying to use the ferries for U.S. military.

KKCR: *I don't know much about boat building. But if I was going to buy a truck, I'd know a little bit about that truck, and I'd know if it was in a wreck and the frame was bent, that's the truck I'm going to avoid buying. Is this somewhat similar—if there's a vessel that large and that important with cargo and our precious families, are we talking about significant risks for those passengers?*

JENKINS: Yes, sir. And like I say, in the past, they fixed—they're gonna fix it to the minimum, and it is very dangerous for people to be on the ship. Because there're certain spots that are going to be on there that are not going to be fixed. And like I say, they're covering up everything with insulation. So, to better view it, they would have to take in one room of the compartment. They would have to pull the insulation completely out of the room to check for the damages that would be in that place. And the short time that they'd been over there, they did not have enough time, in my opinion, to assess the problem and take care of it the way it should have been.

CLEVELAND: Here's something I'm not sure anyone's aware of over there. On the LCS, actually, General Dynamics, who owns Bath Iron Works in Maine, is the lead contractor on the LCS. They have 70 union machinists working in Austal as we speak to do the work on the LCS that General Dynamics is slated to do. We thought it was really funny that Austal would partner with a union contractor to do the work on that LCS, but not want their employees to have the same benefits. ... Training at Austal is actually a joke, in my opinion. They use the Alabama Industrial Training Board to help train the people that they hire in there. They send them through a ten-week course, and then they bring them in there to weld on a doggone ship that is going to be serving our military as well as our commercial passengers. And they're not qualified to do the work.

KKCR: *Given the thickness of the aluminum hull—and I'd like to know what that thickness is—what kind of collision do you think the aluminum hull could withstand?*

JENKINS: The bottom half of the aluminum hull is probably a half-inch thick, and the higher it goes, the thinner it gets. If you know anything about metal, aluminum is one of the lightest materials that there is. If it's done right, it can be strong. But in a collision—it depends on how big of a collision it is—it's like taking an aluminum Coke can and squishing it. It's about the same difference. The roundness of it keeps it good and sturdy, but enough pressure can collapse it.

I'm going to tell you my past experience working with a steel shipyard. We had a cruise ship come in, and the bottom of the steel was probably one inch thick, and it collided with a coral reef. And it looked like you took a can opener and opened it up. That's how bad it damaged the bottom of the ship.

KKCR: *Just peeled it away?*

JENKINS: Yes, sir. And that was a steel ship. Depending on how big the debris is in the water, if you hit the aluminum, yes sir, it can give some major destruction to it.

KKCR: *And so if it did strike a whale, the whale would probably suffer some pretty significant damage and the Superferry as well.*

JENKINS: Yes, sir, because the Superferry is supposed to run between 40 and 46 miles an hour on water, so at that high rate of speed, it's like hitting a large animal with your car. It's going to destroy pretty much what it hits, and as in a whale, it will kill him if not cut him in half.

* * *

Only days after the broadcast of the above interview, Wayne Jenkins lost his job at Austal USA. Comments started appearing on Internet blogs attempting to further undermine Jenkins, claiming that his status as a "disgruntled worker" destroyed any credibility he might have had.

However, Jenkins's allegations were corroborated by an earlier report conducted by the U.S. Navy, no less, on Austal's faulty work at the same shipyard. In August 2007, Sean Reilly had reported for the Newhouse News Service *that the Navy, in corrective action reports filed between May 2005 and May 2007, listed botched welds and employees doing work on a Littoral Combat Ship for which they were not qualified.*

Austal's own inspector also found problems during manufacturing. Kristin Hashimoto, of the Big Island Weekly, *reported on May 1, 2008, that Teresa Hart, a certified "level two" inspector specializing in ultrasonics, and magnetic particle and liquid penetrants, was hired by Austal to provide "quality assurance" (even though there was no quality assurance department). Hart said, "Even when they were trying to hire me, they told me they didn't want a quality assurance department or manager."*

Hart noticed problems with some of the Alakai's *welds while it was under construction. They "just weren't right," she said. "… [T]here were welds missing, that's a pretty big deal, and I thought, well, surely they'll bring somebody in and they'll catch it. It's never normal to miss a weld." Hart told a supervisor about them at the time but was told that her work was restricted to another ship. As her clamors about quality control grew louder, she was terminated in March 2007, five months after she was first brought onboard. "They told me I wasn't a team player," said Hart. [Eds.]*

Governor Lingle *President Bush*

Epilogue and Afterthoughts

Koohan Paik and Jerry Mander

1. Do We Hate Ferries?

WE WERE REPEATEDLY ASKED this question during the year we worked on this book. Let's clarify the point: We *don't* hate ferries. Actually, we quite *love* ferries. One of us (Jerry) grew up with the Staten Island Ferry, which he continues to ride when in New York. We both also love the ferry that runs past Alcatraz from San Francisco to Marin County and use it often, and even the one across the bay to Oakland whenever we have the chance. We love the ferry from Seattle to Bainbridge Island, and the ferries from Vancouver through the small islands north of there. We love the ferries of Venice, of Ireland, and the overnight ferry from Naples to the Aeolian Islands, as well as the small ferries *among* those islands and also the nearby Greek islands. Ferries bring you close to nature and the sea, they are great for people-watching, they are indeed neighborly, you can relax and talk, and you can eat and drink—unless you run into a bad sea, which happens a fair amount in Hawai'i—and then there's this most outstanding fact: You don't have to get on an airplane, which we *do* hate!

We even love the concept of ferries connecting the Hawaiian Islands and, like everyone we know, had a positive reaction to the idea when we first heard about the Superferry. But then, we learned the rest of the story (which you have just read) and realized that the central problem with this project was that it was created to serve some *other* causes—profit for absentee owners, political ambitions for local politicians, militaristic visions—and it had little or nothing to do with the needs of local communities, sustainable economies, or environmental concerns of the more ecologically intact outer islands. The corporation's oft-stated concern for the community never rose above public relations. The people of the islands were never asked whether they wanted it and were never listened to when they tried to make their views known about the size and scale of the operation or environmental concerns.

This was not the neighborly experience—connecting islands and bringing people closer—that most ferries in the world actually provide. This one in Hawai'i is utterly out of scale for its stated purposes, and it has been introduced and operated with extreme disdain for the views of people on the islands.

As for costs, any boat that uses 12,000 gallons of fuel on a round trip will certainly need to raise prices eventually, and probably repeatedly, to cover the rapidly rising costs of fuel. The company can only sell bargain tickets at a loss for so long. This is a commercial enterprise; eventually, ticket prices could be on par with Hawaiian Airlines, if not higher.

In our opinion, an interisland ferry in Hawai'i should probably be operated as a public utility, like the bus service or the water department, to ensure that the welfare of the people in the islands and the protection of the wildlife on land and in the sea are at the top of the list of priorities, not an afterthought. It should be run by the state, as are almost all the ferries listed above, so its purpose would remain clear—not primarily as a business to make a huge profit, but instead to provide a useful service, while doing no harm. That way, those cut-rate fares could remain.

Let's remember, it is not as if Hawai'i taxpayers are not *already* substantially paying for the Superferry, a private business that has been beneficiary of a wide variety of state services. As Maui Tomorrow Executive Director Irene Bowie pointed out at the August 2008 Oversight Task Force meeting, state moneys have funded much more than just the $40 million in changes to accommodate the ferry at all four harbors. Citizens' dollars have also been spent on: *1)* numerous legislative attempts to pass bills that would override the DOT's exemption of environmental review; *2)* at least 12 DOT public meetings to receive input that an environmental review would have evaluated; *3)* purchase of land at Kahului Harbor to accommodate the ferry's need for wharf space; *4)* relocation of other shipping companies at Kahului Harbor; *5)* the special meeting of the Environmental Council to review the DOT exemption decision; *6)* expenses involved with the multiple citizen lawsuits against the DOT and their ongoing appeals (including the Attorney General's defense efforts, in several lower courts and in the State Supreme Court, plus the court-ordered payments to the citizens who brought the court cases and won at the Supreme Court); *7)* Governor Lingle's expenditures in composing her "Unified Command"— payment to various state departments, the Coast Guard, and the Kauaʻi Police Department; *8)* the special legislative session to pass Act 2; *9)* the yearlong operations of the Act 2-mandated Oversight Task Force; *10)* preparation of the Act 2-mandated "rapid risk assessment" (a "substitute" EIS to serve as a stand-in until Belt Collins concludes its own EIS); *11)* preparation of the Belt Collins "EIS;" *12)* preparation of the state auditor's investigation on why the administration exempted Superferry from doing an EIS; *13)* daily tugboat service at Kahului Harbor; *14)* inspectors from the Department of Agriculture, and of Land and Natural Resources, to screen vehicles and monitor ferry employees' screening; and *15)* projected costs for Big Island operations anticipated to begin in 2009.

And, should the project eventually fail, *that* would activate the unconscionable $140 million loan guarantee from MARAD, leaving U.S. taxpayers *everywhere* to foot the bill. So much for free enterprise.

If the boat is eventually picked up by the military in some capacity—as we think it eventually will be, perhaps sooner rather than later, judging by all the military-required features it is installing on its second ship, the *Koa*, before it gets into the water—then all those infamous, expensive harbor improvements pushed by Governor Lingle will have been wasted, and Hawaiʻi's taxpayers will be holding the bag on that. Then you have the massive costs of additional public services to handle overflow tourism and the pollution impacts to the parks, beaches, and water. Already, panicked Maui residents are fearing extinction of certain species, in the wake of inspections that revealed that, each month during the summer of 2008, hundreds of pounds of seaweed and reef fish had been plundered by Superferry riders.[106] Add all that up, and it is far from certain that a commercial ferry service like Superferry is less expensive for the state than a smaller-scale ferry service run by a government agency.

---

[106] For details, see Superferry Oversight Task Force reports at *http://hawaii.gov/dot/harbors/hawaii-inter-island-large-capacity-ferry-vessel-oversight-task-force.*

But, let's say most people would rather the ferry continue to be privately owned and operated. Then, please, let's at least try to keep the ownership *local*—not an absentee owner from New York, 6,000 miles away—so there is a degree of local accountability beyond only in monetary terms. We must *never*, ever again let a private owner of a public service tell us he can't slow the boat down in whale calving grounds because it will affect anticipated profits, as was publicly repeated by John Garibaldi, among others, on many occasions. How *disgraceful* that they continue to get away with that, and that the governor backs them!

If the Hawai'i ferry was not constructed to make large-scale profit, it could probably better serve the real needs of the local people, as well as tourists and small businesses. Without the necessity to achieve such high revenues and without military contracts in view, the boats would be built *smaller* and run *slower*. As indicated, operators would be required to slow down to acceptable speeds in wildlife zones, or steer clear of them entirely, instead of refusing to do so, as now. And the boat would not need four giant jet engines using 6,000 gallons of marine diesel per run. Perhaps it could be modeled on New York Harbor's Circle Line ferry, which is a solar- and wind-powered electric hybrid ship that transports up to 600 passengers.

We also believe that a Hawai'i interisland ferry should *not* carry private cars. Most of the Hawaiian islands are already choking from cars, especially the outer islands, which are far too small to handle them. (This is true even of the Big Island, which isn't so small. But there is no place to expand the existing road system that would not be environmentally devastating.) One *could* make a case for the transport of small visitor buses, or small trucks—for those small farmers the Superferry disingenuously hawked. But more private cars? We don't think so, especially not on tiny islands like Kaua'i. We cannot keep supporting the fantasy that there can be more and more visitors to these islands, more and more cars, more and more growth. These are *islands*. We are killing them. If tourists do come, as they will, there need to be better ways of arranging their transportation, with some combination of public transport services, just as is accomplished with great success on many other islands in the world—hotel shuttles, small buses between attractions, jitney services, car-share programs, bike-share programs, as well as rental cars when necessary. Such a combination would not have nearly the environmental impact as the arrival of 200 *added* cars rolling off a boat every day, or twice per day.

But most important, all such decisions—about how and whether to even try to accommodate more tourism, or whether to have a ferry service at all—and all decisions about its construction, and how it operates, should be consciously made by the people of each of the islands served by it. *And nothing at all should happen* before all issues of wildlife impact, effects on shorelines and coral reefs, and effects on rural culture and agriculture are vetted by a thorough Environmental Impact Statement, of at least equal intention and strength as the standards set by the National Environmental Policy Act and the corresponding Hawai'i act. The so-called EIS mandated by Act 2 is a farce: yet another grim fraud on the people. We hope that current lawsuits will eventually stop the Superferry from continuing to operate until it can meet strict environmental standards. On the other hand, there are some who believe it could never pass a proper EIS anyway, a further explanation for the intense resistance of the company to do any environmental review at all.

2. THE VILLAIN OF THE PIECE

After a year of working on this project, we are left with a few indelible impressions and some questions. The single most vivid impression has to do with the appalling cynicism, arrogance, and self-interested behavior of Governor Linda Lingle. As far as we are concerned, she is the villain of the piece, far more so than the Superferry company, or any federal or state government agency officials or Secretary Mineta or Senator Inouye or former director of the Hawaii DOT Fukunaga—all of whom behaved extremely poorly. More even than John F. Lehman, despite his indifference to local values, his absentee string-pulling, his military adventurism, and his well-known right-wing instincts. John Lehman and his business, J. F. Lehman and Co., and their Hawaii Superferry were, after all, just doing what corporations do. They try to further the institution above all other values; they try to get around laws that stand in their way; they try to get government agencies to help them rather than regulate them; they try to make more money; and they try to tie all their interests together, in this case into a military package. Corporations and corporate actors are not motivated by morals or public interest; they are intrinsically amoral. Only profits matter. Lehman is a classical capitalist, albeit one with far too much access and influence in high places. But, in the end, he is only doing his thing. He did what he was supposed to do—though he should never have had the opportunities in the first place.

Linda Lingle, by contrast, didn't have to turn out this way. Government officials are not inherently motivated to put corporate profits first. She is an elected public official. We put our trust in public officials, though they often later turn against us. Her early years showed signs of an intelligence and progressive spirit that promised better things for her (and our) future. We have never met her, yet it is clear enough to us that she abandoned her concern for the public because of a combination of her growing right-wing Republican ideology—that business growth is far more important than democratic process, environmental sustainability, or anything else—and because of personal ambition.

For Lingle, the Superferry's advent coincided with her first years in office. It presented her with an unusual opportunity to quickly expand her Washington, D.C., connections and options, especially with powerful Republicans. She had already obsequiously called President Bush "the greatest president ever."[107] And suddenly a stupendously "lucky" break floated into her lap: a close business and personal relationship with John F. Lehman. A key figure in the John McCain campaign, and close to many other very prominent figures in Washington, Lehman was the perfect *insider* for whom Lingle could now do big favors; it meant a lot more for her future than making the people of the outer islands happy. And, aside from the campaign donations she received from the company, as mentioned earlier, she was suddenly front and center with John McCain, even introducing his running mate, Sarah Palin, at the 2008 Republican National Convention.

Was it any accident she was called on to sing the vice-presidential candidate's praises in the national media? In fact, one wonders how close Lingle herself may have gotten to actually *beating out* Palin for the nomination—Lingle's experience and story are almost identical: a few years as governor of a discontiguous state, after several terms as a feisty, small-town mayor—though Palin's Miss America-style

---

[107] Dave Shapiro, "State GOP is off and running," in *Honolulu Advertiser*, May 8, 2002.

allure might have been the final determining factor. One can now anticipate that Lingle will achieve a high position in a McCain administration, if he wins, and in any case that we will soon see much more of her on the national stage. Unless, that is, we can all somehow manage to broadcast, as widely as possible, the concealed aspects of the Hawaii Superferry story—how it was used as a stepping stone in her career, at the expense of her constituents, economic sustainability, the authority of the State Supreme Court, and the whales and myriad other creatures.

3. Unanswered Questions

As you have read, we went to considerable lengths to spell out all the apparent military possibilities that have been largely hidden by the HSF company and by Governor Lingle. Not only is there the highly likely interisland transport of Stryker vehicles and other military equipment and the efforts to have the *Koa* include a fold-out vehicle ramp, an onboard wastewater treatment plant, and water desalination facilities to match broad military standards, there is the much more elaborate tale of the efforts of the Superferry's builder and subordinate note holder, Austal USA. For Austal, the stakes are gigantic. By using virtually the same design as the Superferry, the company is potentially in line for billions of dollars in military contracts, as we have described. As a result, one subtheme of the whole story has been the crucial need to get the Superferry operational in order to demonstrate the viability of the boat's design. John Lehman's Superferry company and Linda Lingle have gone out of their way to avoid any legal processes—such as the irksome EIS requirement—that might keep the ship from running. But here's a question we never managed to answer in this book: *Why are they doing this?* It is obvious why Austal would want and need the boat to stay in the water. *But why is it so important to Lehman and the Superferry company?*

While working on this project we spent a fair amount of time looking for financial connections among Austal, the Superferry Corporation, and J. F. Lehman and Co. Do the latter two stand to benefit financially if Austal wins these prodigious contracts? As we go to press, we still don't know the answer to that. We do know that Lehman has bought a shipyard next door to Austal—and as we have mentioned, there is the theoretical possibility that, in the case of a contract, Austal would ask Lehman's new company, Atlantic Marine Holding Company, to participate in production aspects. There is also the possibility that some of Lehman's other military-related companies could gain contracts. These include Elgar Electronics, which manufactures electrical power test and measurement equipment for military and commercial uses, and Atlantic Inertial Systems, a leading niche supplier of highly engineered guidance, stabilization, and navigation products and systems for aircraft, weapons, and land systems applications. All the above certainly seem eligible for contracts, though we don't have evidence that they will get them.

Another possibility we mentioned in the book is that John Lehman is not trying to make more money but is simply a deep believer in his oft-expressed military visions for a vast, aggressive U.S. naval presence in the Pacific. This is what he stood for when he was Secretary of the Navy, and since. He believes in the very strong projection of U.S. military power in a region the United States has dominated for the last century, as Haunani-Kay Trask and Kyle Kajihiro have described in Chapters 16 and 17. It may simply be patriotism, by Lehman's understanding of it, and hopes for the fulfillment of his dreams—his little Superferry exploring the nooks and crannies of Pacific harbors in the cause of military superiority. Maybe he cares more about that than money. Time will tell.

4. The Spirit of Nawiliwili

In August 2008, the first anniversary of the Nawiliwili uprising, a small, informal reunion took place among some of the protesters from the previous year. It was a quiet affair: a picnic, a jam-making contest, a few reminiscences, and a little symbolic armada in the harbor.

It had been nearly a year since the Superferry announced that it had *abandoned* plans to continue service to Kaua'i. Some of the protesters initially took that as a "victory," believing that their success was permanent. Alas, this was a sign of just how spontaneous the original protests had been, among people unfamiliar with the rigor and reality of long-term environmental campaigns. So in the interim, there has been little effort to maintain the opposition fervor or continue to organize the citizens around it. In the meanwhile, however, the Superferry has hired a slick new CEO, Admiral Fargo, who has slowly been making contacts with business interests on Kaua'i and, with help from the right-wing local newspaper, has begun to push the cause of a return. On the very day of the anniversary of the triumph at Nawiliwili, the newspaper reported that Fargo was increasingly "talking story," as he put it, with Kaua'i citizens.

The handwriting is on the wall. To repeat what David Brower famously said, "There are no victories in environmental struggles, only holding actions." Corporations never give up. They just wait for things to quiet down and for attention to turn away. The people of Kaua'i are slowly becoming aware that they will again have to get organized, perhaps sooner rather than later, and begin reviving the "Spirit of Nawiliwili," as some call it. This time, the company will be better prepared for the opposition, as will the governor and the police, especially now that the federal court has upheld the Coast Guard's authority to enforce a security zone off-limits to protesters. Of course, there is also the likelihood that the ferry's supporters will be armed with a completed sham EIS prepared by Belt Collins under the phony conditions of Act 2. The only purpose of that entire exercise was to keep the boat running; as earlier chapters explained, Act 2 has been worded to ensure that there can be no environmental-impact finding that could threaten the boat's viability. The conclusion will be that it is okay to resume operations—yet another phony piece of the charade intended to vindicate the project.

The future quality of life in Hawai'i probably depends on whether the people of Kaua'i, Maui, the Big Island of Hawai'i, and the other outer islands can mount a continued resistance to all this pressure. On the Big Island, the boat's next targeted destination, citizens are already expressing concern about the grand scheme of military buildup, of which the Superferry is a small but vital part. In July 2008, the Hawai'i County Council passed a resolution by 8–1 to halt all B-2 practice bombing and all live firing exercises at Pohakuloa Training Area until the depleted uranium can be found and removed. Although the council has no authority over PTA, lawmakers nonetheless wanted to send a message to the Army that Hawai'i County is extremely concerned about the effects of depleted uranium.

Meanwhile, on October 14, the Hawai'i Supreme Court announced it would accept a legal challenge to the constitutionality of Act 2, which had passed at the urging of Governor Lingle, circumventing the earlier Supreme Court ruling demanding an

Environmental Impact Statement. This is a potentially very important development, and could threaten Superferry's continued service. The ruling is expected in early 2009.

Then on October 28, Admiral Fargo suddenly broke the news that Superferry was delaying the start of its service to the Big Island for a year, and seeking to lease the boat to either military or commercial operators in other locales. Fargo also indicated that Maui service would be cut back. He blamed the difficult economic times as not being propitious for building up a market for the launch of new services. However, many observers are speculating that the real financial crunch may be back in New York, at the offices of J. F. Lehman and Co., which, like most other major Wall Street enterprises, may be eager to convert commercially doubtful long-term investments into short-term cash and profit to get itself through the crisis. If so, then all of Governor Lingle's efforts on behalf of the corporation, including the expenditure of tens of millions of dollars of public tax monies, will have gone for naught. Once again, it becomes clear that if Hawai'i really needed a ferry service, that a *publicly*-owned, *non*profit, *slower* moving, environmentally sensitive ferry operation would have been the viable choice for any Hawai'i transport service—not a high-speed, cost-ineffective vessel privately operated by military investors 5,000 miles away (though that would not have helped Lingle's greater national ambitions). In any case, this is good news for the whales and sea turtles.

Perhaps these late developments will add needed time for Hawai'i's citizens to refocus on the kind of future they want: one infused with the rural, nature-based, traditional qualities for which the islands are famous, an embracing environment that has sustained the people so well, or one dominated by rapidly advancing commercialism, overcrowding, and rampant development—while suppressing the living Earth. It remains to be seen. As has been said many times, the price of democracy is eternal vigilance.

Koohan Paik Jerry Mander
Kilauea, Kaua'i *San Francisco, California*

October 30, 2008

Acknowledgments

IN CHINESE, the identical character means both "crisis" and "opportunity." In the case of the Hawaii Superferry, this correlation certainly proved true—on Kaua'i, in particular. Without the Superferry, the people of Kaua'i never would have had the rich opportunity to join together to create a powerful community, nor would communities of the neighbor islands have started forging alliances for this common cause.

Earlier in this book we cited some "heroes" of this struggle, and others who presented powerful public testimonies. Most of these people came into our lives as a direct result of the uprising at Nawiliwili. Without their involvement, the inspiration for this project would have never coalesced.

But there are also many others who have not yet been mentioned, but who have also inspired us, and have shown sincere support and friendship. Warm thanks to Fred Dente for his unflagging enthusiasm, and Marj Dente for making available to us her extensive newspaper archive. Thanks also to Aunty Nani Rogers for offering her invaluable thoughts on the text. Emmett Aluli and Davianna MacGregor gave us helpful guidance at an early stage, as did Liko Martin, and Uncle Abel Simeona and Simbra Kanaka'ole from Ka'u, on the Big Island. Mililani Trask contributed her mana'o about Hawai'i's political history. Kai and Maria Mander gave useful comments on the early texts, Natasha Murphy provided research help at key moments, and Miyoko Sakashita contributed legal advice.

Warm mahalo also to Andrew Cabebe, Peter and Mimi Buckley, Claire Hope Cummings, Caren Diamond, Ron Dixon, Sharon Goodwin, Claire Greensfelder, Sandra Herndon, Jim Huff, SH Jarvis, Terri Keko'olani, Cheryl Lovell-Obatake, Judie Lundborg, Tony Lydgate, Yari Mander, Hale Mawae, Wes Nisker, Ruth Paik, Aukai Peter, Janos Samu, Aunty Louise Sausen, Mary Sewell, Lee

Swenson, Jay Taylor, Anne Thurston, and Wendy Raebeck. Very special thanks also to Janet Ashkenazy, Nancy, and Boo-boo.

Of course, we are also indebted to the hundreds of people whose names we do not know, though we would recognize them if we saw them, and they would recognize us, from all the public hearings, the events at Nawiliwili, and the evening Governor Lingle visited. Mahalo to us all for giving each other strength.

We are so grateful to Mayumi Oda, for her information and support, and most of all for permission to reproduce her powerful painting on the cover of this book, celebrating the Hawaiian spirit. And finally, a big mahalo to our publisher, Arnie Kotler, for his keen insights, expansive energy, and Buddha heart.

E malama i ka ʻaina; e malama kekahi i kekahi.
Let us care for the land; let us care for each other.

Photographs

Introduction (page viii): *Honolulu Star-Bulletin*/Tom Finnegan

Part One (page 38): Carl Wright

Page 57: Carl Wright

Portraits in Chapter 4: Koohan Paik
Portrait of Pua Laʻa Norwood: Jonathan Jay
Portrait of Kalalea Kaʻuhane: Kamahalo Kaʻuhane

Page 116: © *iStockphoto.com*/Joy Powers

Part Two (page 126): Joe Martin

Part Three (page 206): *aapi.smugmug.com*/J. Hodson

Page 216: Canarias Conservación

Page 290: Reuters/Jason Reed

Index

Abercrombie, Neil, 176
ABN-Amro Bank, 151
acoustic buoys, 219
Act 2, special legislative session, 35, 107, 109, 178–179, 181–184, 193–194, 202, 204, 234–243, 293, 299-300
   Oversight Task Force, 192, 203
Administrative Procedures Act, 232
Aegis Missile Defense, 282
Aila, William, 119
Aipoalani, Dayne, 87, 165, 178
Air Force Optical Tracking Station, 282
aircraft carrier strike group, 282
Akaka, Daniel, 22, 176
Akaka, Moanikeala, 117
Alakai. *See* Hawaii Superferry
Albertini, Jim, 118
algae growth and bloom, 214
alien species, 97, 100–102, 153, 174, 276
   See also invasive species
aloha 'aina, 86-87
Aloha 'Aina organization, 283
Aloha Airlines, 196
aloha spirit, 46–47
American Classic Cruise Lines, 131
   See also U.S. Maritime Administration (MARAD), and Title XI of Merchant Marine Act
American Friends Service Committee, 53, 143–144, 283
Anderson, Michelle, 147
Apoliona, Haunani, 58
Arakawa, Alan, 147
Arinaga, Clayton, 57, 171
Army Strategic Target System (STARS), 279
asymmetric warfare, 258
ATA, 196
Atlantic Marine Holding Company, 15, 34, 157, 163, 248, 298
Atooi. *See* Polynesian Kingdom of Atooi
August, Joel, 153, 156-157, 158, 161-162, 185, 235
Austal USA
   confirmation of contract for Superferry design, 162–163
   Engineering Project of the Year Award, 195

   formal agreement with HSF, 134
   interview with workers, 196, 284–289
   Jenkins firing, 198, 288
   and Joint High Speed Vessel design contract, 191
   and *Koa*, 200
   launch of *Alakai*, 159
   launch of LCS *Independence*, 199
   lawsuit for racial discrimination against, 195, 196
   and Lehman's purchase of Atlantic Marine Holding Company, 15, 34, 157, 248, 298
   Lerchbacker's concerns about HSF costs and scale, 159–160, 253–254
   and origins of HSF, 9
   partnership with General Dynamics, 133, 135, 152, 255, 259, 262, 263
   and stop-work order, 183–184
   and winning bid for prototype of LCS, 152
'awa, 103
Awana, Bob, 17, 132, 142, 186, 190, 238

Bainbridge Island ferry, 113
Baker, Roz, 18, 181
banana republic, 6, 7, 130
Baptiste, Bryan, 57, 78, 82–83, 87, 171
Barber's Point Naval Air Station, 282
Barca, Nicolai, 89
barge at Kahului Harbor
   breaking, 185, 186, 190
   as means to avoid EIS, 141, 201
Bayonet Constitution, 265
Belt Collins and Environmental Assessment, 174–175
Belt Collins hearings (2008), 107–124, 195–196
   Hilo, 117–120
   Kaua'i, 108–117
   Kona, 120–121
   Moloka'i, 121–124
   overview, 107–108
Bernard, Hannah, 37, 209
Bikini, 32
Bissell, Gabriel, 270
Blake, Teddy, 185
Blank Rome LLC, 200

Bonaparte, Josephine, 80
Bowie, Irene, 227, 292
bow-mounted cameras, 212
Brice-O'Hara, Sally, 57, 171
Brosnan, Pierce, 23
Brower, Andrea Noelani, 67, 183
Brower, David, 27, 55, 299
Browning, Bob, 254, 287
Brownlee, Les, 138
Buchanan, Laurie, 124
Bush, George H. W., 268, 278
Bush, George W., 12–13, 15, 143–144, 279
Bush, Laura, 176

Campbell, James, 136
Canary Islands, 210, 215–216, 218
Caparida, Judy, 122–123
Cardoza, Joseph, 149, 151, 165, 169, 173–175, 184–185, 193, 225, 231
Carillo, Manuel, 215
Carter, Raeamma, 113
Case, Steve, 135
Catania, Raymond, 84–85
Cayetano, Ben, 137
ceded lands, 266, 273
Certificate of Public Convenience and Necessity.
  See Public Utilities Commission
Cheney, Dick, 12
Child Welfare Services, 84–85
China, military threat from, 33, 245, 255
Chun, Dennis, 195
Clark, Vern, 258
Cleveland, Swan, 196, 284, 286–288
Clinton, Bill, 17, 279
Coast Guard. *See* U.S. Coast Guard
cobalt-60, 275
cocaine, 103
Cohen, Dan, 142
commercial sexual exploitation, 275–276
Committee on Present Danger, 13
"Conditions of Operation" requested by environmentalists, 179–180
Connaughton, Sean, 85, 161, 166
Conrow, Joan,
  10, 19, 33, 37, 165, 195, 244
"Consequences for Violation," 56
  See also security zone, Nawiliwili Harbor
contraband, 97, 98, 103, 120, 192, 202–203, 223, 227
contraband rocks,
  74-75, 82, 169, 202, 221–223

coqui frogs, 102, 117, 120, 224
costs of building *Alakai*, 159–160, 253
costs of HSF to taxpayers, 201, 292-293
  See also financing of HSF
Cottingham, David, 18, 144
The Creation: An Appeal to Save Life on Earth, 84
cultural impact of HSF. *See* Hawaiian culture, HSF impact on

Davy Crockett recoilless gun, 166
Declaration on the Rights of Indigenous Peoples, 87
Department of Land and Natural Resources (DLNR), 72, 204, 213–215, 222, 227
  Division of Conservation and Resource Enforcement (DOCARE), 215
Department of Transportation (USDOT), federal, 137
Department of Transportation (DOT), Hawaiʻi
  and dividing HSF project into parts, 230
  and Fukunaga, 17
  and EIS recommendation,
    11, 139-140, 188-189
  and Governor's push for exemption,
    190, 197
  and Kahului Harbor EA,
    136, 146-147, 161-162
  and Kahului Harbor expansion, 102
  and legislature encouraging accommodation of, 135
  lobbying of, by HSF, 131, 229
  opposition to EIS, 239–240
  permitting HSF to sail after Supreme Court ruling, 42, 164, 231-233
  and public meetings
    Belt Collins public hearing (2008), 108-124
    as required by legislature,
      154-155, 155-156
  and request for tugboat services, 190
  and Supreme Court ruling that DOT erred, 231-232, 240
  See also Kahului Harbor Master Plan 2025; *Sierra Club v. DOT*
DePledge, Derrick, 18, 188, 249
depleted uranium, 132–133, 166, 194, 201–202, 270–271, 299-300
deTreaux, Karlos, 20
Diamond, Richard, 19
Dick, Timothy, 9–10, 13, 131, 149, 154

INDEX   305

Dinner, David, 114
direct-action activism, 54
   See also protests
disaster relief personnel, 110
DMZ-Hawai'i/Aloha 'Aina, 283
drugs, illegal. See illegal drugs
Duffy, James, 163

E. K. Noda and Associates, 137, 146, 153
EA. See Environmental Assessment
Earth Island Institute, 27
Earthjustice, 20, 138, 158, 159
Eastwood, Clint, 23
Ebeye, 32
ecological impact of HSF.
   See environment, HSF impact on
Edens-Huff, Ka'iulani, 20
Einstein, Albert, 264
EIS. See Environmental Impact Statement
Eisenhower, Dwight, 269
Elgar Electronics, 248, 298
endangered species,
   29, 120, 265–266, 270, 276, 280
Endangered Species Act (ESA),
   18, 98, 137, 211–212, 225
   and "Section 7" consultation,
      144-145, 154
Enewetok, 32
English, Kalani, 18, 154, 181
environment, HSF impact on
   effect of jet engines on harbor bottom,
      214
   Hawaiian monk seals, 213
   HSF as ecological crisis, 26–31
   indirect environmental impacts, 214–215
   invasive species, 223–225
   and Oversight Task Force,
      192, 202–204, 226–227, 292
   overview, 209–210
   seabirds, 213
   turtles, 8, 212–213, 232
   See also contraband; endangered species;
      invasive species; whales
Environmental Assessment (EA)
   Belt Collins and, 174-175
   DOT demand for, 139–141, 188–190
   exemption from,
      136–137, 146–147, 228–235
   Fukunaga stonewalling on, 180
   Garibaldi on, 10, 146, 147, 167, 173, 174
   Hoeppner on, 63–64

   HSF operation concurrent with,
      60, 164, 185, 193
   and MARAD loan guarantee, 14, 60,
      144, 145, 146, 148, 166, 167, 197
   Maui environmental groups' challenges
      on, 149, 151, 153-154, 156-158, 161-
      162, 168, 170-171, 174, 193, 230-235
   Morita complaint on, 168-169
   and Oversight Task Force, 226
   requirement for at federal level.
      See National Environmental Policy
      Act (NEPA)
   and Sierra Club v. DOT, 233, 236
   Taylor on, 83–84
   Yukimura on, 59–60
   See also Environmental Impact
      Statement (EIS); Act 2,
      special legislative session
Environmental Council,
   19, 160, 239–240, 301
Environmental Impact Statement (EIS)
   demand for by state senators, 145–146
   DOT demands for, 139–141, 188–189
   exemption from,
      142, 146, 148, 160, 188-190
   fraudulent nature of Act 2's requirement
      of, 21, 35-36, 107-108, 109-111,
      234-235
   Garibaldi on,
      10, 146, 147, 167, 173, 174
   Hawai'i Supreme Court ruling on,
      20, 35, 60, 64, 107, 163–164, 168,
      169-170, 175, 205, 230-233
   Hoeppner on, 62–64
   Kaua'i County Council resolution on,
      41, 147
   Kaufman on, 98
   and MARAD loan guarantee,
      14, 17–18, 140–141, 143–148,
      151-152, 154, 166-167, 197, 231
   Maui environmental groups' challenges
      on, 149, 151, 153–154, 168,
      170-171, 174, 193, 230-235
   "no action alternative," 35, 107–108
   and Senate Bill 1276, 160, 161
   and Senate Bill 1785, 239
   for Stryker Brigade, 136, 193
   See also Act 2, special legislative session;
      Environmental Assessment (EA)
Erythrina gall wasp, 224
Executive Order 07-10,
   210–213, 215, 226
   See also operating conditions issued
      by Lingle

Fargo, Thomas
    and LCS program, 33–34
    replacing Garibaldi as CEO,
        15–16, 198, 247
    and "talk story" with Kaua'i mayoral
        candidates, 55, 299
fascism, 268–269
Faye, Mike, 160
Federal Impact Aid, 277
Federal Office of Technology Assessment,
    100
federal Title XI Loan Guarantee.
    See MARAD loan guarantee
ferry service that serves public, 294-295
financing of HSF,
    131–133, 135, 143, 148–152
financing for military upgrade,
    200-201, 293
Finding of No Significant Impact
    (FONSI), 162, 223, 229–230
fire ants, 113, 120, 225
fireweed, 120
First Amendment rights, 203, 232-233
First Nations, 87
Fischel, Lloyd, 156
Fox, Michael, 76–78
Freedom, 259, 261–262
Friends of Haleakala National Park,
    151, 153, 221, 231
Friends of Kamalani and Lydgate Park, 76
Friends of the Earth, 27
Fukunaga, Barry
    as DOT Deputy Director of Harbors,
        139–140
    and EIS, 188–189
    and FONSI exemption letters, 230
    initial good intentions of, 17
    legal stonewalling by, 180
    and Morita demand to obey Supreme
        Court ruling, 168
    overturning of ruling on EIS, 164
    promotion to Lingle chief of staff,
        186, 189

Garfield, James A., 265
Garibaldi, John
    denial of military aspects of HSF,
        10, 155, 193
    on EIS requirement, 10, 174
    and HSF employee layoffs, 175
    and HSF speed, 180
    "outreach" on Kaua'i, 185–186
    on PR aspects of Nawiliwili incident, 47
    on refusal of EIS, 140, 146
    replaced by Fargo, 15, 198
    request for state loan, 143, 149–150
gathering and hunting rights, 214
Geller, Larry, 19
General Dynamics,
    133, 135, 152, 246, 259, 261, 262
    as manufacturer of the Stryker tank,
        156
Gillmor, Helen, 151
Ginoza, Lisa, 171
glassy-winged sharpshooter, 101, 225
Global War on Terror (GWOT), 162
Goddard, Charles, 191
Goodwin, Kip, 43
governor of Hawai'i. See Lingle, Linda
Ground-Based Midcourse Defense, 282
Grove Farm Company, 135, 151
Guam, 32, 270, 282

H-3 Freeway, 279
Halawa Coalition, 279
Halawa Valley, 279
Hale-o-Papa Heiau, 279
Hall, Isaac
    and Act 2 appeal, 193, 205
    and EIS exemption, 147, 160
    and lawsuits re HSF operation
        concurrent with EA, 149, 151,
        153–154, 174-175
    and overview of Maui environmental
        groups' challenges on EIS, 20,
        230–231
    and Supreme Court ruling on EIS,
        163, 169, 205
Hamilton, Charles S. II, 261
hanabata days, 52–53
Hanama'ulu Beach, 25
hapu'u ferns, 118
Harada, Ka'ohu, 108–109
Haraga, Rod, 140
Harden, Cory, 119–120
Harman, C. Alexander, 247
Hart, Teresa, 289
Hashimoto, Kristin, 289
Hawai'i (state)
    governor of. See Lingle, Linda
    history of, 6–9, 265
    militarization of, 264–283
    military importance of, 53–54

overview, 22–29
  as *piko*, 53–54
  See also military presence in Hawai'i
Hawai'i Bee Keepers, 224
Hawai'i Environmental Policy Act (HEPA), 11, 35, 58, 64, 107, 168, 172, 189, 228–229, 234–235
  See also Hawai'i Revised Statutes, Chapter 343
Hawai'i Invasive Species Council (HISC), 224
Hawai'i Island
  attitude toward HSF, 147
  call for delay of HSF launch, 158
  public hearing with senators (2007), 177
  public hearing with Belt Collins, Hilo (2008), 117–120
  public hearing with Belt Collins, Kona (2008), 120–121
  public meeting with DOT (2006), 155–156
Hawai'i Revised Statutes, Chapter 343, 83–84, 109–111, 228–229, 234-235
  See also Hawai'i Environmental Policy Act (HEPA)
Hawaii Superferry (HSF)
  afterthoughts on, 291–300
  agricultural inspections of, 226-227
  announcement of start-up date, 146
  arrival in Honolulu, 162
  and audit of Lingle's administrative actions, 188, 194, 197, 230
  background of, 9–10
  and breaking of Kahului docking barge, 185, 190
  and canoe club displacement, 104–106
  Cardoza lifts injunction against, 184–185, 235
  central characters, 9–20
  Certificate of Public Convenience and Necessity, 97, 136, 143, 168–169
  and chemical pollutants, 119
  commencement of construction, 135
  concern over size of, 159–160, 252-253
  concerns of interisland shipping firms, 141
  construction begins, 135
  construction issues, 192, 255–263, 284–289
  and contraband, 97-98, 103, 120, 192, 202–203, 223, 227
  and contraband rocks, 74-75, 82, 169, 202, 221–223

  cracks in rudder of, 191
  current status of, 20–21, 54–55, 297-300
  and deadline threats, 141, 146, 173
  doubled schedule to Maui, 187, 190, 198
  in dry dock, 192, 194–195, 285
  employee layoffs, 175, 194
  financing of, 131–133, 135, 143, 148–152
  financing for military upgrade, 200–201, 293
  and Finding of No Significant Impact, 161-162, 223, 229–230
  first roundtrip to Maui after dry dock, 186–187
  first sea trials of *Alakai*, 161
  formal agreement with Austal USA, 134
  fuel efficiency of, 252–254
  "H-4" as nickname for, 100-101, 147
  Hawai'i Island attitude toward, 147
  heroes and supporters of, 17–20
  interview with Austal USA workers, 196–197, 284–289
  and invasive species, 102, 113, 117, 124, 179–180, 184, 220–225
  Lingle on, 150
  Kaua'i attitude toward, 49–53, 188, 199
  Koa, 160, 200
  launch of *Alakai*, 159
  legislation to establish, 135
  lobbying expenses, concealment of, 197
  lobbying for military features on, 200–201
  Maui attitude toward, 36, 49–50, 147
  Moloka'i attitude toward, 36, 50–51
  and national security, 60, 61–62, 85
  O'ahu attitude toward, 51–53, 69, 77
  overview, 3–21
  passengers stranded by, 166
  petition against, 41, 63, 69, 157
  as prototype for Littoral Combat Ship, 10, 152, 244-246, 255
  and safety, 75, 80, 90
  seasickness on, 187, 190, 196
  and small business operations, 77
  and traffic concerns on Kaua'i, 72, 79,
  and traffic concerns on Maui, 102, 185, 231
  and TRO, 164, 165, 232
  and tugboat service, 190, 293
  See also environment, HSF impact on; Environmental Assessment; Environmental Impact Statement;

308 INDEX

Hawaiian culture, HSF impact on;
  legal cases involving HSF; military
  aspects of HSF; National Marine
  Fisheries Service (NMFS); Nawiliwili
  Harbor incident
Hawaiian Airlines, 10, 131, 252
Hawaiian Canoe Club, 104–105, 139
Hawaiian culture
  aloha spirit, 46–47
  HSF impact on, 138–139, 205, 222–223,
    226–227, 264–267, 273–274
  Lingle on, 176
  overview, 23–28
  and Stryker Brigade, 138–139, 158, 197
Hawaiian Islands Humpback Whale
  National Marine Sanctuary,
  99, 114–115, 120, 150, 192, 226–227
Hawaiian monk seals, 209, 213, 232
Healy Tibbits Builders, Inc., 195
Hellreich, Miriam, 176
Hemmings, Fred, 165
Hempey, Daniel,
  20, 37, 107, 167–168, 228
HEPA. *See* Hawai'i Environmental
  Policy Act
heroin, 103
Hewlen, Timoteo, 86
Higa, Marion, 188, 194, 197
High Speed Connector service. *See* Joint
  High Speed Vessel (JHSV) program
Hill, Claire, 73–76
Ho, Diane, 139
Hoeppner, Rich, 18, 62–64, 78, 157
Hokama, Riki, 156
Holman, Craig, 176
Holocaust, 94
Holter, Lance, 37, 183, 220
Hooser, Gary
  and Act 2, 181, 236–243
  and audit of Lingle's administrative
    actions, 178, 194
  on concealment of lobbying expenses,
    197
  and demand for public meetings,
    154-155
  and EIS exemption, 160, 166-167
  and opposition to HSF, 18, 37
Houck, Richard, 204
HSF. *See* Hawaii Superferry
humpback whales. *See* whales
Hunter, Duncan, 245, 250

'Ilio'ulaokalani Coalition, 138–139
  See also Earthjustice
illegal drugs, 72, 79, 90, 103
imu pohaku. *See* contraband rocks
Independence, 199
Information Systems Facility, Schofield,
  267
Inouye, Daniel K.
  and benefits of HSF, 134
  and campaign contributions from HSF,
    176
  and Cokie Roberts statement, 22–23
  and congressional earmarks to Hawai'i,
    16–17
  and financing for HSF, 153
  and H-3 Freeway, 278–279
  and MARAD loan guarantee, 144
  and militarization of Hawai'i, 264
  and Stryker Brigade, 9, 131–132
Inouye, George, 79–80
interisland shipping, 141
International Fund for Animal Welfare
  (IFAW), 219
invasive species, 102, 113, 117,
  124, 179–180, 184, 220–225

J. F. Lehman and Co.
  background of, 12
  and Fargo, 198
  and possible financial gain from Navy
    contracts, 248–251, 255, 297-298
  investment in HSF, 34, 136, 143,
    148–149, 151, 153, 155, 162, 247
  and purchase of Atlantic Marine
    Holding Company, 157, 248, 298
  and rapid buildup of Navy fleet,
    246–247, 298
  See also Lehman, John F.
Jackson, Gail, 120
Jay, Jonathan, 185, 196, 284
Jenkins, Wayne, 196, 198, 254, 284–289
Joint High Speed Vessel (JHSV) program
  Austal USA contract for preliminary
    design of, 191
  and Fargo, 15–16
  HSF as prototype for, 10
  and rapid buildup of Navy fleet,
    33–34, 244–246
  purpose of, 249–250

Ka'ena Point, 282
Kaeo, Kaleikoa, 272

Kahana Sunset Owners Ass'n. v. County of Maui (1997), 230
Kahoʻolawe, 277–278
Kahului Harbor
  barge at, 141
  EA, 136-137
  expansion of, opposition to, 102-106, 111, 139
  and impact of HSF engines on, 214
  and purchase of land at, 292
  rally, 187
  traffic, 161-162, 185
Kahului Harbor Coalition
  and chronology of HSF legal challenges, 230–235
  and EIS exemption, 136, 146–147, 161–162
  and federal lawsuit demanding EIS, 151
  and Hawaiʻi Supreme Court ruling on EIS, 163
  and lawsuits re HSF operation concurrent with EIS, 149, 153, 156–158, 170-171, 177, 184, 193
Kahului Harbor Master Plan 2025, 153, 162
Kajihiro, Kyle, 19, 37, 53, 143–144
Kamaka family, 279–280
Kanuikapono Hawaiian Charter School, 57, 65
Kauaʻi
  attitude toward HSF, 49–53, 147, 188
  lawsuits by environmental groups, 167–168, 233-234
  meeting with Garibaldi, 185–186
  Nawiliwili Harbor incident, 41–46, 92–96, 165–166, 232, 233, 298–300
  pubic hearing with Belt Collins (2008), 108–117
  public hearing with senators (2007), 176–177
  public meeting with DOT (2006), 155–156
  public testimony (2007), 47–49, 56–91, 171
  rejection of petition by Lingle, 63, 157
  support of Senate Bill 1276, 160
  testimony of citizens, 56–91
Kauaʻi County Council EIS resolution, 41, 147
Kaufman, Greg, 98–100, 174
Kaʻuhane, Kalalea, 86
Kauka, Sabra, 57
Kealoha, Keone, 109–111
Kennedy, Rick, 261

Khashoggi, Adnan, 23
Kim, Harry, 177
Kingdom of Atooi. *See* Polynesian Kingdom of Atooi
Kipuka, 138
Kissinger, Henry, 13, 238
KKCR radio, 19–20, 37, 196, 198, 284–289
Kliks, Michael, 224
Koa, 160, 200
koa wood, 117
Kokeʻe, 282
Kokubun, Russell, 19, 181
Krekel, Tig, 247
Kubasik, Christopher E., 257
Kuloloio, Leslie "Uncle Les," 155-156
Kwajalein, 32

Lapetina, Abbie, 80–81
Law, Torri, 68, 167
legal cases involving HSF, 228–235
  Act 2, floor remarks by Hooser, 236–243
  Act 2, special legislative session, 234–235
  Hawaiʻi Supreme Court intervention, 231–233
  lawsuits by environmental groups, Kauaʻi, 167–168, 233-234
  lawsuits re HSF operation concurrent with EIS, 149, 151, 153–154, 156–158, 161–162, 168, 174, 193, 230–235
  new appeals, 233–234
  overview, 228–231
  Sierra Club v. DOT (2007), 230–231, 233, 236
  Wong v. Bush, 232
Lehman, John F.
  appointed chair of HSF board, 148–149, 154
  background of, 12–15, 16, 34
  as businessman, 294–295
  on environment, 161
  and expanded Pacific fleet, 34, 149, 246
  initial involvement in HSF of, 136
  and Lingle, 95
  and Maritime Administration (MARAD) loan guarantee, 167
  and McCain, 204
  and military aspects of HSF, 33–34, 85, 246–247
  named chair of HSF board, 153
  and purchase of Atlantic Marine Holding Company, 15, 34, 157, 248, 298
  See also J. F. Lehman and Co.

Lehman Brothers, 12
Lerchbacker, Alan, 159–160, 253–254
Lili'uokalani, 265
Lind, Ian, 19, 197
Lingle, Linda
    advancement in national politics, 35, 295–297
    and audit of HSF administrative actions, 188, 194, 197, 230
    background of, 10–12
    and bias toward corporate interests, 72, 112
    and campaign contributions from HSF, 34–35, 175–176
    chastised by Oshiro, 180–181
    chastising demonstrators, 165-166
    and EIS exemption, 149, 188, 190
    elected governor, 10, 132
    and "emergency" security zone provisions, 169-170
    Hooser's call for investigation of, 178
    lack of concern for outer island HSF issues, 45
    legal stonewalling by, 194, 199
    letter supporting HSF ghostwritten by Garibaldi, 143
    promotion of Fukunaga, 140, 186, 189
    and public testimony, Kaua'i (2007), 47–49, 56–91, 171
    and "Unified Command," 56–57, 169-171
    as "villain," 295–297
    visit with Laura Bush, 176
    See also Act 2, special legislative session
Littoral Combat Ship (LCS) program
    Austal USA/General Dynamics partnership for, 133, 145, 152, 246, 259, 261, 262
    as boondoggle, 204, 244-251
    and Fargo, 15–16
    Freedom, 259, 261-262
    future of, 249–250, 263
    HSF as prototype for, 10, 15, 133, 152, 183-184, 207, 244-246, 255
    and launch of *Independence*, 199
    and Navy stop-work order, 183–184
    and rapid buildup of Navy fleet, 33–34, 244–247, 298
lobbying
    expenses for, concealment of, 197
    for military features on HSF, 200–201
Lockheed Martin, 133, 259

maile, 89, 103
Makaha Ridge, 282
Makua Valley, 60, 278, 283
Malama Kaua'i, 67, 109, 183
Malu 'Aina Center for Non-Violent Education and Action, 118
Mander, Jerry, 3, 22, 129, 173, 291
Manu, Ruth, 121–122
MARAD. *See* U.S. Maritime Administration
marine life, HSF impact on.
    See environment, HSF impact on
Marine Mammal Protection Agency, 144, 145, 148
Martin, Liko, 54
Maui
    announcement of doubled schedule to, 187–190, 198
    attitude toward HSF, 36, 49–50, 147
    breaking of Kahului docking barge, 185, 186, 190
    contraband from, 202, 221–223, 227
    first HSF roundtrip after dry dock to, 186–187
    lawsuits by environmental groups, 149, 151, 153–154, 156–158, 161–162, 174, 193
    off-loading rate at Kahului, 185
    protests, 45, 139, 187
    public hearing with PUC (2004), 98–106, 142
    public hearing with senators (2007), 177
    public meeting with DOT (2006), 155–156
Maui County Farm Bureau, 101
Maui Land and Pineapple Company, 135, 151
Maui Tomorrow
    and chronology of HSF legal challenges, 230–235
    and Conditions of Operation, 179–180
    and EIS exemption, 147, 221
    and federal lawsuit demanding EIS, 151
    and Hawai'i Supreme Court ruling on EIS, 163
    and lawsuits re HSF operation concurrent with EIS, 149, 153, 157–158
    legal challenge to Act 2, 187
    meeting with Garibaldi, 141-142
Mayer, Dick, 19
McCain, John, 14, 204, 296
McCreary, Richard T., 260–261, 263
McNeil Wilson Communications, 167
Meyers, Greg, 168

miconia, 124, 224
Mijares, Scott, 69–71
Mikulina, Jeff, 184
militarization of Hawai'i and Pacific, 264–283
military aspects of HSF
  confirmation by Austal USA, 162
  confirmation by Connaughton, 85, 166
  confirmation by MARAD, 161
  denial by Garibaldi, 10, 155, 193
  first public citation of, 136
  and military importance of Hawai'i, 53–54
  overview, 7–8, 33–34
  as prototype for Littoral Combat Ship, 10, 152, 244-246, 255
  and U.S. Pacific military history, 31–33
  See also lobbying, for military features on HSF
military presence in Hawai'i, 264–283
  and economic dependency, 277
  and environmental contamination, 270–271, 274–275
  expansion of, 203, 266-268, 280-283
  and militarization of youth, 276–277
  overview, 264–283
  past resistance to, 277–280
  and prostitution, 275–276
  and taking of land, 264-268, 273
  threats to cultural survival, 273–274
  threats to native ecosystems and endangered species, 276
Mineta, Norman, 17, 137, 144, 295
Mintz, Louis N., 247
Mission Support Training Facility, 267
Mixon, Benjamin, 197
Miyashiro, Lloyd, 116
Moloka'i
  attitude toward HSF, 36, 50–51
  public hearings with Belt Collins (2008), 121–124
Moloka'i-Maui Invasive Species Committee, 124
mongoose, 81, 120, 221
Moniz, Jaymie, 142
Monk Seal Watch Program, 213
Morita, Hermina, 18, 78, 165-166, 168–169, 174, 180

Na 'Imi Pono, 138–139
Na Kai 'Ewalu Canoe Club, 104
Naeole, Iokepa, 104–106

National Defense Features program, 200-201
National Environmental Policy Act (NEPA), 11, 14, 35, 137, 138–139, 158, 229
National Humpback Whale Sanctuary. *See* Hawaiian Islands Humpback Whale National Marine Sanctuary
National Marine Fisheries Service (NMFS), 144-145, 213, 219
  and Section 10 "incidental-take" permit, 154, 179
National Oceanic and Atmospheric Administration (NOAA), 99
National Park Foundation Leadership Summit, 176
natural resources, HSF impact on, 97-98, 103, 117–118, 179, 184, 266-267, 276
  See also contraband; invasive species
Nature Conservancy, 89
Navy. *See* U.S. Navy
Navy University Affiliated Research Center (UARC), 281–282, 283
Nawiliwili Harbor incident, 41–46, 92–96, 165, 298–300
NEPA. *See* National Environmental Policy Act
New World Order, 268–269
night-vision equipment, 212
9/11 Commission, 13
Nixon, Richard, 13
"no action alternative" on EIS, 35, 107–108
No Child Left Behind Act, 276
Nohili burial sites on Kaua'i, 279
North, Joe, 261–262
Northwest Hawaiian Islands, 32
Norwest Equity Partners, 151
Norwood, Pua La'a, 72–73

O'ahu
  attitude toward HSF, 21, 51–53, 69, 77
  and contraband, 222–223
  and depleted uranium, 166, 194
  and invasive species, 221, 224
  military presence on, 265–268, 272, 281
  military training sites on, 278–280
  and natural resources, 103, 214
  and O'ahu-centric media, 43
  toxic chemicals on, 274–275
  See also Stryker Brigade
Obama, Barack, 22–23
O'Halloran, Terry, 194, 249

312   INDEX

operating conditions issued by Lingle, 184
ʻopihi, 79, 89, 103, 117, 202, 227
ordnance, unexploded, 274
Oshiro, Marcus, 180–181, 199–200
Ota, John, 118–119
Oversight Task Force,
  195, 202–204, 226–227
  See also Act 2, special legislative session

Pa, Robert, 87–88, 178
Pacific Missile Range Facility (PMRF),
  8, 60, 279, 282
Pacific Whale Foundation,
  98, 114–115, 174
Paik, Koohan,
  22, 41, 129, 173, 226, 252, 270, 291
Palin, Sarah, 12, 204, 296
Papahanaumoku (Papa), 273, 278
Parker, Jeffrey, 101–103
Parsons, Brad, 19
Pearl Harbor, 8, 274–275
People for the Preservation of Kauaʻi,
  60, 157, 233–234, 239
pest movement. *See* invasive species
Pfeiffer, Michelle, 23
Pier 19 renovation, Honolulu, 133
pigs, wild, 221, 224
piko, 53–54
Pilago, Angel, 177
Pohakuloa Training Area (PTA),
  8, 166, 265–267, 270–271, 280
Polynesian Kingdom of Atooi,
  20, 50, 87–88, 178
Potter, Kim, 114–115
Pratt, Lloyd Imuaikaika, 65–66
Project for the New American Century, 13
protests
  on Kauai. *See* Nawiliwili Harbor incident
  on Maui, 186–187
  overview, 5–6
  against Stryker Brigade, 133–134
public hearing with senators (2007),
  176–177
public hearing with Belt Collins (2008)
  Hilo, 117–120
  Kauaʻi, 108–117
  Kona, 120–121
  Molokaʻi, 121–124
  overview, 107–108
public hearing on Maui with PUC (2004),
  98–106, 142
public hearings on Stryker Brigade

  location, 159
public meeting with DOT (2006),
  155–156
public testimony on Kauaʻi with Lingle
  (2007), 47–49, 56–91, 171
  See also individual names
Public Utilities Commission
  Certificate of Public Convenience and
    Necessity, 97, 136, 142, 168-169
  and compliance of environmental
    regulation, 60
  HSF application, 9, 136
  hearing on Maui for Certificate of
    Public Convenience and Necessity
    (2004), 98-106, 142
  hearings on four islands, 142
  and internal DOT document, 189
  and legislature encouraging
    accommodation of HSF, 135
  and Morita complaint against, 168
  and protests by interisland shipping
    companies, 141
Punohu, Anne, 89–91

Queen Elizabeth II, 217
Quigley, Craig R., 260

radioactive waste, 275
  See also depleted uranium
ramp on vessel, 142, 159–160, 190,
  200–201, 246, 297
Reagan, Ronald, 238, 256
Reciprocity Treaty of 1887, 265
Reeser, Don, 221
Reilly, Sean, 289
Reserve Officer Training Corps (ROTC),
  276–277
Ritter, Fabian, 215
Roberts, Cokie, 22–23, 54
rocks, contraband, 74–75, 82, 169, 202,
  221–223
Rose, Katy, 20, 115–117, 196
Roughead, Gary, 245, 260
Rumsfeld, Donald, 15, 138, 258

Sacher, Jeff, 19
Sawyer, George A., 247
Say, Calvin, 176
Sea Fighter, 250
sea mammals, 8, 119
  See also whales
seabirds, 213

seasickness, 187, 190, 196
"Section 7" consultation (under Endangered Species Act), 144-145, 154
security zone, Nawiliwili Harbor, 12, 65, 67, 68, 70–71, 90, 167, 169-170, 203, 228, 232-233
  "Consequences for Violation," 56
Senate Bill 1276, 160, 161
Senate Bill 1785, 239
Shapiro, Dave, 199–200
Shirley, John W. "Bill," 247
Shooltz, Michael, 36, 92
Shore, Teri, 37, 217
Sierra Club
  and chronology of HSF legal challenges, 230–231
  and EIS exemption, 147, 221
  and federal lawsuit demanding EIS, 151
  and Hawai'i Supreme Court ruling on EIS, 163
  and lawsuits re HSF operation concurrent with EIS, 149, 156-157
Sierra Club v. DOT (2007), 230–231, 233, 236
  See also Supreme Court of Hawai'i
Sinkin, Lanny, 170, 203, 232–233
Slay, Carolyn, 284
sonar, 99, 212
Souki, Joseph, 145–146, 161, 176
Spain, 9, 131
special legislative session.
  See Act 2, special legislative session
Star Wars Defense, 282
STARS (Army Strategic Target System), 279
State of Hawai'i Environmental Council, 19, 160, 239-240
Strategic Defense Initiative (SDI), 282
Stryker Brigade
  cultural impact of, 138–139, 158, 197
  and Daniel Inouye, 16, 131–132
  and depleted uranium, 85, 111, 117
  and determination of inadequacy of air transport, 138
  EIS for, 136, 159, 193, 281
  final decision to base on O'ahu, 197
  on O'ahu, 156, 280–281
  protests against, 133–134
  public hearings on location of, 159
subsistence fishing and gathering, 214
Sullivan, Paul E., 257, 259, 261
Summerall, Charles, 277

Superferry Oversight Task Force.
  See Oversight Task Force
Superfund sites, 274
Supreme Court of Hawai'i
  accepts legal challenge to Act 2, 205, 300
  and Act 2, special legislative session to overturn Supreme Court ruling, 11-12, 20, 173-174, 177-179, 181-184
  appeal of *Sierra Club v. DOT* at, 151, 230-231
  and DOT, 41-42, 164
  and defiance of *Sierra Club v. DOT* decision, 164, 169, 231-234
  and expense to state of *Sierra Club v. DOT*, 293
  and Hall, 20
  and influence on lower court, 175
  and Lingle, 35, 41-42
  Sierra Club v. DOT, 11-12, 35, 64, 163, 169, 231-233, 240
  and *Sierra Club v. DOT* decision, regarding segmenting project by island, 168, 230
  and state Environmental Council, 19, 160
surfers at Nawiliwili Harbor, 5, 42, 44–45, 92-96
sustainability, 51–53, 72, 109, 122, 215
SWAT teams, 44
Sylva, Mahelani, 20

Takamine, Victoria Holt, 139
target missiles, 282
Taubman, Philip, 33, 37, 255
Tavares, Charmaine, 187, 190, 204
Taylor, Ken, 83–84
Temporary Restraining Order (TRO), 88, 164, 165, 170, 232
Tepley, Lee, 19
terrorism laws, 12, 170, 203, 232
  See also security zone, Nawiliwili Harbor
Theater High-Altitude Area Defense, 282
Theater Security Cooperation (TSC), 162
Thielen, Laura, 171
Thompson, Loren, 257
Thousand Friends of Kaua'i, 114, 167–168, 172, 233–234, 235
toxic chemicals, 274–275
traffic concerns. *See* Hawaii Superferry (HSF), traffic concerns on Kaua'i; Hawaii Superferry (HSF), traffic concerns on Maui
Trask, Haunani-Kay, 37, 264

Trujillo, Jimmy, 20, 196, 284
Tsutsui, Shan, 18, 154, 181
tugboat service, 190, 293
turtles, 8, 212–213, 232

"Unified Command," 56–57, 169-170, 171
uranium, depleted. *See* depleted uranium
Uranium Medical Research Center, 271
U.S. Army
  Army Strategic Target System
    (STARS), 279
  See also Stryker Brigade
U.S. Coast Guard
  appeal to bar protesters from Nawiliwili,
    170, 203, 232
  citizens' experience with,
    68, 73, 86, 87–88, 95
  and "Consequences for Violation," 56
  and Nawiliwili Harbor incident, 42
  See also security zone, Nawiliwili Harbor
U.S. DOT, 137
U.S. Marine Corps' Third Marine
  Expeditionary Force, 162
U.S. Marine Mammal Commission,
  144-145
U.S. Maritime Administration (MARAD)
  and American Classic Cruise Lines
    loan guarantee, 131
  and confirmation of military role of
    HSF, 161, 166
  and HSF loan guarantee,
    14, 17–18, 140–141, 143–148,
    151-152, 154, 166–167, 197, 231
  reasons for EIS exemption, 148
  and Title XI of the Merchant Marine
    Act, 101, 143
U.S. National Marine Fisheries Service,
  98, 144–145, 148, 154
  and U.S. DOT as authority over, 137
U.S. Navy
  aircraft carrier strike group, 282
  and control of Pacific Basin coastlines,
    31–34
  and extension of lease on Westpac
    Express, 162
  and High Speed Connector service, 162
  and rapid buildup of Pacific fleet,
    244–254
  See also Joint High Speed Vessel
    program; Littoral Combat Ship
    program
U.S. Pacific military history, 31–33
U.S. Trust Territory, 31

Valenciano, Randal, 60, 167-168, 172, 189
Varroa bee mite, 221, 224, 225, 227
Voluntary Intermodal Sealift Agreement
  (VISA), 161

Waikane Valley, 279–280
Wakea, 273, 278
Wescott, Greg, 100–101
Wescott, Masako, 103
Westpac Express, 33–34, 133, 152, 162, 244
whales
  and Act 2, special legislative session, 184
  in the Canary Islands,
    210, 215–216, 218
  Garibaldi on, 180
  and HSF "incidental-take" permit,
    154, 179
  and HSF service after dark, 187
  Jackson on, 120
  Kaufman on, 98–100, 174
  latest findings on vessel-whale collisions,
    215–216
  Ota on, 118–119
  and Oversight Task Force, 226–227
  Potter on, 114–115
  and "Section 7" consultation, under
    Endangered Species Act,
    144-145, 154
  speed limits in eastern seaboard
    whale zones, 202
  whale-ship collisions, 209–212, 217–219
  See also Hawaiian Islands Humpback
    Whale National Marine Sanctuary
White, Rick, 112
White, Terry, 131, 142, 156
Whitlock, Ned, 113
wild pigs, 221, 224
Wilson, Christie, 18
Wilson, E. O., 84
Wilson, Juan, 19, 111–112, 120, 191
Winter, Donald C., 257, 263
Wong v. Bush, 232
World Shipping Council, 202
www.islandbreath.org, 111

Yamane, John Sydney, 77
Yates, Chris, 18, 145, 147–148, 151-152
Yukimura, JoAnn, 18, 58–61, 171, 185

Zoodsma, Barb, 211

About the Authors

KOOHAN PAIK is a journalist, media-literacy educator, and award-winning filmmaker based on Kaua'i. Her work focuses on preservation of culture and language, such as her 2006 short film, *La Vendemmia*, which documents Sicilian winemaking traditions that are no longer practiced. She is also the writer and director of a Hawaiian-language docudrama based on the literary classic *The True Story of Kaluaikoolau*, a tale of the legendary Native freedom fighter during Hawai'i's annexation period. Her films have been exhibited at the Paris Museum of Modern Art; the Berlin International Film Festival; Yonsei University, Seoul; the London Institute of Contemporary Arts; the Whitney Museum of American Art; and many other venues worldwide. Her articles on sustainability and colonialism have been published in *WorldWatch* magazine, *Slow* (journal of the Slow Food movement), and in the book *Paradigm Wars: Indigenous Peoples' Resistance to Globalization*, as well as *asianamericanfilm.com*, among other periodicals. She has taught filmmaking to students of all ages and backgrounds, including indigenous Hawaiian youths from the island of Ni'ihau. Recently, she has delved into the agit-prop potential of YouTube, as seen in *Greensumption*, a send-up of ecomarketing campaigns, and *Discover Kaua'i*, widely credited for galvanizing Kaua'i's current wave of antidevelopment activism. This is her first book.

JERRY MANDER is director of the International Forum on Globalization (IFG), a San Francisco "think tank" focused since 1994 on exposing the negative impacts of economic globalization. Mander was trained as an economist in the 1950s (Columbia University), but his early career was as president of a major commercial ad agency, Freeman, Mander & Gossage, and then as founder of the country's first *nonprofit* ad agency in 1971, Public Media Center, which ran advertising and publicity campaigns for Sierra Club, Greenpeace,

Friends of the Earth, and various indigenous and antiwar groups. These campaigns included the celebrated Sierra Club campaigns (with David Brower) that kept dams out of the Grand Canyon, established a Redwood National Park, and stopped production of the Supersonic Transport (SST). During the 1980s, Mander also assisted Native Hawaiian campaigns on behalf of the Pele Defense Fund (Big Island) and the Protect Kahoʻolawe ʻOhana. He is author or editor of several bestselling books, including *Four Arguments for the Elimination of Television*, *In the Absence of the Sacred*, *The Case Against the Global Economy* (with Edward Goldsmith), *Alternatives to Economic Globalization* (with John Cavanagh), and *Paradigm Wars: Indigenous Peoples' Resistance to Globalization* (with Victoria Tauli-Corpuz). He has been called "the patriarch of the anti-globalization movement" (Andrew Revkin, environmental writer, *New York Times*, 2007).

About the Contributors

HANNAH BERNARD has been employed as a marine biologist since 1983. She has worked as a research scientist (fishery biologist) with the National Marine Fisheries Service and Hawaiʻi Wildlife Fund (marine biologist) specializing in protected marine life for sixteen out of twenty-four years as a marine biologist. Much of her work has been the study of marine life, including threatened and endangered marine species in the ocean waters in and around Maui. She is a member of the Sierra Club's Hawaiʻi Marine Wildlife and Habitat Committee, in addition to being a member of the Pacific Scientific Review Group, a regional scientific and management advisory group to the National Marine Fisheries Service empowered by mandate through the Marine Mammal Protection Act, and a member of the Pacific Cetacean Offshore Gillnet Fishery Take Reduction Team, also mandated by law. She is also the cofounder and president of the Hawaiʻi Wildlife Fund.

JOAN CONROW has been working as a journalist since 1980 and was formerly a staff writer for the *Honolulu Star-Bulletin* and *Honolulu Advertiser* and a freelance correspondent for Reuters. Her articles have been published in many local, regional, and national newspapers and magazines. She also writes creative nonfiction and fiction. She has lived on Kaua'i since 1987.

DANIEL HEMPEY has been practicing law since 1990. A former public defender, he has tried hundreds of cases to verdict. Hempey has served as a judge pro tempore in Alameda County, California, and is currently a partner at Hempey & Meyers, LLP in Lihue, Kaua'i. His clients have included multinational corporations, small businesses, individuals, and nonprofit organizations, in cases ranging from constitutional inverse condemnation, civil rights litigation, and contract disputes to the defense of homicide cases. He has prevailed in numerous appeals in the Hawai'i appellate courts, including the reversal of a murder conviction by the Hawai'i Supreme Court. Hempey & Meyers honors an extensive pro bono component, which generally focuses on indigenous Hawaiian rights, animal protection, and cases seeking to enforce environmental compliance for the protection of common resources. Along with his partner, Greg Meyers, Hempey was the lead attorney in the case to stop the Superferry from using Kaua'i's Harbor until it had completed an EA that the State Supreme Court said was required.

LANCE HOLTER is chair of the Maui Sierra Club. Since 1981, he has resided on Maui, where he has been involved in extensive community service, including work with the Ka Hale A Ke Ola Homeless Center, the Maui Coastal Algae Bloom Studies, the Maui Board of Realtors Shoreline Setback Committee, and the Kaho'olawe Ocean Management Plan Technical Review, among others. In 2008, he cochaired the Hawai'i Democratic Party State Convention Environmental Committee, and he served as chair of the Democratic Party for Maui County from 2007 to 2008.

GARY HOOSER, a Democrat, represents Kaua'i and Ni'ihau in the Hawai'i State Legislature. He is the founder and former owner of Wai'oli Properties, a real estate and development company, and H&S

Publishing. In 1997, he was named "Business Person of the Year," by the Rotary Club of Kapaʻa, and in 1995, the Kauaʻi Chamber of Commerce named him "Entrepreneur of the Year." His community activities include membership in the Rotary Club, involvement with the Kauaʻi Filipino Chamber of Commerce, and a position on the board at Island School, in Kauaʻi.

KYLE KAJIHIRO is the program director for the American Friends Service Committee in Hawaii. He works on demilitarization, environmental justice, and Kanaka Maoli human rights issues. He has been involved in immigrant worker organizing, community mural projects, antiracist/antifascist activism, the Central America Solidarity movement, Hawaiian sovereignty solidarity efforts, and community radio and television. He has traveled to and participated in various international solidarity delegations and conferences, including those in Vieques, Tonga, Korea, Japan, Guam, the Marshall Islands, Ecuador, China, and various cities in the United States, to discuss peace and demilitarization issues in Hawaiʻi.

MICHAEL SHOOLTZ is a 61-year-old semiretired banker and developer of high-rise office buildings on the mainland. He holds an M.B.A. from the University of Michigan and has been a resident of Kauaʻi since 2000. He hopes to learn to surf.

TERI SHORE is program director at Turtle Island Restoration Network. In this role, she directs all aspects of conservation, policy, and advocacy campaigns for sea turtles and sustainable fisheries in California, Texas, Costa Rica, and Papua New Guinea—all key nesting or foraging habitats for endangered sea turtles. Previously, as campaign director for Sea Turtle Restoration Project, she directed the national campaign that achieved a sea-turtle marine reserve closed to shrimp fishing in Texas waters and advanced the turtle-safe shrimp certification program. She also worked for seven years as campaign director for the Clean Vessels Program at Friends of the Earth (previously Bluewater Network) to advocate for cleaner marine vessels, from passenger ferries to cruise liners and commercial oceangoing ships. In that capacity, she was involved with the marine industry, legislators, regulators, environmental groups, and public health advocates to achieve stringent ferry-emissions standards and new pollution laws for cruise ships and ocean-going vessels in California, as well as the United States as a whole, and internationally. Shore is also a journalist who has authored environmental articles and reports. She serves on the board of the Sierra Club San Francisco Bay Chapter Backpack Section and is a past president of the California Alpine Club.

PHILIP TAUBMAN, Washington bureau chief for the *New York Times*, is the author of *Secret Empire: Eisenhower, the CIA, and the Hidden Story of America's Space Espionage*.

HAUNANI-KAY TRASK is a Native Hawaiian activist, writer, and academic. She is a professor of Hawaiian studies with the Kamakakuokalani Center for Hawaiian Studies at the University of Hawai'i at Manoa and has represented Native Hawaiians at the United Nations and various other global forums. Trask is the author of several books of poetry and nonfiction, including *Light in the Crevice Never Seen* and *Eros and Power: The Promise of Feminist Theory*, which is a revised version of her Ph.D. dissertation; and *From a Native Daughter: Colonialism and Sovereignty in Hawai'i*, which is a collection of essays on the Hawaiian sovereignty movement. She is also producer of the award-winning film *Act of War: The Overthrow of the Hawaiian Nation*.

Koa Books publishes works on personal transformation, progressive politics, and native cultures.

Please visit www.koabooks.com for information about recent and forthcoming titles.

Koa Books
932 Hendersonville Road #104
Asheville, NC 28805
www.koabooks.com

Koa Books is a book imprint of Chiron Publications.

www.ChironPublications.com

www.ingramcontent.com/pod-product-compliance
Lightning Source LLC
Chambersburg PA
CBHW020349170426
43200CB00005B/112